Legacy of Suppression

Legacy of Suppression

Freedom of Speech and Press in Early American History

Leonard W. Levy

The Belknap Press of Harvard University Press

Cambridge, Massachusetts   1960

To the Memory of My Father
ALBERT LEVY
1896–1958

ᴥᔰ Preface

This book presents a revisionist interpretation of the origins and original understanding of the First Amendment's clause on freedom of speech and press. I have been reluctantly forced to conclude that the generation which adopted the Constitution and the Bill of Rights did not believe in a broad scope for freedom of expression, particularly in the realm of politics.

I find that libertarian theory from the time of Milton to the ratification of the First Amendment substantially accepted the right of the state to suppress seditious libel. I find also that the American experience with freedom of political expression was as slight as the theoretical inheritance was narrow. Indeed, the American legislatures, especially during the colonial period, were far more oppressive than the supposedly tyrannous common-law courts. The evidence drawn particularly from the period 1776 to 1791 indicates that the generation that framed the first state declarations of rights and the First Amendment was hardly as libertarian as we have traditionally assumed. They did not intend to give free rein to criticism of the government that might be deemed seditious libel, although the concept of seditious libel was — and still is — the principal basis of muzzling political dissent. There is even reason to believe that the Bill of Rights was more the chance product of political expediency on all sides than of principled commitment to personal liberties. A broad libertarian theory of freedom of speech and press did not emerge in the United States until the Jeffersonians, when a minority party, were forced to defend themselves against the Federalist Sedition Act of 1798. In power, however, the Jeffersonians were not much more tolerant of their political critics than the Federalists had been.

This has been a difficult book to write, because the facts have dictated conclusions that violate my predilections and clash with the accepted version of history. But just as my personal preferences as to current policy do not depend on what passed for wisdom in the eighteenth century, my views as a scholar do not depend on my civic convictions nor on historical convention. I have tried to heed Maitland's advice by putting myself back into the "twilight" where the past must be taken on its own terms. Lord Chief Justice Reeves, in the preface to his *History of English Law to the Time of Elizabeth* (1783), regretted that "modern writers, in discoursing of the ancient law, were too apt to speak in modern terms and generally with a reference to some modern usage." Reeves attempted to forget the changes wrought by time so that the "laws of the time would then be learned in the language of the time . . . and exhibited in the true colours in which they appeared to persons who lived in those respective periods." In this spirit, I have sought "merely to show," as Ranke put it, "how things actually were."

The difficulty is that much of history lies in the interstices of the evidence and cannot always be mustered and measured. Moreover, legal history is in large part the history of ideas, and ideas emerge, grow, and become part of men's mental baggage in mysterious ways, colored by the environment and conditioned by the climate of opinion.

The historian, lacking a spectrograph to discern color and a thermometer to measure climate, sticks rigorously to the tangible evidence at the risk of losing the spirit of the time he seeks to reconstruct. What was left unsaid or undone may have been as important as what was said and done, yet is unrevealed in the documentary remains of the past. Certain ideas, I am sure, must have been "in the air" at the time, but the fact is no longer susceptible to proof.

I am keenly aware of the limitations of my skeptical approach toward my materials: believe nothing unless proved beyond reasonable doubt by the evidence. Take, for example, the two major libertarian propositions of the later eighteenth century, that truth is a defense against a charge of criminal libel, and that the jury should have the power of deciding the questions that judges reserved to themselves: whether the defendant's intent was malicious and whether his words had the seditious tendency alleged. That these libertarian propositions were "in the air" is beyond doubt. But most of the scraps of evidence that can be gathered on the subject tend to show that it was not the intention in America to modify the common law by incorporating these propositions within the meaning of free-press guarantees. Yet I am certain that if the American people at any time between the Zenger case and the ratification of the First Amendment would have held a referendum, they would have overwhelmingly cast their ballots in favor of the two propositions. Working with the "evidence," however, leads to the conclusion that this certainty on my part is utterly unprovable; according to the evidence, the issue was, at best, unsettled.

On the other hand I do believe that the preponderance of the evidence reliably settles a major issue that may be stated in the form of different but related questions: was it

the intention of the generation from the Revolution to the
First Amendment to supersede the common law by repudiating the Blackstonian concept that freedom of the press
meant freedom from prior restraint? by rejecting the idea
that government may be criminally assaulted, that is, seditiously libeled, merely by the expression of critical opinions that tended to lower it in the public's esteem? by
abandoning alleged distinctions between "liberty" and "license"? by abolishing the power of government to punish
words that do not directly incite to acts in violation of
law?

These questions define the issue confronted in this book.
I am not contending that the Framers of the First Amendment did not have a high regard for the open discussion
of public matters. Indeed, neither in America nor in England did the common law actually prevent widespread discussion of affairs of state by the common people. Nor am
I arguing that there was no intention to modify the common law in any respect. As I have indicated, it may well
have been the intention, though unprovable, to permit defendants to plead truth as a defense and to let juries decide
the whole of the issue in trials for seditious libel. Whether
that was the intention is not, however, the main issue.
Murder remains a crime even if a defendant may plead
self-defense and a jury may rightfully consider his plea.
My concern, in brief, is whether it was the intention, as
Zechariah Chafee, Jr., has affirmed, "to wipe out the common law of sedition, and make further prosecutions for
criticism of the government, without any incitement to
law-breaking forever impossible in the United States of
America." [1]

[1] *Free Speech in the United States* (Cambridge, Mass., 1948),
p. 21.

This accepted understanding of the Framers' intentions has become what Locke called a "received hypothesis," held as a result of learned and traditional convictions. Such convictions are not easy to abandon, as Locke testified:

> Would it not be an insufferable thing for a learned professor, and that which his scarlet would blush at, to have his authority of forty years' standing, wrought out of hardrock Greek and Latin, with no small expenses of time and candle, and confirmed by general tradition and a reverend beard, in an instant overturned by an upstart novelist? Can any one expect that he should be made to confess, that what he taught his scholars thirty years ago was all error and mistake, and that he sold them hard words and ignorance at a very dear rate? [2]

Locke's words have steeled me against the possibility of being condemned as an apostate from libertarianism, or what is even worse, being hailed as a convert to the "new conservatism" that has recently been fashionable among many historians. I do not write history from the standpoint of any ideological tong. Nor is it my intention to play the debunker who relishes smashing popular idols and myths. I would be delighted if this book were proved to be wrong. Right or wrong, however, its revelations do not dim my faith in the essential spirit of Milton, Locke, Jefferson, or, for that matter, Zechariah Chafee, Jr., and other heroes of civil libertarianism who are sometimes criticized in the following pages. That they may have been occasionally wrong or perhaps inconsistent proves only that they were human, subject to error and even blinded now and again by prejudice, like the rest of us. But the thrust of their thinking is of perduring nobility, for the principles to which they were dedicated will always stand for an

[2] *An Essay Concerning Human Understanding*, ch. 20, sect. 11.

ever-broadening recognition of individual liberty. So too, the fact that the First Amendment was not originally intended to mean what it has become to mean does not derogate from the statesmanship of its Framers, who formulated its language in words of such breath, however ambiguous, that we have been able to breathe a liberality of meaning into it, in keeping with the ideals of our expanding democracy.

Leonard W. Levy
Dean of the Graduate School
Brandeis University

ᴥᴦ Acknowledgments

It is a pleasure to acknowledge the encouragement that I have received from Justice Felix Frankfurter, Professor Henry Steele Commager of Amherst College, Professor Richard B. Morris of Columbia University, Mr. Howard Jay Graham of the Los Angeles County Law Library, Mr. Henry Allen Moe of the Guggenheim Foundation, Professors Mark Howe and Paul Freund of Harvard Law School, and my colleagues, Professors Max Lerner and John P. Roche of Brandeis University. Professors Freund and Roche, who read this manuscript in entirety, offered suggestions that helped to correct errors of fact and judgment. Professor Roche, by his conversation and writings, contributed much to my own thinking. But my deepest obligation, by far, is to Professor Howe. He gave selfless hours of patient, oral criticism and Socratic questioning which he supplemented with detailed notes on revision that proved to be invaluable. I deeply appreciate his counsel, criticism, and confidence. That I sometimes have not concurred in the judgments of those for whom I have the very highest regard does not lessen my sense of debt to them nor diminish the value of their advice.

I am very grateful to the John Simon Guggenheim Memorial Foundation for the fellowship that enabled me to take a year's leave of absence from Brandeis University. The Fund for the Republic also provided aid. Abram L.

Sachar, the President of Brandeis University, and John P. Roche, the Dean of Faculty, generously assisted with a grant-in-aid of research as well as a leave of absence. Mr. Benjamin Swig of Los Angeles, a patron of scholarship, indirectly provided support and encouragement. My thanks are also due to Mrs. Rosamonde Morrison, my cheerful and accurate typist, and to the librarians at Harvard, particularly to Carolyn E. Jakeman and her staff at Houghton Library, who were most cooperative in searching for obscure tracts for me to examine. The editors of the *William and Mary Quarterly* have given permission to use the substance of an article that I originally published in their periodical.

Finally, I wish to acknowledge the special assistance offered by the ladies of my family, Elyse, Wendy, and Leslie, each of whom in her inimitable fashion contributed, sometimes in subtle ways, to the writing of this book.

This book would have been dedicated to Justice Felix Frankfurter but for the transcendent claims of my father's memory.

❧ Contents

Legacy of Suppression

CHAPTER ONE

৽ Seditious Libel versus Freedom of Expression

The proposition has been conventionally accepted in both law and history that the Framers of the First Amendment had a very broad understanding of freedom of speech and press and intended to abolish the common law of seditious libel. James Madison himself, the "father" of the Constitution and of the Bill of Rights, explicitly argued that proposition,[1] and it has been reiterated in our own time by our greatest judges, as well as by distinguished constitutional historians and lawyers.

Justice Holmes, for example, with Justice Brandeis concurring, declared, "I wholly disagree with the argument . . . that the First Amendment left the common law as to seditious libel in force. History seems to me against the notion."[2] More recently Justices Black and Douglas stated, "But the First Amendment repudiated seditious libel for

[1] "Madison's Report on the Virginia Resolutions" (1799–1800), in Jonathan Elliot, ed., *The Debates in the Several State Conventions on the Adoption of the Federal Constitution . . . and Other Illustrations of the Constitution* (Philadelphia, 1941, 2nd ed., rev.), 4:561–567.

[2] Abrams v. United States, 250 U.S. 616, 630 (1919).

this country." [3] Professor Henry Schofield, in his original
and influential essay on freedom of the press in the United
States, noted that under the English common law many
political publications in the colonies before the American
Revolution were considered seditious and even treasonable.
"One of the objects of the Revolution," Schofield concluded, in a statement quoted with approval by the Supreme Court, "was to get rid of the English common law
on liberty of speech and of the press." [4] Professor Zechariah
Chafee, Jr., author of the standard work on this subject,
alleged, "The First Amendment was written by men to
whom Wilkes and Junius were household words, who intended to wipe out the common law of sedition, and make
further prosecutions for criticism of the government, without any incitement to law-breaking, forever impossible in
the United States of America." [5] Numerous others have
supported the same proposition.[6] They have, however, in

[3] Beauharnais v. Illinois, 343 U.S. 250, 272 (1951). See also the
opinion of Justice Jackson in the same case at p. 289.
[4] Henry Schofield, *Essays on Constitutional Law and Equity*
(Boston, 1921), 2:521-522, reprinting the essay, "Freedom of the
Press in the United States," originally published in *Proceedings* of
the American Sociological Society, 11:67-116 (1914). For the opinion of the Supreme Court, see Bridges v. Cal., 314 U.S. 252, 264
(1941), *per* Justice Black for the majority.
[5] Chafee, *Free Speech in the United States* (Cambridge, Mass.,
1948), p. 21.
[6] See, *e.g.*, Theodore Schroeder, *Constitutional Free Speech*
(New York, 1919), p. 98; Leon Whipple, *Our Ancient Liberties*
(New York, 1927), pp. 93-94; Giles J. Patterson, *Free Speech and
a Free Press* (Boston, 1939), pp. 101-102, 125-128; Osmond K.
Fraenkel, *Our Civil Liberties* (New York, 1944), pp. 64-65; Francis
Biddle, *The Fear of Freedom* (New York, 1951), pp. 55-56; James
Morton Smith, *Freedom's Fetters: The Alien and Sedition Laws
and American Civil Liberties* (Ithaca, 1956), pp. 427-431; John
Kelly, "Criminal Libel and Free Speech," *Kansas Law Review*,
6:310 (1958); and C. Herman Pritchett, *The American Constitu-*

Mrs. Malaprop's phrase, "anticipated the past" by succumbing to an impulse to recreate it so that its image may be seen in a manner consistent with our rhetorical tradition of freedom, thereby yielding a message which will instruct the present. The evidence suggests that the proposition is more presuppositious than plausible, or if plausible, unprovable.[7]

We may even have to confront the possibility that the intentions of the Framers were not the most libertarian and their insights on the subject of freedom of expression not the most edifying. But this should be expected since the Framers were nurtured on the crabbed historicism of Coke and the narrow conservatism of Blackstone. The ways of thought of a lifetime are not easily broken. The Declaration of Independence severed the political connection with England but the American states continued the English common-law system. If the Revolution produced any radical libertarians on the meaning of freedom of speech and press, they were not present at the Constitutional Convention or the First Congress which drafted the Bill of Rights. But to understand that scholars and judges have

---

tion (New York, 1959), p. 430. For a similar view by an older and very eminent authority, Judge Thomas M. Cooley, see his *Treatise on the Constitutional Limitations Which Rest Upon the Legislative Power of the States*, ed. V. H. Lane (Boston, 1903, 7th ed.), pp. 613–615.

[7] A few writers have agreed with this conclusion, but their dissent from the Holmes-Chafee-Schofield thesis seems equally presuppositious since they offered no or slight evidence to support their view. See Edward S. Corwin, "Freedom of Speech and Press under the First Amendment: A Resumé," *Selected Essays on Constitutional Law*, ed. Douglas B. Maggs *et al.* (Chicago, 1938), 2: 1060–1063; W. R. Vance, "Freedom of Speech and of the Press," *Minnesota Law Review*, 2:259 (1918); and Thomas F. Carroll, "Freedom of Speech and of the Press in the Federalist Period: The Sedition Act," *Michigan Law Review*, 18:636–637, 649–650 (1920).

betrayed a penchant for what Professor John P. Roche calls "retrospective symmetry," [8] by giving to present convictions a patriotic lineage and tradition — in this case, the fatherhood of the "Framers" — is no reason to be distressed. We may miss the comforting assurance of having the past's original intentions coincide with present preferences. Yet the case for civil liberties is so powerfully grounded in political philosophy's wisest principles, as well as the wisest policies drawn from experience, that it need not be anchored to the past.

No citizen, and certainly no jurist worthy of his position, would or should conclude his judgment on either a constitutional question or a matter of public policy by an antiquarian examination of the original meaning of the freedom of speech-and-press clause. What passed for wisdom in the era of the Framers may very well have passed out of date with the growth of libertarianism in America. But antiquarianism, although the vice of the jurist, is its own reward to the historian who, without the need of finding a tradition that is liberal or otherwise, seeks to know the past. We know very little, though, about the original understanding of the First Amendment's provision that "Congress shall make no law . . . abridging the freedom of speech, or of the press . . ." The meaning of no other clause of the Bill of Rights at the time of its framing and ratification has been so obscure to us. Historians, whether libertarian or not, have taken for granted that the Framers meant one thing or another, without inquiring into the evidence. One can do wonders with "insights" and inferences, depending upon one's predilections, but clear and prepon-

[8] Roche, "American Liberty: An Examination of the 'Tradition' of Freedom," in M. R. Konvitz and C. Rossiter, eds., *Aspects of Liberty* (Ithaca, 1958), p. 130.

derant proof has not been offered to elevate past generaliza-
tions beyond the level of a guess.

The sources, particularly for the period 1787–1791, are
unfortunately almost silent on the matter under inquiry.
The reason for the scantiness of the evidence goes far to
explain why it is so difficult to ascertain the Framers' understanding of freedom of speech. That freedom had almost no history as a concept or a practice prior to the First
Amendment or even later. It developed as an offshoot of
freedom of the press, on the one hand, and on the other,
freedom of religion — the freedom to speak openly on
religious matters. But as an independent concept referring
to a citizen's personal right to speak his mind, freedom of
speech was a very late development, virtually a new concept without basis in everyday experience and nearly unknown to legal and constitutional history or to libertarian
thought on either side of the Atlantic prior to the First
Amendment. The very phrase, "freedom of speech," until
the last quarter of the eighteenth century referred primarily
to a parliamentary, not a civil, right:[9] the legislator's im-

---

[9] The phrase "freedom of speech" used in connection with the
right of the citizen to speak his mind was extremely rare in the
seventeenth century. Professor Mark Howe has called my attention to the appearance of the phrase in "A Proclamation against
excesse of Lavish and Licentious Speech of matters of State" issued
by James I on Dec. 24, 1620. The king's point was that "freedome
of speech" did not extend to matters of state which "are no
Theames, or subjects fit for vulgar persons, or common meetings
. . ." In 1644 William Walwyn advocated "freedom of discourse"
and Milton "freedom of speaking." Milton in 1673 referred again
to "freedom of speech" in the sense of a personal rather than a
parliamentarian's right. In the eighteenth century this usage of
freedom of speech was more frequent but still rare before 1776. It
was employed by "Tory Author" and by "A Young Gentleman
of the Temple" in 1712, by John Trenchard and William Gordon
collaborating as "Cato" in 1721, by an anonymous defender of

munity from punishment for anything said by him in his official capacity during a legislative session. The phrase originated in Anglo-American history in the struggle of Parliament to achieve the privilege of free debate, and in that sense it has a history separate from the history of free speech as a civil liberty.[10]

I Freedom of speech could not become a civil liberty until the truth of men's opinions, especially their religious opinions, was regarded as relative rather than absolute; until kings and parliaments were sufficiently strong and stable to be able to ignore political criticism; and until the people were considered the source of sovereignty, the masters rather than the servants of the government. There could be no toleration of dissent when Catholics, Anglicans, and Puritans were profoundly convinced that the precise shade of belief which each respectively professed must be established as England's only true religion and that all be compelled to accept it for their own salvation as well as for the good of God and the nation. Heresy and nonconformity were severely prosecuted as crimes from the time the Inquisition was introduced in England and continued as

---

"Craftsman" in 1731, by James Alexander in 1737, by James Parker in 1740, by Bishop Hayter in the late 1750's, and by William Bollan in 1766. The books and tracts by all these persons, together with citations to their work, will be discussed in Chapters Three and Four.

[10] On the parliamentary right, see J. E. Neale, "The Commons' Privilege of Free Speech in Parliament," in R. W. Seton-Watson, ed., *Tudor Studies* (London, 1924), pp. 257–286; Zechariah Chafee, Jr., *Three Human Rights in the Constitution of 1787* (Lawrence, Kan., 1956), pp. 4–89; Harold Hulme, "The Winning of Freedom of Speech by the House of Commons," *American Historical Review*, 61:825–853 (July 1956); and Hulme's *The Life of Sir John Eliot* (New York, 1957), pp. 47–48, 59–60, 248–252, 307–338, and 365–368.

crimes after the nationalization of the church under Henry VIII. Whether the government was Catholic or Protestant, Anglican or Puritan, the compulsion of conscience for the sake of uniformity necessitated restraints on freedom of speech and press regarding religion. The Reformation, moreover, by making the monarch the head of the established church, converted every religious question to a political one and suffused government policies with religious overtones. As a result, nonconformity and heresy became virtually indistinguishable from sedition and treason. Criticism of the church affected the state and vice versa. Not only was criticism dangerous; it was necessarily wrong when emanating from inferior subjects against their masters. The danger was particularly great for several centuries after the emergence of the national state, when the life of the monarch was in jeopardy and the peace and security of the state were precarious. Freedom of religious and political expression was feared as a means of triggering conspiracies, internal disorders, wars, revolutions, or some other disastrous train of events that might pull down church and state.

Just as many torts or private wrongs became crimes, or offenses against the king's peace, so too certain libels, once only civilly redressable, became the objects of criminal retribution. As early as 1275 Parliament outlawed "any false news or tales whereby discord or occasion of discord or slander may grow between the king and his people or the great men of the realm . . ." The statute was re-enacted in 1379 for the prevention of the "subversion and destruction of the said realm" by means of false speech.[11]

[11] Van Vechten Veeder, "History of the Law of Defamation," in *Select Essays in Anglo-American Legal History*, comp. and ed. by a Committee of the Association of American Law Schools (Boston, 1909), 3:453–454.

Punishment was to be meted out by the king's council sitting in the "starred chamber." These were the earliest statutes making dangerous utterances a crime, and together with the ecclesiastical laws against heresy and other religious crimes they began the long history of the suppression of opinions deemed pernicious.

The invention of printing, of course, magnified the danger of such opinions. The crown claimed an authority to control printing presses as a right of prerogative. A system for the censorship of heretical manuscripts, long established by the English church and approved by Parliament, was taken over by Henry VIII and soon applied by him to writings on any subject. The manuscript of any work intended for publication had to be submitted to crown officials empowered to censor objectionable passages and to approve or deny a license for the printing of the work. Anything published without an *imprimatur* was criminal. Under Elizabeth the system of prior restraints upon the press was elaborately worked out, with the administration of the complex licensing system divided between three crown agencies: the Stationers Company, a guild of master publishers chartered to monopolize the presses and vested with extraordinary powers of search and seizure; the Court of High Commission, the highest ecclesiastical tribunal, which controlled the Stationers Company and did the actual licensing; and the Court of Star Chamber which issued the decrees defining criminal matter and shared with the Court of High Commission jurisdiction over the trial of offenders. The agencies for enforcement changed during the Puritan Revolution, but the licensing system continued. Under the Restoration, the system was based principally on an act of Parliament, rather than royal prerogative; it con-

tinued until 1694.[12] But the expiration of the system at
that time did not remotely mean that the press had become
free. It was still subject to the restraints of the common
law.

One might publish without a license, but he did so at
the peril of being punished for libel. The point of departure for the modern law of criminal libels was Sir Edward
Coke's report of a Star Chamber case of 1606, in which the
following propositions were stated. A libel against a private
person might be punished criminally on the theory that it
provokes revenge and therefore tends, however remotely,
to a breach of the peace. But a libel against a government
official is an even greater offense "for it concerns not only
the breach of the peace, but also the scandal of government . . ."[13] The essence of the crime as fixed by the
medieval statutes was the falsity of the libel, but the Star
Chamber ruled in 1606 that truth or falsity was not material, and ruled too that the common-law courts also possessed jurisdiction over criminal libels.

Four major classes of criminal libel emerged from subsequent decisions in the common-law courts. Blasphemous
libel, together with laws against heresy and the establishment of a state church, made freedom of expression on matters of religion a risk. The law of obscene or immoral libel
crimped literary, artistic, and other forms of personal expression. So did the law of private libel which protected

[12] For an excellent discussion of the licensing system from its
origins in England to its demise in 1694, see Fredrick S. Siebert,
Freedom of the Press in England, 1476–1776 (Urbana, 1952), chs.
2–3, 6–12.

[13] *De Libellis Famosis,* 3 Coke's *Reports* 254 (1606), quoted in
Sir James Fitzjames Stephen, *A History of the Criminal Law of
England* (London, 1883), 2:304–305.

individual reputations by making possible civil suits for
damages; but a private libel could also be prosecuted by
the state to prevent supposed bad tendencies to a breach
of the peace. By far the most repressive class of libel, however, was seditious libel. It can be defined in a quite elaborate and technical manner in order to take into account
the malicious or criminal intent of the accused, the bad
tendency of his remarks, and their truth or falsity. But the
crime has never been satisfactorily defined, the necessary
result of its inherent vagueness. Seditious libel has always
been an accordion-like concept. Judged by actual prosecutions, the crime consisted of criticizing the government:
its form, constitution, officers, laws, symbols, conduct,
policies, and so on. In effect, any comment about the government which could be construed to have the bad tendency of lowering it in the public's esteem or of disturbing
the peace was seditious libel, subjecting the speaker or
writer to criminal prosecution.

Underlying the concept of seditious libel was the notion,
expressed by Chief Justice Holt in Tuchin's case (1704),
that "a reflection on the government" must be punished because, "If people should not be called to account for possessing the people with an ill opinion of the government,
no government can subsist. For it is very necessary for all
governments that the people should have a good opinion of
it." [14] Through the seventeenth century, certain seditious
libels which were construed as revealing an intention to
"compass" or imagine the death of the king were punished
as treason. In 1663, for example, William Twyn, for printing a book that endorsed the right of revolution, was held
to have compassed the king's death; Twyn was sentenced

[14] Rex v. Tuchin, Howell's *State Trials*, 14:1095, 1128 (1704),
quoted in Stephen, *History of the Criminal Law in England*, 2:318.

to be hanged, cut down while still alive, and then emasculated, disemboweled, quartered, and beheaded — the standard punishment for treason.[15] Algernon Sidney also paid the penalty for treason; his offense was the writing of an unpublished treatise on government discovered in his study.[16] Treason as a purely verbal crime, unconnected with some overt act beyond the words themselves, died out after the execution of Mathews in 1720, convicted under a special statute rather than at common law.[17] Utterances once held to be treasonable became wholly assimilated within the concept of seditious libel. As a lesser crime or misdemeanor, seditious libel was punished less severely: by imprisonment, fines, the pillory, and whipping. But prosecution for seditious libel became the government's principal instrument for controlling the press; according to Professor Siebert's excellent study of freedom of the press in England, "convictions for seditious libel ran into the hundreds" in both the seventeenth and eighteenth centuries.[18]

[15] Rex v. Twyn, Howell's *State Trials*, 6:513, 536 (1663).
[16] Rex v. Sidney, Howell's *State Trials*, 9:818 (1683), discussed by Stephen, *History of the Criminal Law in England*, 2:409–411.
[17] Rex v. Mathews, Howell's *State Trials*, 15:1323 (1719).
[18] Siebert, *Freedom of the Press*, p. 365. Siebert's estimate of the number of eighteenth-century convictions for seditious libel is probably exaggerated. Referring to the period 1700–1730, he says at p. 382, "Only occasionally was it necessary for the government to crack the whip of seditious libel to remind printers and publishers of their proper function." Of the period 1730–1760, he says at p. 381, that it "witnessed the beginning of the revolt of juries and the failure of prosecutions. . . ." A conviction in 1754 he describes as "the first to be obtained from a London jury in twenty-seven years." (*Ibid.*, p. 383.) There was a wide disparity between the number of informations filed for seditious libel and the actual number of prosecutions; there was also a disparity between the number of prosecutions and the actual number of convictions. The number of informations undoubtedly "ran into the hundreds." Being arrested, called into court, and forced to pay costs on the

The procedure in prosecuting a seditious libel was even more objectionable, in the minds of the libertarian theorists, than the fact that the accused could be punished for words alone.[19] From 1662 until a century later the secretary of state possessed the power of ferreting out seditious libels by issuing warrants which authorized a search of the homes and offices of all suspects and the arrest of anyone on the mere suspicion of being implicated in the writing, publishing, or circulation of such libels. General warrants, whose use was severely restricted in felony cases, were employed promiscuously in cases of seditious libel, a misdemeanor. Search, seizure, and arrest were used as a means of harassing antiadministration writers and editors against whom the evidence might not warrant a trial. But the government was not restricted to trying only those indicted or presented by a grand jury. The attorney-general might proceed against all misdemeanors by an information, that is, by determining the libelous character of a publication, bringing it to the attention of the Court of the King's Bench, and securing a warrant for the arrest and trial of the offender. Prosecuting by information rather than by indict-

dismissal of the information could have an intimidating effect even if the prosecution proceeded no further. Convictions, in other words, were not necessary for the law of seditious libel to operate oppressively.

[19] My account of the law of seditious libel and the procedure of prosecution is based on a great number of the tracts and books discussed in Chapters Three and Four. Particularly useful were [Anon.], *State Law: Or, the Doctrine of Libels, Discussed and Examined* (London, n.d., [1729], 2nd ed.), 136 pp.; [John Raynor], *A Digest of the Law concerning Libels. By a Gentleman of the Inner-Temple* (Dublin, 1778), 139 pp.; and Father of Candor, *A Letter Concerning Libels, Warrants, the Seizure of Papers, and Sureties for the Peace of Behaviour* (London, 1771, 7th ed.), reprinted in *A Collection of Interesting Political Tracts* (probably edited by J. Almon) (London, 1773), 1:1–164.

ment bypassed the Englishman's beloved institution, the grand jury, which in felony cases stood between him and the government. At the trial of a seditious libel, the defendant was not even judged by his peers in any meaningful way. Despite the ambiguity of earlier practice the judges in the eighteenth century permitted juries to decide only the fact of the publication. That is, the only question which the jury passed upon was whether the defendant did or did not publish the remarks charged against him and whether they carried the innuendo as alleged. The judges reserved exclusively for themselves as a matter of law the decision on the crucial question whether the defendant's remarks were maliciously intended and of a bad tendency. The judges also refused to permit the defendant to plead the truth as a defense. Indeed, they proceeded on the theory that the truth of a libel made it even worse because it was more provocative, thereby increasing the tendency to breach of the peace or exacerbating the scandal against the government. As a result of these rules applicable to criminal or crown libels, a man might be arrested on a general warrant, prosecuted on an information without the consent of a grand jury, and convicted for his political opinions by judges appointed by the government he had aspersed.

Thus the disappearance of the prior restraints which had been imposed by the licensing system until 1694 did not meaningfully free the press. Theoretically one might say or print what he pleased, but he was responsible to the common law for allegedly malicious, scurrilous, scandalous, or derogatory utterances which supposedly tended towards the contempt, ridicule, hatred, scorn, or disrepute of other persons, religion, government, or morality. Blackstone, the oracle of the common law in the minds of the American Framers, summarized the law of crown libels as follows:

where blasphemous, immoral, treasonable, schismatical, seditious, or scandalous libels are punished by the English law
. . . the liberty of the press, properly understood, is by no
means infringed or violated. The *liberty of the press* is indeed essential to the nature of a free state; but this consists
in laying no *previous* restraints upon publications, and not
in freedom from censure for criminal matter when published. Every freeman has an undoubted right to lay what
sentiments he pleases before the public: to forbid this is to
destroy the freedom of the press: but if he publishes what
is improper, mischievous, or illegal, he must take the consequences of his own temerity. . . . But to punish (as the
law does at present) any dangerous or offensive writings,
which, when published, shall on a fair and impartial trial [20]
be adjudged of a pernicious tendency, is necessary for the
preservation of peace and good order, a government and
religion, the only solid foundations of civil liberty. Thus the
will of individuals is still left free; the abuse only of that
free-will is the object of legal punishment. Neither is any
restraint hereby laid upon freedom of thought or enquiry:
liberty of private sentiment is still left; the disseminating, or
making public, of bad sentiments, destructive of the ends of
society, is the crime which society corrects.[21]

The common law's definition of freedom of the press
meant merely the absence of censorship in advance of pub-

[20] Blackstone's endorsement of a "fair and impartial" trial was
meaningless to the libertarians of the time, since he explicitly
repudiated one of their two major gauges of fairness, the right of
the defendant to prove the truth of his alleged libel; moreover,
Blackstone ignored the other libertarian gauge of fairness at a
time when it was the principal issue of contention: the right of
the jury rather than of the judge to decide the criminality of the
alleged libel.

[21] Sir William Blackstone, *Commentaries on the Laws of England*
(London, 1765–1769), Book 4, ch. 11, pp. 151–152; or, in the 18th
ed., which I used (New York, 1836), 2:112–113.

lication. But the presence of punishment afterwards, for "bad sentiments," oral or published, had an effect similar to a law authorizing previous restraints. A man who may be whipped and jailed for what he says or prints is not likely to feel free to express his opinions even if he does not need a government license to do so. The common-law definition of freedom of the press left the press at the mercy of the crown's prosecutors and judges. Freedom of discussion and the law of libel were simply incompatible; the first could not coexist with the second.

Speech and press were restrained by Parliament as well as by the common-law courts. Both Lords and Commons combined the functions of prosecutor, judge, and jury, with the result that prosecutions before either House could be more effective than in the courts. In the Woodfall case, for example, the defendant, prosecuted on an information for seditious libel, was saved from a conviction when the jury returned a verdict of "guilty of printing and publishing *only*"; but the Commons, prosecuting him in 1774 for the same offense, imprisoned him and exacted costs of seventy-two pounds.[22] Theoretically Parliament did not prosecute for the common-law crime of libel; its punitive powers were directed against contempt of its authority or reputation by a breach of its privileges. In practice, however, the distinction between a verbal contempt, breaching parliamentary privilege, and the crime of seditious libel could be negligible.

"Parliamentary privilege" was an omnibus term that referred to a bundle of rights which each House claimed and exercised.[23] Among these were freedom from arrest,

[22] Rex. v. Woodfall, Howell's *State Trials*, 20:895 (1770), and Siebert, *Freedom of the Press*, pp. 371–372.

[23] See, generally, Mary Patterson Clarke, *Parliamentary Privilege in the American Colonies* (New Haven, 1943), and Carl Wittke,

access to the executive, passing on the credentials of members, freedom of speech, and the power of punishing both members and nonmembers for violations of privileges. The English Bill of Rights of 1689 secured to members their freedom of speech, after a century-long struggle begun by the Wentworths under Elizabeth and highlighted by the martyrdom of Sir John Eliot. After 1689 the problem was not that Parliament's free speech was infringed, but that Parliament did not permit freedom of speech to nonmembers. The unauthorized reporting of parliamentary proceedings was prohibited. Reflections on either House or any of its members or on the government generally, in other words, seditious libels, were subject to prosecution by the House itself. The guilty parties were summoned, examined, and tried in a summary fashion; their criminal publications were burned by the hangman at the order of the house, the party humiliated, usually on his knees, and forced to pay costs. He could also be imprisoned indefinitely by the Lords, but only for the life of the session by the Commons. Commons and Lords, writes Professor Siebert, after about 1730 were the "principal deterrents to free and open discussion of political questions through the power to punish a printer for what today would be considered harmless discussions of public issues. . . . All in all, Parliament seems to have exerted almost as great a pressure on printers and publishers in the eighteenth century as did the common-law courts." [24] In the colonies, the assemblies were a far greater

---

The History of English Parliamentary Privilege (Columbus, Ohio State University Bulletin, vol. 26, no. 2, 1921).

[24] Siebert, *Freedom of the Press,* p. 368. But in the last quarter of the eighteenth century, Parliament "quietly abdicated its functions as a prosecutor and judge of seditious libels in favor of the attorney general and common-law courts." (*Ibid.,* p. 374.)

menace to freedom of discussion than the common-law courts.[25]

Prosecutions for breach of parliamentary privilege and for criminal utterances certainly fettered speech and press, but could not suppress criticism of the government. In England and her colonies, the king's subjects were so interested in politics and so convinced by their glorious, if largely rhetorical, traditions of freedom that an astonishing degree of discussion existed, considering the restraints. The law in the books and the law in life, it must always be remembered, were not the same. Even a flurry of actual prosecutions could have only a lingering rather than an enduring effect, as in the case of persecution for the cause of conscience. Nevertheless it would be an exaggeration to say that speech and press were free as a matter of common experience, although fettered by the law. It would be closer to the truth to say that freedom of speech and press was so little known that even libertarian theory regarded the right to express seditious sentiments as an intolerable indulgence in licentiousness.

[25] This point is largely the subject of Chapter Two, below.

❧ The American Colonial Experience

The persistent image of colonial America as a society in which freedom of expression was cherished is an hallucination of sentiment that ignores history. The evidence provides little comfort for the notion that the colonies hospitably received advocates of obnoxious or detestable ideas on matters that counted. Nor is there reason to believe that rambunctious unorthodoxies suffered only from Puritan bigots and tyrannous royal judges. The American people simply did not understand that freedom of thought and expression means equal freedom for the other fellow, especially the one with hated ideas.

To be sure, the utmost freedom often existed on the frontier, but the test of free speech is not the right of a man to soliloquize or shout his outrageous ideas from the top of a lonely mountain; it is, rather, his right to speak openly and with impunity among his neighbors. Colonial America was the scene of the most extraordinary diversity of opinion on religion, politics, social structure, and other vital subjects, but every community, particularly outside of the few "cities," tended to be a tight little island clutching its own respective orthodoxy and too eager to banish or extralegally punish unwelcome dissidents. As John P. Roche says so strikingly, "Colonial America was an open society dotted with closed enclaves, and one could generally settle with his co-believers in safety and comfort and exercise the right of oppression." [1]

Where vigorously expressed nonconformist opinions were suffered to exist by the community, they were likely to run afoul of the law. In colonial America, as in England, the common law of criminal libel was strung out like a chicken wire of constraint against the captious and the chancy, making the open discussion of public issues hazardous, if not impossible, except when public opinion opposed administration policy. However, the judiciary in America, particularly in the eighteenth century, was not the agency that menaced those who would disturb an acquiescent public opinion. It is an old saw, of course, and an inaccurate one, that "Colonial times were rife with a continuing struggle between the royal judges and American writers and printers, who demanded freedom to criticize. . . ." [2] There may have been hundreds of trials for seditious libel in England during both the seventeenth and eighteenth centuries, but in America before the Revolution, the number was insignificant, probably not more than half a dozen. The notoriety of the Zenger trial derives in part because it was so isolated a phenomenon. Except for two other cases, an obscure trial of a New Yorker in 1745 for "singing in

---

[1] Roche, "American Liberty: An Examination of the 'Tradition' of Freedom," in M. R. Konvitz and C. Rossiter, eds., *Aspects of Liberty* (Ithaca, 1958), p. 137.
[2] John Kelly, "Criminal Libel and Free Speech," *Kansas Law Review*, 6:306 (1958).

praise of the Pretender," [3] and a prosecution, ending in an acquittal, at about the same time in South Carolina,[4] the Zenger case was the last of its kind under the royal judges. The traditionally maligned judges were, as a matter of fact, virtually angels of self-restraint when compared with the intolerance of community opinion or the tyranny of the governors who, acting in a quasi-judicial capacity with their Councils, were a much more dreaded and active instrument of suppression than the common-law courts. Yet the most suppressive body by far, surpassing even the prerogative court of governor-and-Council, was that acclaimed bastion of the people's liberties: the popularly elected Assembly. That the law bore down so harshly on verbal crimes in colonial America was the result of the inquisitorial propensities of the nonjudicial branches which vied with each other in ferreting out slights on the government. The law of seditious libel, particularly in the eighteenth century, was enforced in America chiefly by the provincial legislatures exercising their power of punishing alleged breaches of parliamentary privilege, secondly, by the executive officers in concert with the upper houses, and lastly, a poor third, by the common-law courts. The latter gathered a very few seditious scalps and lost as many to acquittals; but the Assemblies, like the House of Commons which they emulated, needing no grand jury to indict and no petty jury to convict, racked up a far larger score.

Zealously pursuing its prerogative of being immune to criticism, an Assembly might summon, interrogate, and fix

[3] Julius Goebel, Jr. and T. Raymond Naughton, *Law Enforcement in Colonial New York* (New York, 1944), p. 99 note 178, citing *MS* Minutes, N. Y. Court of Quarter Sessions, 1732–1762, p. 181.
[4] Isaiah Thomas, *The History of Printing in America* (Worcester, 1810), 2:143–144.

criminal penalties against anyone who had supposedly libeled its members, proceedings, or the government generally. Any words, written, printed, or spoken, which were imagined to have a tendency of impeaching an Assembly's behavior, questioning its authority, derogating from its honor, affronting its dignity, or defaming its members, individually or together, were regarded as a seditious scandal against the government, punishable as a breach of privilege. The historian of *Parliamentary Privilege in the American Colonies* concludes, in guarded understatement, "Literally scores of persons, probably hundreds, throughout the colonies were tracked down by the various messengers and sergeants and brought into the house to make inglorious submission for words spoken in the heat of anger or for writings which intentionally or otherwise had given offense." [5]

The practice began with the first Assembly that ever met on American soil, when the Virginia House of Burgesses, in 1620, adjudged a Captain Henry Spellman guilty of "treasonable words" and stripped him of his rank. [6] Cavalier Virginia simply did not tolerate such nonsense as dissent. Governor Berkeley's often quoted statement of 1671 suggests the attitude of the Old Dominion's government. Replying to a query put to him by the Lords Commissioners of Foreign Plantations on the state of religion, he wrote that it might be better and added, "But, I thank God, there are no free schools nor *printing*, and I hope we shall not have these hundred years; for *learning* has brought disobedience, and heresy, and sects into the

[5] Mary Patterson Clarke, *Parliamentary Privilege in the American Colonies* (New Haven, 1943), p. 117.
[6] H. R. McIlwaine and J. P. Kennedy, eds., *Journals of the House of Burgesses of Virginia, 1619–1776* (Richmond, 1905–1915), vol. 1619–1659, p. 15.

world, and *printing* has divulged them, and libels against the best government. God keep us from both!" [7]

In 1660 the House of Burgesses had committed a man for "scandalous, mutinous, and seditious" words; he had criticized the house on a tax matter.[8] Even a member of the Governor's Council was wise to curb his tongue. Colonel Philip Ludwell, who thoughtlessly called Governor Jeffreys a law-breaker, was convicted and heavily fined in 1678 by his fellow councillors for scandalizing the government.[9] In 1682 a printer named Buckner who had the temerity to publish unlicensed the laws of the colony was forced to post a bond of £100 to be forfeit should he ever print anything in the future.[10] Shortly after, Governor Effingham issued a proclamation condemning the "over lycentious-nesse of the People in their discourses" and reminded the public that any remark tending to sedition was criminal.[11] Since seditious utterances were ordinarily tried before local justices of the peace, there is no way of estimating the frequency of prosecutions. Only cases seriously affecting the state were brought to the Council's attention. One such case occurred in 1699 when the Council deputized one of its members to arrest and subject to "condign punishment" four individuals alleged to have stirred up sedition by spreading an "evill opinion" of the government.[12]

[7] Quoted in William Waller Hening, *The Statutes at Large Being a Collection of All the Laws of Virginia (1619–1792)* (Richmond, 1809–1823), 2:517.

[8] *Ibid.*, 2:15. Case of Edward Prescotte, 1660. For related events of an earlier date, see 1:360–361 and 380.

[9] H. R. McIlwaine and W. L. Hall, eds., *Executive Journals of the Council of Colonial Virginia, 1680–1754* (Richmond, 1925–1945), 1:468–478.

[10] Hening, *Va. Statutes*, 2:518, Proclamation of 12 Oct. 1685.

[11] *Executive Journals of the Council*, 1:75.

[12] *Ibid.*, 1:438.

In neighboring Maryland during the seventeenth century there was as little freedom of expression as in Virginia. In 1689 a disaffected group calling itself the Protestant Association, led by John Coode, who had been tried earlier for seditious speech and blasphemy, revolted against Lord Baltimore's proprietary government. In their declaration of reasons for taking up arms, the rebels specified a grievance which suggests that open political debate had been scotched in Maryland. Referring to harsh laws that had been severely enforced, they singled out "especially one that against all Sense, Equity, Reason, and Law Punishes all Speeches, Practices, and Attempts relating to his Lordship and Government, that shall be thought Mutinous and Seditious. . . ." Among the punishments actually meted out had been "Whipping, Branding, Boreing through the Tongue, Fine, Imprisonment, Banishment, or Death," making unsafe the "Words and Actions" of everyone.[13]

A glance at New York and Pennsylvania indicates that speech and press were as unfree there during the seventeenth century as in the South. Prosecutions for "speaking seditious words" began in New York under the first governor and were continuing at the close of the century. In the case of one Peter Chocke, who had denied the governor's authority and called him the worst in the history of the province, the Quarter Sessions Court of Westchester decided that the "words vented by the said Chocke" were so "highly Criminall" as to warrant being tried by the

[13] "The Declaration of the Reasons and Motives for the Present Appearing in Arms of Their Majesties Protestant Subjects In the Province of Maryland," 1689, in Charles M. Andrews, ed., *Narratives of the Insurrections, 1675–1690* (New York, 1915), p. 309. For a few illustrative cases of prosecution against speech, see William Hand Brown, *et al.*, eds., *Archives of Maryland* (Baltimore, 1883–1952), 2:55; 4:309 and 321; 65:15–16.

highest court of the province.[14] The press, of course, was
rigorously restrained by prior censorship. Until the appointment of Governor Burnet, in 1719, every governor
from Dongan's time had been instructed to permit no press,
book, pamphlets, or other printed matter "without your
especial leave & license first obtained." [15]

In 1685, three years after the first settlement under Penn's
proprietorship, John Curtis of Philadelphia was prosecuted
for "speaking treasonable words." [16] A year later began
Pennsylvania's troubles with its first printer, William Bradford. His initial publication, an almanac, was censored
while still in manuscript, and he was warned "not to print
anything but what shall have Lycence from ye Councill." [17]
Penn himself had presided over a Council meeting in 1683
when it was ordered that the laws of the colony should not
be printed.[18] In 1689, Bradford found himself in trouble
for having printed at the request of Joseph Growdon, a
councillor, a copy of the "Frame of Government" of 1682,
with comments by Growdon. The latter, on being interrogated by Governor Blackwell at a session of the Council,
refused, even under threat of censure, to answer any questions concerning the unlicensed publication "of a dangerous
nature." [19] Blackwell, knowing Bradford to be the printer,

[14] Goebel and Naughton, *Law Enforcement in New York*, p. 152.
For other references to cases of seditious speech, see p. 62 notes 12
and 13, and p. 99 note 178.

[15] "Instructions to Governor Dongan," 1686, in E. B. O'Callaghan
and B. Fernow, eds., *Documents Relative to the Colonial History
of the State of New York* (Albany, 1856–1887), 3:375. See also
5:142.

[16] David Paul Brown, *The Forum: Or, Forty Years Full Practice
at the Philadelphia Bar* (Philadelphia, 1856), 1:267.

[17] *Minutes of the Provincial Council of Pennsylvania* (Harrisburg, 1838–1840), 1:115.

[18] *Ibid.*, 1:18.

[19] *Ibid.*, 1:278.

for there were no others south of Boston, summoned him next, only to find him as intractable as Councillor Growdon. Repeatedly invoking the common-law privilege against self-incrimination, as had Growdon, Bradford resisted the governor's alternating cajolery and threats. At one point the suspect stated that he knew of no one's having been appointed Imprimatur, whereupon Blackwell burst out, "Sir, I am 'Imprimatur'; and that you shall know." A moment later he added, "Sir, I have particular order from Governor Penn for the suppressing of printing here, and narrowly to look after your press, and I will search your house, look after your press, and make you give in five hundred pounds security to print nothing but what I allow, or I'll lay you fast." [20] Whether Bradford was forced to post bond in so high an amount is unknown, but he was sufficiently discouraged to give up and return to England. Shortly, however, he was back in Pennsylvania. A year later, his press seized by the government, he was in jail, charged with seditious libel and awaiting trial as a defendant in what was probably the first criminal trial in America involving freedom of the press. [21]

[20] "The examination of William Bradford before Governor Blackwell, att Philadelphia, the 9th of the Second month, 1689, concerning printing the Charter," Framed *MS* hung in hall of New York Historical Society. Reprinted in Brown, *The Forum*, 1:276–279, and in John William Wallace, *An Address Delivered at the Celebration by the New York Historical Society, May 20, 1863, of the Two Hundredth Birth Day of Mr. William Bradford* (Albany, 1863), pp. 49–52. No record of the examination appears in the *Minutes of the Provincial Council of Pennsylvania*.

[21] Matt Bushnell Jones, *Thomas Maule, The Salem Quaker and Free Speech in Massachusetts Bay* (Salem, 1936, 42 pp.; reprinted from Essex Institute Historical Collections, vol. 72, no. 1, January 1936), p. 13, mistakenly claims that Maule's trial of 1696, reviewed below, p. 32, was "the first criminal action involving freedom of the press to be tried in the American colonies." In all likelihood

Bradford had supported a separatist faction among the Quakers led by George Keith, whose heretical views caused his dismissal as headmaster of the Friends' school in Philadelphia. Forbidden to speak at Quaker meetings, he and a follower, Thomas Budd, publicized their position through a number of tracts published by Bradford although without his name on them. In one of these, *An Appeal from the twenty-eight Judges to the Spirit of Truth*, Keith predicted that the name of Deputy Governor Thomas Lloyd "would stink"; he also contended that ministers should not be magistrates and accused them of monopolizing the magisterial power. As a result, Keith, Budd, Bradford, and several of their faction were arrested. The warrant for their commitment alleged their guilt for "Publishing, Uttering, & Spreading a Malitious and Seditious paper . . . Tending to the Disturbance of the Peace and Subversion of the present Government." [22] The prisoners were summarily convicted "without All Hearing or Tryal" by a court composed of eight magistrates, six of whom were the very ministers accused by Keith. He and the other defendants, excepting Bradford and a MacComb who had circulated the tract, were sentenced to humiliation in the public

---

there were probably similar trials, as yet unknown, before Bradford's. As a matter of fact, there were much earlier trials, such as Wheelwright's in 1637, mentioned below, p. 30, involving freedom of speech, as contrasted with freedom of the press, but raising the same broad issues.

[22] The characterization of Lloyd is at p. 6 and the warrant, dated Aug. 24, 1692, is reproduced at p. 4 of *New England's Spirit of Persecution Transmitted to Pennsylvania, And the Pretended Quaker found Persecuting the True Christian-Quaker, in the Tryal of Peter Boss, George Keith, Thomas Budd and William Bradford . . . 1693. Giving an Account of the most Arbitrary Procedure of that Court* (Philadelphia, 1693, printed by William Bradford), 38 pp. Ascribed to George Keith and Thomas Budd.

market place, there to be proclaimed by the common crier as seditious persons, disturbers of the peace, subverters of the government, and enemies to the king.[23] Bradford and MacComb escaped sentence by demanding their rights under Magna Carta to a trial by jury. The judges reluctantly consented, although one of them observed that the prisoners deserved to have their backs lashed instead.[24]

After four months in jail, Bradford came to trial. Keith and his associates were also defendants, new presentments having been made against them for the same tracts under a statute prohibiting defamation of the magistrates. Tried separately, after the others were convicted and fined five pounds each, Bradford managed his case with considerable skill and daring. He immediately challenged two of the jurors on the ground of having prejudged his case since they had been overheard expressing the opinion that the pro-Keith faction were enemies of the government. One of the two jurors, acknowledging the statement attributed to him, requested to be discharged, but the court, the same Quaker magistrates who had presided at the earlier stage of the case, refused. The prosecutor then demanded of Bradford whether he had ever heard any of the jurors say that he had printed the seditious tract, "for that is only what they are to find." [25] In reply, Bradford, for the first time in an American libel trial, raised the contention that the jury was to try the whole of the matter, the criminality of the publication as well as the defendant's responsibility for it.

> Bradford. "That is not only what they are to find, they are to find also, whether this be a seditious paper, or not, &

[23] Proclamation read by the crier, *ibid.*, p. 6.
[24] *Ibid.*, p. 10.
[25] *Ibid.*, p. 33. The trials were held Dec. 6–10, 1692.

whether it does tend to the weakening of the hands of the Magistrate."

Attorney. "No, that is matter of Law, which the Jury is not to meddle with, but find whether W. B. printed it or not, and the Bench is to judge whether it be a seditious Paper or not; for the Law has determined what is a Breach of the Peace, and the penalty, which the Bench only is to give judgment on."

Judge Jennings. "You are only to try, whether W. B. printed it, or not."

Bradford. "That is wrong; for the Jury are Judges in Law, as well as in matter of Fact." [26]

Unable to get a favorable ruling from the court, Bradford continued his own defense, arguing that the tract had not been seditious and that there was no evidence to show that he had been the printer. When the prosecution introduced the frame or form containing the pages set in type, which the sheriff had seized in Bradford's office, the printer demanded that evidence be adduced to prove he had set the type. Thus, Bradford's defense, unlike the later Zenger defense, did not rest on an admission of his responsibility for printing, conterbalanced by a claim that he had a right to print what he pleased if truthful. In other words, the charge of seditious printing raised an issue of freedom of the press which was not argued.

Judge Jennings, in instructing the jury, surprisingly accepted Bradford's point that they might find whether the tract was seditious as well as the fact of his responsibility.[27] The jury deadlocked at nine to three for a conviction, and after forty-eight hours were discharged without having

[26] *Ibid.*, pp. 33–34. Page 33 is misnumbered as p. 31 in the rare tract reporting the trial.
[27] *Ibid.*, p. 36.

reached a verdict. There is a story that Bradford was saved
by a sympathetic juror who, while examining the type-
form that was used to print the tract, accidentally shoved
the bottom of the form with his cane, whereupon it came
apart and all the type collapsed to the floor, and with it, the
prosecution's case.[28]

Bradford asked the court for a release from prison with
his printing tools restored, but he was recommitted to
await a new trial. After about a year had passed from the
time of his arrest, he was suddenly released without a second trial. His rescuer was Governor Fletcher of New York,
who, on the suspension of Penn's charter, had been given
control of Pennsylvania. Fletcher, needing an official press
in New York, prevailed upon the Pennsylvania Council to
restore Bradford's liberty and property,[29] and he promptly
left the City of Brotherly Love for a new career as a royal
printer. In his new home, he established the *New-York
Gazette*, which was the province's only newspaper until
the appearance in 1733 of Zenger's *Journal*. Chastened by
his experiences in Pennsylvania, Bradford allowed his paper
to be a licensed administration organ. When Zenger was
prosecuted for seditious libel, old William Bradford condemned him for having published "pieces tending to set the
province in a flame, and to raise sedition and tumults." [30]
Bradford may have been the first American martyr to the
cause of a free press and the earliest advocate of the jury's
power to decide the law in libel cases; but there is nothing

[28] Brown, *The Forum*, 1:282 and Wallace, *An Address*, pp. 56–57,
both relying on Thomas, *History of Printing in America*, 2:12.
The only primary source for the case, *New England's Spirit of
Persecution*, does not mention this incident.
[29] *Minutes of the Provincial Council of Pennsylvania*, 1:326–327.
[30] Quoted in Thomas, *History of Printing in America*, 2:97.

in his career of consistently failing to champion freedom of the press that justifies awarding him the palm as a doughty exponent of the cause for which he once suffered.

The absence of freedom of speech, especially on religious subjects, in seventeenth-century Massachusetts is so familiar a fact that a mere reminder should suffice. Beginning in 1635 when the legislature, sitting as a court, banished Roger Williams for the crime of disseminating "newe & dangerous opinions, against the aucthoritie [*sic*] of magistrates," [31] the government kept busy by punishing dissidents for sedition, heresy, or both. Between 1637 and 1647, John Wheelwright, Anne Hutchinson, a half-dozen or more of their Antinomian followers, Peter Hobart and others involved in the Hingham affair, Robert Child and his six associates, and Samuel Gorton were all convicted for seditious sermons, petitions, or remonstrances against the civil authority.[32] In 1652, William Pynchon, an assistant, by escaping to England missed the distinction of being the first person to be prosecuted for opinions expressed in print.

[31] Nathaniel B. Shurtleff, ed., *Records of the Governor and Company of the Massachusetts Bay in New England (1628–86)* (Boston, 1853–1854), 1:160.

[32] For a convenient compilation of the original sources concerning all those named but Gorton, see Mark DeWolfe Howe, ed., *Readings in American Legal History* (Cambridge, Mass., 1949), pp. 144–179 and 189–208, especially pp. 148–153, 157, 164, 179, 190, 197, and 202. The original sources on Gorton are Edward Winslow, *Hypocrasie Unmasked, A True Relation of the Proceedings of the Governor and Company of the Massachusetts Bay against Samuel Gorton of Rhode Island* (1646), ed. Howard Millar Chapin (Providence, 1916); and Gorton's "Simplicities Defence against Seven-Headed Policy" (1646), in Peter Force, ed., *Tracts and Other Papers Relating Principally to the Origin . . . of the Colonies in North America* (New York, 1947 ed.), vol. 4, no. 6. John Winthrop, *The History of New England from 1630 to 1649*, ed. James Savage (Boston, 1853), has data on all the cases.

His tract, which had been licensed in England, was adjudged "erronyous and hereticale" by the legislature, which commanded it to be burned by the public executioner.[33] There had been several earlier cases of unpublished manuscript works having been censored or burned.[34] In 1654, the respected first president of Harvard, Henry Dunster, was indicted by a grand jury and convicted for breaching the peace by delivering a sermon on infant baptism.[35] He was the first person prosecuted under common-law process for a religious speech. In 1661, the legislature humiliated another distinguished person, John Eliot, by forcing him to retract "such expressions as doe too manifestly scandalize the goument [*sic*] of England," and ordered his book, *The Christian Commonwealth*, which advocated that rulers should be elected, to be "totally suppressed."[36] The government's persecutions of the Baptists and Quakers that began in the 1650's and lasted through the century were religiously inspired but legally grounded in part on the victims' censure of the government and their tendency to disturb the peace, which was synonymous with seditious utterance.[37] John Wise, "the first great American democrat," with five associates who were named, plus an unspecified number of others identified only as "evil minded and disaffected persons," were tried and convicted for seditious libel in 1687. They had seditiously brought the king's government into hatred and contempt

[33] Clyde Augustus Duniway, *The Development of Freedom of the Press in Massachusetts* (New York, 1906), pp. 32–33.

[34] *Ibid.*, pp. 19, 20, 24, and 29, for the cases of Stoughton, Smyth, Lechford, and Saltonstall.

[35] *Ibid.*, pp. 34–35.

[36] *Ibid.*, pp. 38–39.

[37] See, *e.g.*, the statute of 1656 against the Quakers, quoted in Peleg W. Chandler, ed., *American Criminal Trials* (Boston, 1844), 1:35 and the discussion therein following.

in the minds of the people by daring to declare that a tax
not levied by the Assembly was contrary to Magna Carta
and did not have to be paid. Wise's punishment was suspension from the ministry, a fine of fifty pounds, and the posting of a bond in the extravagant sum of one thousand
pounds to guarantee his good behavior for a year.[38]

One Massachusetts case deserving more extended notice
is that of Thomas Maule, the irascible Quaker merchant of
Salem who has been credited as having won the "first victory for freedom of the press in America. . . ."[39] Maule in
1695 published a book, licensed and printed in New York,
which was so aspersive a commentary on the civil and ecclesiastical rulers of Massachusetts that he was promptly
arrested for "wicked Lyes and Slanders . . . upon Government, and likewise divers corrupt and pernicious Doctrines utterly subversive of the true Christian religion and
professed faith."[40] The sheriff seized all available copies of
his book, and Maule was brought before the lieutenant-governor and Council in Boston "who," he wrote, "put divers
Insnaring Questions to said *Maule*," which he refused to
answer.[41] The Council ordered his books to be burned but
conceded to his demand that he be tried by a jury of his
peers in his own county. His bond, however, was placed

---

[38] "Proceedings Agt. Wise and Others of Ipswich for Misdemeanors," in Robert Noxon Toppan, ed., *Edward Randolph*
(Boston, 1898–1909), 4:171–182. For the phrase characterizing
Wise, see Clinton Rossiter, *Seedtime of the Republic* (New York,
1953), pp. 206 and 225.

[39] Jones, *Thomas Maule*, p. 25.

[40] Theo. Philanthes [Thomas Maule], *New-England Persecutors
Mauld With their own Weapons . . . Together with a brief Account of the Imprisonment and Tryal of Thomas Maule of Salem,
for publishing a Book, entitled, Truth held forth and maintained,
&c.* (New York, 1697, 62 pp.), p. 53.

[41] *Ibid.*, p. 55.

at an astronomical figure, thereby insuring his safekeeping
in jail. Conducting his own defense in a most aggressive
manner before three judges, all members of the Council,
Maule repeated in court the bitter charges he had made in
his book. When he was interrupted by one of the judges
who denounced him as a "horrible Lyar" and admonished
him to silence, he declared fearlessly that he spoke only the
truth and did not fear their punishments since he had been
imprisoned on five former occasions and twice whipped.[42]
His statements in court caused a postponement of the trial
so that he might be reindicted for verbal crimes against the
judges in addition to his published libels.

In late 1696, after nearly a year in jail from the time of
his arrest, he was finally tried. The presiding judge asked
the jury to return a verdict of guilty on ground that the
defendant's book tended to the overthrow of the Commonwealth and the church. Maule, in his defense, said nothing
about freedom of the press. Instead, he made a technically
adroit attack on the insufficiency of the evidence against
him, combined with a clever appeal to the jury's emotional
reaction against the recent witchcraft trials with which he
compared the case against him. He concluded, like Bradford had at his trial, by calling upon the jury to decide the
law over the heads of the judges, his accusers.[43] The jury,
much to the court's dismay, returned a verdict of not guilty.
The foreman, when asked to explain the verdict, declared
that the jury believed that the prosecution should have been
an ecclesiastical rather than a civil affair, a matter to be
decided by a "Jury of divines." [44] Neither the arguments of
defense nor the jury's explanation of the verdict turned on

[42] *Ibid.*, pp. 56–57.
[43] *Ibid.*, pp. 51–62.
[44] *Ibid.*, p. 62.

a regard for freedom of the press. Though this was the first criminal trial in Massachusetts for a printed libel and has been hailed as a precursor of the Zenger case, the participants regarded the cause as a matter of conscience rather than that of a free press. This case and the others which have been reviewed indicate that liberty of expression in principle or practice barely existed, if at all, in the American colonies during the seventeenth century.

By 1763, the situation was substantially unchanged but for the disappearance of the licensing system. A continuation of the case of Massachusetts will illustrate. In 1719 when the governor was still empowered to exercise prior censorship, John Checkley, the most prominent Anglican minister in the Bay Colony, was prevented from publishing a tract critical of Calvinist doctrines.[45] The legislature then enacted a statute, aimed at Checkley, compelling any person "suspected to be disaffected to his Majesty or to his Government" to swear an oath of loyalty. Checkley refused the oath on grounds of conscience and a resentment against being the only person singled out, without any act of disloyalty on his part. For his contumacy he was convicted in 1720, fined six pounds, and bound to good behavior.[46] After a stay in England, Checkley returned to Boston with a stock of his writings defending episcopacy, including the book which he had been forbidden to publish in 1719. The Council declared that the book reflected on the ministers of the Commonwealth and contained "sundry vile insinuations against His Majestys rightfull and lawfull authority & the constitution of the Government of Great Britain." He was indicted in 1724 for having libel-

[45] Duniway, *Freedom of the Press*, pp. 84–86.
[46] Edmund F. Slafter, *John Checkley; or the Evolution of Religious Tolerance in Massachusetts Bay* (Boston, 1897), 1:34–37.

ously published "false Seditious & wicked words," convicted, and fined fifty pounds. On appeal to the Superior Court of Judicature, he was quickly retried and convicted again. The jury returned only a special verdict, finding that he had published the book; the court, reserving to itself determination of its criminality, ruled as a matter of law that Checkley had published a seditious libel. He was fined fifty pounds and costs and obligated to post a bond of double that sum for his future good behavior.[47]

Several printers at about this time were hounded by the government, reminding critics that the indefinable line between liberty of the press and licentiousness made discretion the better part of safety. John Colman in 1720 published a tract on the reasons for the economic distress of the province, with the result that the governor and Council ordered his arrest and prosecution on ground that the tract contained many passages "reflecting upon the Acts & Laws of the Province, & other proceedings of the Government and has a Tendency to Disturb the Administration of the Government, as well as the Publick Peace."[48] The prosecution was dropped without explanation after Colman had been harassed by the necessity of court appearances and the posting of bonds.

A similar incident involved Benjamin Gray the next year when he published an unlicensed tract arguing for bills of credit. The Council voted that he had employed "many Vile, Scandalous, and very Abusive Expressions" reflecting on the government and ordered his prosecution."[49] This time, however, the Council did not proceed by an informa-

[47] *Ibid.*, 1:56–66. The case is also reviewed by Duniway, *Freedom of the Press*, pp. 107–110 and 166–171, and Thomas, *History of Printing in America*, 2:427–428.
[48] Duniway, *Freedom of the Press*, p. 92.
[49] Thomas, *History of Printing in America*, 2:425.

tion, as in Colman's case; it trusted a grand jury to return an indictment, but the jurors, upon hearing Gray's contrite expressions of sorrow for his misdeed and his allegations that he had not intended to affront the government, found no true bill.[50]

It was at this time, 1721, that effective censorship by licensing ended in Massachusetts. Governor Shute, disturbed about the growing licentiousness of the press, attempted to obtain from the General Court endorsement of his instructions from the king that no printed matter be permitted without his prior license. The House, however, rejected the proposed censorship law, though not because of any solicitude for freedom of the press. In their reply to the governor, the representatives agreed that seditious libel should meet with condign punishment, but chided the executive for having permitted libels against the House. It is clear from the House's reply that it rejected the proposed legislation because to have vested the executive with an exclusive licensing power might have made it difficult for the representatives to publish before the people their own criticisms of his policies. Although freedom of the press benefited from this blow against the licensing system, the House was motivated only by a desire to strengthen its own position against executive domination.[51]

The final attempt to enforce prior restraints in Massachusetts ended in failure in 1723. James Franklin of Boston, who founded the unlicensed *New England Courant* and made it a vehicle of political and religious satire, was the unwilling hero of the episode. In 1722, when his paper was less than a year old, he ran a brief notice that the government was outfitting a ship to go after coastal pirates "some-

[50] Duniway, *Freedom of the Press*, p. 94.
[51] *Ibid.*, pp. 94–96.

time this month, wind and weather permitting." The in-
sinuation that effective action was not being adopted as
speedily as possible was galling to the General Court. The
Council promptly arrested him and after a *pro forma* hearing resolved that he had committed "a High affront to this
Government"; whereupon the House, concurring, ordered
his immediate imprisonment for the remaining month of
the legislative session. This summary punishment was a
striking instance of the exercise of parliamentary privilege,
a legislative revenge for an imagined insult. After a week of
close confinement, Franklin humbly petitioned the General
Court for the privilege of using the prison yard, pleading
illness and being "heartily sorry" for his offense. His petition was granted, but he served out the mouth.[52]

The experience did not, however, temper his journalistic
satire. Upon his release the *Courant* continued its policy
of mockery and innuendo. Several stinging pieces in early
1723 provoked the General Court to deal with Franklin
once again. A joint committee was appointed to consider
measures of restraint. The report of the committee,
adopted by both Houses, censured the publisher for having
offended the government by injurious reflections which
disturbed the public peace. He was then ordered never to
print the *Courant* or any pamphlet or paper "Except it be
first Supervised, by the Secretary of this Province," and he
was to post bond to insure his compliance. The irrepres-
sible Franklin disregarded the orders of the General Court
by bringing out the next issue of the *Courant* without
license and with a fresh aspersion; but he discreetly went
into hiding to escape the inevitable warrant for his arrest on

[52] Thomas, *History of Printing in America*, 2:217, reprints the
offensive passage; the orders of the General Court and the prisoner's petition are duplicated in Duniway, *Freedom of the Press*,
pp. 99 and 163, respectively.

a charge of contempt of the General Court. At this point, Franklin made his young brother Ben the new publisher of the paper in order to circumvent obedience to the legislature's command that James Franklin print nothing unlicensed. Upon his eventual capture and imprisonment, the legislature, confident of its case against him, permitted his release under bond and requested an indictment from a grand jury. That was the government's mistake. It should have held him in jail under authority of the General Court for breach of privilege, because the grand jury, probably motivated by a detestation of the licensing system which had ended a generation earlier in England, returned the bill ignoramus. Thus, Franklin went luckily free, and prior restraint of the press was at an end in Massachusetts.[53]

But the press was not free. Only the next year Checkley was convicted for seditious libel. The law of criminal publications remained unaltered; subsequent punishment awaited anyone who "abused" his right to publish his sentiments without license. Thomas Fleet, publisher of *The Evening Post* in Boston, was the next intended victim. His paper was remarkably candid in its comments on a variety of subjects and was denounced as a "sink of sedition, error, and heresy" by the clergy in particular, although he was careful not to asperse government policies. In 1742, however, he printed an item that he had picked up in conversation with a naval officer. Parliament, he reported "had called for all the Papers relating to the war [between England and Spain], and 'twas expected the Right Hon. Sir Robert Walpole would be taken into custody in a very few days." The Council immediately ordered the attorney-general to file an information against Fleet, circumventing

[53] Thomas, *History of Printing in America*, 2:219–222, and Duniway, *Freedom of the Press*, pp. 101–103.

a grand jury, and to prosecute him for his "libelous Reflection upon his Majesty's Administration" tending to "inflame the minds of his Majesty's subjects here and disaffect them to his Government." Fleet, however, immediately produced witnesses to attest to the truth of the news item, and events quickly proved its accuracy. As a result, the prosecution was dropped.[54] The government's intention to circumscribe political reportage was surely evident, though, and newspapers were alerted to the fact that literal accuracy bounded their freedom.

In 1754 the General Court demonstrated once again its power to restrain the press by punishing public criticism as a breach of privilege. A pamphlet with the intriguing title, "The Monster of Monsters," had been anonymously published satirizing the House's debate on a recently enacted and unpopular excise bill — the allegorical monster. The House angrily resolved that the unknown author had perpetrated "a false, scandalous Libel reflecting upon the Proceedings of the House in general, and on many worthy Members in particular, in breach of the privileges thereof."[55] The hangman was ordered to burn a copy of the offensive pamphlet, while warrants went out for the arrest of Daniel Fowle, suspected as the printer, and his apprentice, Joseph Russell. Brought to the bar of the House, the two were easily trapped into confessing their complicity as distributors of the pamphlet. Fowle also implicated his brother, who was also a printer, and a Mr. Royal Tyler, a prominent merchant who later became a member of the Council. Fowle's brother, Zechariah, was

[54] Thomas, *History of Printing in America*, 2:473 and 234, and Duniway, *Freedom of the Press*, pp. 112–115.

[55] Quoted in Daniel Fowle, *A Total Eclipse of Liberty* (Boston, 1755, 32 pp.), p. 11.

arrested but escaped punishment because of illness. Tyler, the probable author, on being interrogated by the speaker of the House, unsuccessfully demanded a lawyer and answered all questions by referring to his privilege against self-incrimination. He was thrown in jail and denied bail, but was unaccountably released after two days, as was Daniel Fowle's apprentice. Daniel was regarded by the House as the chief culprit and was treated accordingly. He was imprisoned incommunicado, denied even the privilege of writing a censored letter to his wife. Although writing materials were prohibited to him, the jailer negligently failed to search his person. He spent the first night on the floor of the bedless, stinking, unheated cell composing a narrative of his suffering. Having caught a "prodigious cold," he was moved to a better cell in the company of "Murderers, Thieves, Common-Cheats, Pick-Pockets, &c." His confinement all the while was grounded merely on a charge of being "Suspected of being guilty. . . ."

After five days of rough treatment, Fowle was brought before the bar of the House again where he was severely reprimanded by the speaker for having published a seditious libel and then was returned to his cell until he should pay the costs of his case. On the sixth day of imprisonment, when the affair had become "the chief Topik of Conversation in Town," Fowle petitioned the speaker for a discharge so that he might nurse his sick wife. The petition was granted on condition that he return when summoned, but public sympathy being with Fowle, the House dropped its charges and let him alone even after he published his tract, *A Total Eclipse of Liberty*,[56] which in pathos and anger told the world about his troubles. The oddest aspect

[56] My account of Fowle's case is based on this tract, cited in the note above. The quoted phrases are at pp. 19, 24, and 26.

of the whole affair is that the supposedly esteemed liberty of the press did not seem to be at stake in the minds of any of the participants. Fowle himself regarded the whole affair as a gross violation of Magna Carta's guarantee of personal liberty and due process of law. Vigorously condemning the proceedings against him as unjust and arbitrary, he quoted Montesquieu to prove the tyranny of one body being accuser, judge, and jury. But he never mentioned liberty of the press or any aspect of freedom of discussion. His complaint was not that his words were deemed criminal, but that he had been treated harshly and denied trial.

In the neighboring colony of New York the open expression of opinion was esteemed as little. Early in the eighteenth century there occurred the trial of Colonel Nicholas Bayard, a leader of the aristocratic party who had been instrumental in securing the conviction and execution of Jacob Leisler. The appointment of a new governor, Lord Cornbury, kindled Bayard's hope of returning to power against the Leislerians who then controlled the government. In an effort to ingratiate himself with Cornbury, Bayard drew up addresses to him, the king, and Parliament, accusing Lieutenant-Governor Nanfan, the chief justice, and members of the Council, of nefarious actions ranging from bribery to oppression. Among those whose signatures Bayard procured were members of the local garrison. Nanfan immediately retaliated by arresting the author of the derogatory addresses on a charge of treason under a statute of 1691 loosely drawn by Bayard himself against Leisler. It provided that anyone who by arms "or otherwise" endeavored to "disturbe the peace" should be deemed a traitor. Bayard was hoist by his own petard; instead of confronting a charge of seditious libel, a mere misdemeanor, he found

himself, in 1702, on trial for his life along with his hench-
man, Alderman John Hutchins. The indictment alleged
their attempt to procure the mutiny of the garrison by
inducing the soldiers to sign false and scandalous lies against
the government, rendering it "cheap and vile" in the eyes of
the people. From indictment to conviction, the case was a
travesty of common-law procedure, a fact which saved the
prisoners' heads, for the prosecution was condemned as
illegal on appeal to the Privy Council. If the government
of New York had been content with a charge of seditious
libel, it could have made the conviction stick.[57]

The government had even less luck with its prosecution
of Francis Makemie and John Hampton, Presbyterian ministers who were arrested for unlicensed preaching with intent to "spread their *Pernicious Doctrine* and *Principles*, to
the disturbance of the Church by *Law Established*, and of
the *Government* of this *Province*." [58] Although Hampton
was imprisoned with Makemie, he was not presented to the
ground jury by the attorney-general, probably because he
had not aggravated the offense, as had Makemie, by publishing his unlicensed sermon which was "reputed a Libel"
by the governor. While the two were in jail, they applied
for a release to the courts, stating that Cornbury had refused to recognize their certificates from Virginia and
Maryland certifying that they had complied with the provisions of the 1689 Act of Toleration. The judiciary, however, never received their petition; it was pocketed by
the attorney-general, "asserting it to be a Libel against

[57] Rex v. Bayard, Howell's *State Trials*, 14:471–516 (1702).
[58] *A Narrative of a New and Unusual American Imprisonment
of Two Presbyterian Ministers: And Prosecution of Mr. Francis
Makemie*, 1707, by a Learner of Law, and Lover of Liberty. Reprinted in Force, ed., *Tracts and Other Papers*, vol. 4, no. 4, p. 24.
The anonymous author was probably Makemie himself.

Ld. Cornbury." At the trial, the prosecution presented a case of seditious and unlicensed preaching, while the defense argued that the Act of Toleration extended to the colonies and protected the rights of conscience. The jury of New Yorkers returned a verdict of not guilty, influenced very possibly by the popular opposition to the assumption in the indictment that the Church of England was the established church of the province.[59]

The acquittal scored a victory for religious toleration and freedom of religious speech. But no speech reprehending the government was tolerated, at least not before the Zenger case. Before then the legislature showed its mettle by punishing for breach of privilege the occasional hardy critic who dared to scandalize its dignity by offensive comment. Between 1706 and 1720 there were four such cases, one of which involved the arrest of nine citizens and another of seventeen grand jurors for seditious reflections on the Assembly.[60] In two of these four cases the victim of the Assembly's wrath was one of its own members, Lewis Morris in 1710 and Samuel Mulford in 1720. Representative Mulford's troubles began in 1716 when he was first expelled from the Assembly for a speech against unequal representation in which he asked whether the government was carried on for the benefit of the people or was arbitrary, illegal, and oppressive. Governor Hunter, the object of some of Mulford's choicest adjectives, instituted a common-law prosecution against him for "a false and Malitious Libel, against the Government . . . tending to alienate the

[59] On this point, see Sanford H. Cobb, *The Rise of Religious Liberty in America* (New York, 1902), pp. 337–341.

[60] *Journal of the Votes and Proceedings of the General Assembly of the Colony of New-York, 1691–1765* (New York, 1764–1766), 1:211 (1706), 1:283 (1710), 1:411 (1717), and 1:443 (1720).

affections of the Subjects from the Government. . . ." [61]
The Assembly then relented and petitioned the governor
to quash the prosecution on the theory that a speech on the
floor was privileged — except of course when the member
aspersed the Assembly, in which case it alone might take
appropriate action. Hunter replied that the prosecution was
not for the speech in the Assembly but for its publication
by Mulford. The case, however, never came to trial. Mulford went directly to England where he secured from
the Lords of Trade an order commanding Hunter to cease
the criminal proceedings against him.[62] In 1720 Mulford
was back in the Assembly where he again unburdened himself in an accusation that the representatives had gotten the
colony deeply in debt and ought to be cleaned out by the
people. His "rash Expression" was solemnly deemed to be a
reflection upon the House, which after examining him before its bar voted that he be summarily expelled. Mulford's
case indicates that free speech, which originated as a parliamentary privilege, did not extend to criticism of the legislature even by a member.

The Zenger case in 1735 gave the press freedom to
print as far as the truth carried and a jury's emotions might
be sympathetically swayed, if the truth was directed away
from the House. Prior license had long disappeared for any
publication except that revealing the votes and proceedings
of the General Assembly. This information of the most
vital public interest could be printed only after first being
submitted to the speaker for his examination and signature.

[61] The sources are printed in O'Callaghan and Fernow, eds.,
Documents Relative to the Colonial History of New York, 3:363–
371, which includes Mulford's speech; his defense in court begins at
p. 372.
[62] *Ibid.*, 3:383 and 5:505.

Beginning in 1745,[63] this order was repeated at each session down to the Revolution. The governor, too, was finicky about publications concerning him, as James Parker, the official printer, came to know. During King George's War, in 1747, Governor Clinton sharply criticized the Assembly for its insufficient appropriation of defense funds, and the Assembly, angrily retorting that his remarks tended to the "subversion" of its rights, drew up a long remonstrance in its defense. Clinton then commanded Parker not to print the remonstrance in the proceedings of the Assembly because it scandalized him. The printer, caught between contending forces either of which could destroy him, helplessly turned to the House for instructions, giving it a rare opportunity to masquerade as the self-appointed defender of the free press. Unanimously the legislators voted

That it is the undoubted Right of the People of this Colony, to know the Proceedings of their Representatives . . . That any Attempt to prohibit the printing or re-printing, any of the Proceedings of this House, is an infringement of the Privileges of this House, and of the People they represent . . . That his Excellency's Order to forbid the printing or re-printing the said Remonstrance, is unwarrantable, arbitrary and illegal, and . . . tends to the utter subversion of all the Rights and Liberties of this House, and of the People they represent.[64]

The Assembly then ordered Parker to print its remonstrance and deliver ten copies to each member so that the people might be apprised of their representatives' "firm Resolution to preserve the Liberty of the Press . . ." [65] Confronted by this popular stand, Clinton shrewdly took

[63] *Journal of the General Assembly of New York*, 2:65.
[64] *Ibid.*, 2:193. See also pp. 173 and 192.
[65] *Ibid.*, 2:198.

no action against Parker; there was no sense in further antagonizing the Assembly from which adequate defense measures were still to be wheedled.

The legislature's professed commitment to the principle of a free press was abandoned a few years later, in 1753, when the printer, Hugh Gaine, deeming the king's instructions to the new governor and the latter's speech to the Assembly a matter of public interest, published them in his *New York Mercury*. The Assembly, upon learning that Gaine had "presumed" to print part of its proceedings without license, summoned him to its bar and demanded to know by what authority he had dared to breach its privileges. Gaine, who was apparently astonished and intimidated by the turn of events, most abjectly humbled himself. He had done wrong, he claimed, only out of ignorance but was profusely sorry for having given offense and "humbly asked their pardon." Mollified by this proper display of contrition, the Assembly magnanimously released him after censure, a warning, and exaction of the costs of the case.[66]

In 1756 James Parker, who had been the center of the earlier episode when the Assembly's conflict with the governor dictated the tactic of posturing as a friend of liberty of the press, was the next victim of parliamentary privilege. He had published in his *New-York Gazette* an article on the distressed condition of the people in Orange and Ulster Counties which the House took to be "greatly reflecting" upon it and calculated "to irritate the People of this Colony against their Representatives. . . ." Parker and his associate, William Weyman, were voted to be guilty of a "high misdemeanour" and contempt of authority. Taken into custody by the sergeant-at-arms of the House, they were

[66] *Ibid.*, 2:358–359.

interrogated before the bar. A most cooperative witness, Parker revealed that the offensive article had been written by the Reverend Hezekiah Watkins of Newburg. The publishers confessed their fault for printing the article, denied any intention of giving affront, promised to be more circumspect in the future, and humbly begged the pardon of the honorable House. Notwithstanding this submission to authority, the Assembly kept the prisoners in jail for a week before discharging them. The Reverend Watkins, who was promptly arrested, admitted his authorship but pleaded that he had acted out of a mistaken zeal for the welfare of the people rather than from a disrespect for the House. He was heartily sorry and pleaded to be forgiven, but was jailed anyway. The next day, however, he was formally reprimanded before the bar of the House and discharged after paying the costs.[67]

In 1758 the speaker of the House received a letter from one Samuel Townsend, a justice of the peace in Queen's County, asking legislative relief for certain refugees quartered on Long Island. The speaker, presenting the House with the letter, termed it "insolent," whereupon that body commanded Townsend's appearance. When he daringly failed to show up, he was cited for contempt, and a warrant was issued for his arrest. Hauled before the bar he was examined in the usual intimidating fashion, but showed no signs of repentance. The Assembly then voted that because his letter reflected on its "Honour, Justice and Authority," he was guilty of a "high Misdemeanour and a most daring Insult." The gloomy prison provoked Townsend to reconsider his position. He forthwith sent the House a petition expressing his deep sorrow for having written the letter by which he had inadvertantly cast reflection on the House.

[67] *Ibid.*, 2:487–489.

He promised faithfully to avoid every occasion of exposing himself to such misdeeds in the future and asked for the House's "Compassion." Moved by this respectful submission from a judge, the Assembly immediately released him from jail and discharged him after an official reprimand from the speaker.[68]

As New York approached the revolutionary controversy, its press was only as free as its legislature permitted. In practice, all political comment was tolerated so long as criticism did not touch the people's representatives in any way. The failure of the common-law prosecutions against Bayard, Mackemie, and Zenger made the courts a mere formal threat against unfettered discussion. The actively suppressive power was exercised by an unlimited discretion in the legislature to move against supposed breaches of parliamentary privilege. The frequency of the cases and the incidence of punishment were scarcely great enough to suggest tyranny, but the arbitrary exercise of legislative prerogative was more than sufficiently restrictive to have a smothering effect on the free expression of opinion on legislative measures and matters.

The point on which all libertarian theorists had been united was the salutary influence of freedom of speech and press as a check on evil or incompetent rulers and the stimulus to responsible government which open discussion might provide. But in New York, as in Massachusetts, the legislature did not allow this libertarian theory a chance to be put into practice. A royal governor, his policies, and his administration were almost always fair game for popular disapprobation; the Zenger case proved that but hardly more. In the struggle of the colonial assembly for independence from the governor, most antiadministration criticism played

[68] *Ibid.*, 2:551–555 *passim.*

into the hands of the legislature and the popular party. Freedom of the press was, in other words, a useful instrument for the expansion of legislative prerogative, but in any clash between parliamentary privilege and liberty of discussion, the former was the unexceptioned superior. This fact recalls the statement of the popular party representatives, John Morin Scott and William Livingston, in their New York journal printed by James Parker: any publication which they deemed injurious to the country verged on treason, making "groundless and trifling" the plea of freedom of the press.[69] Parker himself summarized the matter when he wrote that one might say anything on condition that he does so with a just regard for the laws — [70] and the laws provided for the punishment of seditious libel and breach of parliamentary privilege. The scope of permissible free expression was recognized as so narrow that none of the several defendants before the New York General Assembly even attempted to justify themselves by reference to liberty of the press. Perhaps they realized the claim would have been "groundless and trifling."

The experience with freedom of speech and press in Pennsylvania was hardly different. Licensing lasted till at least 1722 as the case of Andrew Bradford indicates. He had followed his father, old William Bradford, into the printing business and founded Pennsylvania's first newspaper, the Philadelphia *American Weekly Mercury*. Shortly after the second anniversary of the paper, in 1722, he printed a brief pamphlet by an anonymous author and then carried it as an article in his paper. The subject was the "dying Credit of the Province." Summoned by the Council to explain the aspersive innuendos against the government,

[69] See below, pp. 141–142.
[70] *Ibid.*

Bradford lamely declared that he had no knowledge of the offensive piece which must have been accepted and run off by one of his journeyman printers without his knowledge. If freedom of the press mattered, the way to defend it was not to state how "very sorry" he was for the publication of the piece "and for which he humbly submitted himself and ask'd Pardon of the Govr. and the Board. . . ." On behalf of the Council, the governor ordered, "That he must not for the future presume to publish anything relating to or concerning the Affairs of this Government, or the Government of any other of his Majesty's Colonies, without the permission of the Governour or Secretary of this province. . . ." [71] There is an interesting sidelight to the incident. Among the members of the Council laying down this order, which was utterly irreconcilable with any principle of a free press, was the man who later gained fame as the stalwart defender of the press, Zenger's counsel, Andrew Hamilton.

A year later there occurred one of those rare common-law prosecutions for seditious speech. Two men were arrested for derogatory comments about the king. One added to his contempt by affronting the magistrates in a declaration that he was not bound to obey either the House of Hanover or the House of Hanover's judges. The first prisoner confessed his guilt, but the second was contumacious and his sedition had to be proved at a trial. Judge Robert Asheton informed the jury that "it is greatly imprudent and presumptuous, for private persons to intermeddle with matters of so high a nature; and it will be impossible to preserve the peace, unless subjects will quietly submit themselves to those whom Providence has placed over them . . . what severity can be too harsh for those

[71] *Minutes of the Provincial Council of Pennsylvania*, 1:143.

who thus despise dominions, and speak evil of dignitaries? who curse, asperse, and deny their supreme, true, and lawful and *undoubted* sovercign." Upon conviction the individual who had confessed was sentenced to two hours in the pillory with a paper fixed on his breast and another on his back with the words: "I stand here for speaking contemptuously against my sovereign Lord, King George." He was also fined twenty marks sterling and costs. The other defendant was sentenced to the pillory for two hours on each of two days and afterwards, on each day, "you *shall be tied to the tail of a cart, and be drawn round two of this city squares,* and then you shall be *whipped on your bare back, with forty-one lashes,* and be imprisoned till you have paid the charges of prosecution."[72] A sentence like this did not have to be repeated to have a lingering cautionary effect on the tongues of citizens.

Andrew Bradford was again in trouble with the Council in 1729. His *Mercury,* it seems, had published a letter, signed "Brutus," which the authorities considered to be a reflection on the king and the government of Great Britain, calculated "to incite the Inhabitants of this Province to throw off all subjection to the regular and established powers of Government." The Council added that the letter constituted "a wicked & seditious Libell" that had been published under mistaken notions of liberty. Bradford was jailed, his home and printing shop searched for evidence of the author's identity, and the attorney-general was ordered to commence a prosecution against the printer. He saved his skin, however, by naming the author as a Parson Campbell of Long Island and pleaded sheer innocency of the bad tendency of the letter. Although he was recommitted

[72] Quoted in Brown, *The Forum*, 1:262–265 *passim*. Brown cites no primary source in the case, nor have I been able to locate any.

to jail, there to ponder the perils of publishing, his coopera-
tion with the authorities and his abject apologies won his
discharge. The records do not indicate the fate of the mysterious Long Island parson.[73] They do indicate, however,
that the recorder of the Council and one of those who conducted the examination of Bradford and committed him to
prison was Andrew Hamilton.

Bradford and Hamilton were, as a matter of fact, enemies
for many years and attacked each other through the pages
of the *Mercury* and Franklin's *Pennsylvania Gazette*.[74]
During the Zenger trial, Andrew Bradford had good reason
to emulate his father, Zenger's rival and publisher of the
administration organ, the *New-York Gazette*, in applauding
the prosecution. The younger Bradford was also the American publisher of "Remarks on Zenger's Tryal" by the
West Indian lawyers who attacked the validity of Hamilton's argument for the defense.[75] Bradford did his best to
disabuse the public of the notion that Hamilton deserved
his reputation as a champion of a free press. A "single
Attempt on the side of Liberty," he editorialized, should
not obscure a long record of enmity to the cause of the
press. Bradford had more in mind than Hamilton's participation in the Council orders which had restrained him.
Replying to a "Panegyrick" on Hamilton which appeared
in Franklin's paper, Bradford accused him of hypocrisy and
added the following tale to the evidence:

A Person that has cruelly harassed and imprisoned a Printer,
and again caused him to be assaulted and knock'd down in

[73] *Ibid.*, 1:285–286, and *Minutes of the Provincial Council of
Pennsylvania*, 3:392.

[74] See Anna Janney DeArmond, *Andrew Bradford, Colonial
Journalist* (Newark, Del. 1949), ch. 4, "The Bradford-Hamilton
Controversy."

[75] See below, p. 134.

the open Street, meerly for copying an English Print, or inserting in his News-Paper, some general Invectives against a particular Vice, which by a foreign Innuendo, or consciousness of Guilt, the Person [Hamilton] applied to himself, can no more merit the Character of a sincere Advocate for the Liberty of the Press, than a venal Hireling for a fulsome Harangue does the Name of a Cato. . . .[76]

The Council, or upper house, by no means outdid the Assembly as a defender of the proper bounds of freedom of the press. The most glaring instance of the Assembly's exercise of its punitive powers occurred in 1758 in relation to the Smith-Moore case.[77] William Moore, the Anglican chief judge of the Court of Common Pleas for Chester County, had a record of opposition to Quaker principles on the subject of defensive war. In late 1757 on the charge that he had been unjust in his capacity as judge, he was summoned for examination by the Quaker-dominated Assembly. Moore itcrated his innocence and denied the authority of the House to try him for his conduct as a judge, particularly since the charges against him were cognizable at common law, thus creating the possibility of double jeopardy. The Assembly continued its investigation anyway, and in an address to Governor Denny, published in the *Pennsylvania Gazette*, demanded Moore's removal from office on ground of oppression and corruption. The judge, having been accused in the public press, prepared a defense which he asked the *Gazette* to publish. The printer dis-

[76] *American Weekly Mercury*, April 13, 1738, quoted in DeArmond, *Bradford*, p. 106. See also pp. 110–111.

[77] Reported at great length in *Votes and Proceedings of the House of Representatives of the Province of Pennsylvania (1682–1776)*, in Gertrude MacKinney and Charles F. Hoban, eds., *Pennsylvania Archives*, 8th ser. (n.p., 1931–1935), vol. 6, chiefly at pp. 4677–4716. For another case involving scandalous reflection on the Assembly, see 6:4615.

creetly requested and inexplicably received permission from the speaker of the house to run Moore's reply, which was copied also by the other Philadelphia newspaper, the *Pennsylvania Journal*. Moore then approached his friend and future son-in-law, the Reverend William Smith, for help. Smith, one of the most prominent Anglicans in the province and president of the University of Pennsylvania or, more properly, provost of the College and Academy of Philadelphia as it was then called, was an extremely influential person among the large German-speaking population of the city. He had been instrumental in founding a German-language newspaper, and Moore requested his good offices in seeing to the translation and publication of his reply to the legislature. Smith's compliance was his undoing, for the members of the House had been waiting for a pretext to revenge themselves upon him for his outspoken advocacy of a more aggressive campaign against the French. Early in 1758, the sergeant-at-arms of the incoming assembly arrested both Smith and Moore for their crimes against the preceding assembly.[78]

Three of Smith's friends were summoned to testify on his complicity in publishing Moore's newspaper account. The first examined, Dr. Phineas Bond, refused to answer

[78] *Votes and Proceedings*, 6:4619–4620, 4637, 4645, and 4677–4678. See also Horace Wemyss Smith, *Life and Correspondence of the Reverend William Smith* (Philadelphia, 1879), who discusses the case at 1:167–187, an account valuable for data on the background of the case and for its reproduction of Smith's letters and other primary sources. William Renwick Riddell's "Libel on the Assembly: A Prerevolutionary Episode," *The Pennsylvania Magazine of History and Biography*, 52:176–192, 249–279, and 342–360 (1928), is chiefly concerned with the antagonism between the House and the governor and also with the legal power of the House to imprison for contempt. The account in Albert Frank Gegenheimer, *William Smith* (Philadelphia, 1943), pp. 139–148, contains nothing of value and is undocumented.

any questions. He was assured that the Assembly was not seeking to incriminate him, yet he remained obstinate. Finally he was offered immunity against prosecution for any testimony he might offer in relation to the alleged seditious libel by Smith and Moore. When Bond persisted in his role as a silent witness, the Assembly voted him to be in "high Contempt" and committed him to jail for an indefinite period. After a few hours behind bars, Bond reconsidered his position and informed the Assembly that he proposed to disclose that which "he had apprehended himself obliged by the Ties of Honour and Friendship to conceal. . . ." He and Smith's other friends then gave damaging testimony and were discharged.[79]

Judge Moore, after five days of imprisonment, was summoned to the bar of the House for a hearing. He admitted his authorship of the newspaper address against the Assembly, but denied its competency to try him, particularly on the charges relating to his conduct as a magistrate. He was tried anyway, on two counts: judicial misconduct and libeling the House, the constitution, and the government. Upon conviction for the second count, he was pronounced guilty of "false, scandalous, virulent and seditious Libel," the common hangman was commanded to burn copies of his offensive publication, and the sheriff was ordered to hold him in jail indefinitely or until such time as the Assembly might authorize his discharge. The sheriff was additionally commanded that "he do not obey any Writ or *Habeas Corpus,* or other Writ whatsoever, that may come to his Hands for the Bailing and Discharging the said *William Moore.* . . ."[80]

This suspension of the writ of habeas corpus was as

---

[79] *Votes and Proceedings,* 6:4678–4680, 4681–4682.
[80] *Ibid.,* 6:4683–4689. The quotation is at 6:4689.

arbitrary a deprivation of personal liberty as any American legislature might dare attempt. If the word tyranny seems too harsh to describe the case, it is only because in England no writ covered a commitment by either House of Parliament. But the Pennsylvania Assembly was not Parliament, even though it aped the empire's great legislature. Parliament literally and constitutionally possessed unlimited powers. *Lex parliamenti* superseded *lex terrae.* In America however, the very concept of constitutionalism meant a government of regularized and distinctly limited powers, invalidating the notion of legislative prerogative. The constitutional theory underlying the American Revolution denied that the highest authority in the land was a legislature from whose acts no appeals could be had. The Assembly's absolute denial of habeas corpus, especially as to the misdemeanor of a seditious libel in the form of a breach of privilege, comported more with the conduct of a Stuart despot than with supposed American principles of law and government that antedated the revolution by at least a century.

With Judge Moore in jail, the Assembly turned to the provost of the college. He was brought before the bar of the house and formally charged with "being a Promoter and Abettor of the Writing and Publishing a Libel, entituled, *The humble Address of William Moore. . . .*" Smith requested counsel, a copy of the charges against him, and discharge from prison so that he might prepare his defense. He was permitted counsel, a copy of the charges, and time to prepare his defense, but was denied liberty even under bond.[81] Governor Denny and the Assembly, meanwhile, exchanged a series of long, recriminatory messages on the justice and legality of the Assembly's prosecu-

[81] *Ibid.,* 6:4691-4692.

tions of Smith and Moore. At one point the governor raised the question whether the present Assembly might take cognizance of a libel addressed to the previous one, but the House aggressively repudiated all challenges to its authority.[82] To buttress its case against Smith, it summoned Anthony Armbruster, the printer of the German-language paper that had published the libel. For seeming prevarication and refusal to answer certain questions repeatedly put to him, Armbruster was committed to jail, to be held indefinitely in close confinement. After one day of imprisonment, he docilely submitted to the will of the Assembly, begging its pardon and giving direct answers to all questions. The Assembly then voted, *before* Smith's trial commenced, "Resolved, by a great Majority, That the said William Smith is guilty of promoting and publishing the libellous Paper entituled, *The Address of* William Moore *to Governor* Denny." [83]

The mock trial before a kangaroo court, acting as accuser, judge, and jury, began almost a week later and was marked by extraordinary procedure even for an Assembly, a body not noted for judicial regularity. Libertarian theorists had raised the cry of "Star Chamber law" when royal judges reserved to themselves the question whether a publication was libelous. But not even under Star Chamber procedure was the question of libel decided in advance of the trial. The nearest analogy to the procedure in Smith's case occurs in Wonderland at the trial of the Knave of Hearts for stealing the tarts; the sentence "Off with his head!" preceded both trial and verdict. To make certain that there could be no slip-up, the Pennsylvania Assembly

---

[82] *Ibid.*, 6:4649–4654, 4680–4681, 4683–4685, 4693–4696, 4697–4698, 4708–4714.
[83] *Ibid.*, 6:4704–4705.

also decided prior to the trial that the prisoner would not be permitted to dispute its power and authority to punish persons guilty of "Libels against the Government," nor to argue that Moore's publication was not a libel. Smith's counsel requested and was denied leave to argue that a libel on one Assembly could not be punished by a succeeding one, or to enquire whether the publication charged did constitute libel. Smith was permitted only to defend himself against the charge on which he had already been adjudged guilty: abetting that libel.[84]

The trial ran its course from a predetermined end to a foregone conclusion. Smith was sentenced to jail until he should give "Satisfaction" to the Assembly for his offense. His counsel immediately moved that he be allowed the privilege of an appeal to the king, that he be furnished with transcripts of the proceedings of the Assembly, and that he be released on bail pending decision on the appeal. But the Assembly refused the motion, answering that appeals could be had to the king and Privy Council only from "inferior Courts" but never from the "Judgments of the House of Assembly, relating to Breach of Privilege, and Contempt to the House. . . ." [85] Smith had only to purge himself of his offense by due submission to the authority of the Assembly and confess his error, if he desired his freedom, declared the speaker. At this point the prisoner arose and replied with deep feeling that he was innocent of any crime and "could not in Conscience make any Acknowledgments, or profess Sorrow and Contrition to the House for his Conduct; and, striking his Hand upon his Breast, assured them, no Punishment they could inflict, would be half so terrible to him, as the suffering his Tongue

[84] *Ibid.*, 6:4703–4704.
[85] *Ibid.*, 6:4715.

to give his Heart the Lie." [86] According to another version
of his reply, he also declared that he thought it his duty
"to keep the Dutch press as *free* as any other in the province"; he is said, also, to have invoked, at least in passing,
freedom of the press in his defense.[87] If so, he was the only
American with the temerity or imagination to confront a
legislature with that defense on a charge of breach of
privilege. Smith's impassioned statement moved several persons in the audience to break into applause, resulting in
their prompt arrest. They were later released after being
forced to ask the Assembly's pardon.[88] Smith himself was
returned to prison, committed indefinitely on a command to
the sheriff that he should not, at his peril, obey a writ of
habeas corpus.

The prisoners, Smith and Moore, vainly petitioned the
chief justice of the highest court of the province for a writ
of habeas corpus. The court ruled that the petitioners,
having been committed by the House for a breach of privilege, could not be granted the writ nor be bailed during
the sitting of the House. The governor also refused to inter-
cede. Not until the Assembly recessed were the prisoners
freed, after more than three months of imprisonment. But
when the Assembly reconvened within three weeks, they
were again arrested and imprisoned. Fortunately for them
the Assembly shortly adjourned for the summer. Governor
Denny, who had repeatedly resisted requests from the
Assembly to remove Judge Moore from office, now convened his Council for a full hearing of the charges; the
Council unanimously ruled that Moore was "perfectly

[86] *Ibid.*
[87] Quoted in Thomas, *History of Printing in America*, 2:340;
see also Smith, *Life of Smith*, 1:174–175.
[88] *Votes and Proceedings*, 6:4715–4725 *passim.*

innocent." But when the Assembly met once again in the
fall, it characterized the action of the governor and Council
as a "Design to overthrow the Constitution, and enslave
the People, by depriving their Representatives of their most
essential Rights, Powers, and Privileges. . . ." A week after
this statement, the Assembly continued its unprecedented
behavior by reordering the imprisonment of both Smith
and Moore, but the sergeant-at-arms could not find either.
Two months later an incoming Assembly convened and
promptly demonstrated that it had been infected by its predecessor's contagion of harassment. Moore, from some-
where in hiding, had published another libel on the representatives, and an order went out for his arrest and Smith's,
on a warrant from the speaker. The sergeant-at-arms even-
tually reported that Moore had "absconded" while Smith
had "lately embarked for England." Undaunted, the Assembly for the fifth time ordered Moore's arrest.[89]

Smith had fled to England as the only means of appealing
his cause to the Privy Council. His efforts to obtain justice
there were opposed by the official agent of the Pennsylvania Assembly, Benjamin Franklin, one-time printer and
reputed champion of a free press. When the Privy Council
finally ruled on the case, in 1759, it decided that Moore's
published statement had indeed been a seditious libel upon
the Assembly; but, since it had been published after the
adjournment of the Assembly against which it had been
directed, no subsequent Assembly had jurisdiction to consider the offense. Only the Assembly that had been libeled
might take action during the life of its session. In addition,
the Privy Council ruled that the power of the House of

[89] *Votes and Proceedings,* 6:4792, 4799, 4825, 4839, 4855, 4894,
4930. See also Riddell, "Libel on the Assembly," *Pennsylvania
Magazine,* 52:251, 262 *et passim;* Smith, *Life of Smith,* 1:180, 187.

Commons to imprison for contempt in the form of a libel
or breach of privilege was not possessed by "these inferior
Assemblies in America"; nor could they suspend the writ
of habeas corpus in such cases without invading both "his
Majesty's Royal Prerogative, and the Liberties of the People." The latest warrants for the rearrest of Smith and
Moore were thus rendered void, enabling them to return to
Philadelphia in safety, eighteen months after their night-
mare had begun.[90] So ended an episode which together
with others of a similar nature[91] demonstrated the American
legislature's regard for freedom of the press and civil liberty
generally. Incidentally, the future conduct of "these inferior
Assemblies in America" indicated that they had an equal
regard for the opinion of the Privy Council on the point
that they possessed no powers of imprisoning for seditious
contempt.

In the South, conditions were about the same as in the
Middle and New England colonies. A detailed survey of
Southern cases would be repetitious; the cast of characters
differed but the plot was unchanged except in one respect.
There were fewer cases, but not because a greater freedom
prevailed. On the contrary, there seems to have been more
acquiescence and less press activity. Virginia, for example,

[90] *Votes and Proceedings*, 6:5092; Riddell, "Libel on the Assembly," *Pennsylvania Magazine*, 52:263, 342, 343; and Gegenheimer,
William Smith, p. 148.

[91] In addition to the earlier cases which have been reviewed,
there were others contemporary with the Smith-Moore affair. See
Clarke, *Parliamentary Privilege*, p. 120, citing a manuscript journal
of the Rhode Island legislature, for the imprisonment by both
Houses of a citizen who damned the Assembly. The New Hampshire Assembly also jailed a man for the same offense in 1754. See
Clarke, p. 120, citing *New Hampshire Provincial Papers*, 6:240-241.
Clarke, at p. 107 and again at p. 120, refers to earlier New Hampshire cases involving breach of privilege by scandalous utterance.

had no press until 1729 and no newspaper until 1733. Printing came to the Carolinas and Georgia even later and everywhere in the South was introduced under government auspices, closely controlled until the outbreak of the revolutionary controversy in the 1760's. There was not even a competitor to the government press in Virginia until 1766.[92] In both Virginia and South Carolina in the 1740's there appear to have been single instances of prosecutions for criminal libel in the common-law courts but neither case ended in a conviction. William Parks, the royal printer of the Virginia *Gazette*, was acquitted of the charge of seditious libel upon a member of the House of Burgesses after proving in court that the member had once been convicted of sheep-stealing as alleged.[93] The South Carolina case, which involved a libel on the established church by three defendants, one of whom was the famous evangelist, George Whitefield, never even came to trial.[94]

Although the royal judges in the South compiled no record of suppressing criminal utterances, the governors, Councils, and lower Houses did better. The Burgesses of Virginia, for example, punished ten men in 1705 for signing a seditious paper and would have taken punitive action again in 1710 had an anonymous author been located.[95] Governor Spotswood of Virginia made his bid against the disseminators of "Seditious principles . . . or other Insinuations tending to the disturbance of the peace" when he issued a proclamation in 1711 threatening "the Loss of Life or Member" or imprisonment for anyone daring to

[92] See Thomas, *History of Printing in America*, vol. 2, under the heads of the individual colonies.
[93] *Ibid.*, 2:143–144.
[94] *Ibid.*, 2:156.
[95] *Journals of the House of Burgesses of Virginia*, vol. 1702–1712, pp. 148 and 230.

commit the heinous crime.[96] The upper House was active too in 1714 when prosecuting a justice of the peace for "many Seditious Speeches" and again in 1720 against a minister charged with "uttering false and Scandalous Speeches" against the crown.[97] In 1758, when the Pennsylvania Assembly moved against the provost of the provincial college, the House of Burgesses in Virginia was also wielding its power to punish a breach of privilege, this time against a professor of philosophy of the College of William and Mary. Professor Rowe had indiscreetly declared at a friend's house, unaware that another of the guests was a member of the legislature, that as a minister of the Anglican Church he would refuse to administer sacraments to any "Scoundrels" in the legislature who would vote for settling the salaries of the clergy in cash instead of tobacco. For his "scandalous and malicious" utterance that highly reflected on the honor of the House of Burgesses, Rowe was arrested, forced to beg pardon, and discharged on paying costs.[98] None of the available evidence for the South, or elsewhere, for that matter, suggests that freedom of speech or press existed before the revolutionary controversy.

No cause was more honored by rhetorical declamation and dishonored in practice than that of freedom of expression during the revolutionary period, from the 1760's through the cessation of hostilities. The irony of the period might best be portrayed by a cartoon depicting the tarring and feathering of a Tory speaker under a banner run up by the patriots inscribed, "In Liberty's Cause." Yankee

[96] *Executive Journals of the Council of Colonial Virginia*, 3:586–587.
[97] *Ibid.*, 3:364 and 527.
[98] *Journals of the House of Burgesses of Virginia*, vol. 1758–1761, pp. 16, 17–18.

Doodle's Liberty Boys vociferously claimed for themselves the right to free expression which they denied their opponents.

The revolutionary controversy with England did wonders for the expansion and vitality of the colonial press, because the patriot leaders discovered the secret of propaganda. The press, along with pulpit, platform, and parliamentary forum, became an enormously effective vehicle for advertising the Whig position, and so long as England maintained control of the situation, the revolutionary journalists, whose newspapers doubled in number between 1763 and 1775, unceasingly urged the value of open debate. Cato, Zenger, Andrew Hamilton, and Wilkes became continental heroes, extolled for their supposed defense of unfettered political discussion. The royal judges and their common law of seditious libel were identified with Star Chamber tyranny on the slightest suggestion that patriot propagandists were licentiously abusing their privileges of free speech and press. With the instruments for the administration of justice in the hands of the crown, Whig leaders employed extralegal instruments, particularly threats and mob violence, to checkmate any efforts of the government to suppress seditious libel.[99]

Not that the royal governors, usually with the support of their councils, did not have legitimate cause for retreating in self-defense to the royal courts. Royal authority and parliamentary measures were treated with a merciless contempt and abuse that passed all bounds of fair debate. Fair debate was, however, a prized value with the revolutionary

[99] For detailed treatments of the subject of this paragraph, see generally Philip Davidson, *Propaganda and the American Revolution, 1763–1783* (Chapel Hill, N. C., 1941), and Arthur M. Schlesinger, *Prelude to Independence: The Newspaper War on Britain, 1764–1776* (New York, 1958).

party. Josiah Quincy, Jr., writing as "Nedham," laid down its standard when he endorsed "propriety of language" by asserting that the man who acts from principle will "treat all villains with words and actions correspondent to their crimes." Knaves could not be dignified by civility. "FACT is a test of just sentiment. TRUTH is an external standard of propriety in language." Then, in a demonstration of his own adherence to this standard, Quincy declared, "Thus I have considered Mr. Hutchinson as degrading the highest station in the law to the lowest office of the inquisition; as descending from the rank of CHIEF JUSTICE to that of a COMMON INFORMER: an informer against 'particular persons and the province in general:' — yes, — the *dark* assassin of private *characters* and HIS NATIVE COUNTRY." The piece concluded with an invective describing Governor Hutchinson as "the first, the most malignant and *insatiable* enemy" of America who had "committed greater public crimes, than his life can repair or his death satisfy. . . ." [100] Little wonder that the royal authorities wistfully hoped that a few convictions for seditious libel might have a salutary effect in restraining an extravagance of language which exacerbated an incendiary situation.

The royal courts, however, proved to be even more futile in the crisis than they had been in the preceding decades. Except for the convictions of Bayard in 1702, reversed on appeal, of the two Philadelphians who had repudiated the House of Hanover in 1723, and of Checkley in 1724, no common-law prosecutions for seditious utterance had yet been unsuccessful in the eighteenth century. Even in the preceding century, the defendants in the two most notable cases involving freedom of the press, Bradford and Maule,

[100] Quoted in Joseph T. Buckingham, *Specimens of Newspaper Literature* (Boston, 1852), 1:187 and 191.

had not been convicted. It is no surprise, then, that during the crisis years preceding the battle of Lexington, only one indictment could be wrangled from a grand jury — and it came to nothing.[101] The authorities tried to do better, but only half-heartedly. The danger of touching off a riot because of an unpopular prosecution was too great a risk to be taken. In New York, for example, after the passage of the Stamp Act, Lieutenant-Governor Colden informed Secretary Conway in England that the provincial newspapers were brimming with a hate "exciting the people to disobedience of the Laws and to Sedition." But he agreed with his Council "that considering the present temper of the people this is not a proper time to prosecute the printers and Publishers of the Seditious Papers. The Attorney General likewise told me that he does not think himself safe to commence any such Prosecution."[102] A month later Colden reported that James Parker was suspected to be the printer of an incendiary paper but it was imprudent even to make an inquiry into the matter for fear of "raising the Mob which it is thought proper by all means to avoid." [103] By way of contrast the Assembly never doubted its power to suppress sedition. At the height of the Stamp Act crisis, a letter purporting to come from anonymous members of the

---

[101] MacDougall's case, discussed below, pp. 78–85. J. M. Smith, *Freedom's Fetters: the Alien and Sedition Laws and American Civil Liberties* (Ithaca, 1956), at pp. 426-427 claims that a "method used to crush colonial opposition to ministerial policies was an accelerated use of the law of seditious libel." Aside from the fact that colonial opposition to ministerial policies was not crushed at all, none of Smith's authorities offers evidence to support his generalization. It is true, however, that a distinguished roster of historians subscribes to the views expressed in *Freedom's Fetters*.

[102] Sept. 23, 1765, in *Documents Relative to the Colonial History of New York*, 7:759.

[103] Oct. 12, 1765, to Conway, *ibid.*, 7:767.

Sons of Liberty, signing themselves "Freedom," was delivered to the clerk of the House instructing the members on the measures to be taken and accusing them of not supporting "public Liberty." The Assembly, with the support of the radical leaders,[104] promptly voting the letter to be "Libellous, Scandalous, and Seditious," called upon the governor to offer a reward of fifty pounds for the discovery of the author or authors.[105] Fortunately for the authors, they were not caught.

Nowhere was the failure of common-law process more evident than in Massachusetts where Chief Justice Hutchinson doggedly sought to persuade grand juries to return indictments for seditious libel. In one charge, early in 1767, he urged a grand jury to take note of the fact that libeling a person in public print was a crime of high nature, "and it is more mischievous still, when it is pointed against all Authority." He added that he knew "no more dangerous Symptom in any State" than when its rulers were slandered and the authority of the government despised. The grand jury ignored him.[106] Later in 1767, the chief justice undertook to define freedom of the press, stating:

> Pretty high Notions of the Liberty of the Press, I am sensible, have prevailed of late among us; but it is very dangerous to meddle with, and strike at this Court.

[104] Carl Lotus Becker, *The History of Political Parties in the Province of New York 1760–1776* (Madison, Wis., 1909), p. 39.
[105] *Journal of the General Assembly of New-York*, 2:787. Becker, p. 40, explains that although the Assembly opposed the Stamp Act and had approved of the resolutions of the Stamp Act Congress, "it was especially opposed to having political matters referred to the unenfranchised for decision." It was even more opposed to being criticized.
[106] Josiah Quincy, Jr., ed., *Reports of Cases Argued and Adjudged in the Superior Court of Judicature of the Province of Massachusetts Bay, Between 1761 and 1772* (Boston, 1865), pp. 236–237.

The Liberty of the Press is doubtless a very great Blessing; but this liberty means no more than a Freedom for every Thing to pass from the Press without Licence. — That is, you shall not be obliged to obtain a Licence from any Authority before the Emission of Things from the Press. Unlicenced Printing was never thought to mean a Liberty of reviling and calumniating all Ranks and Degrees of Men with Impunity, all Authority with Ignominy. — To carry this absurd Notion of the Liberty of the Press to the Length some would have it — to print every Thing that is Libellous and Slanderous — is truly astonishing, and of the most dangerous Tendency.[107]

Hutchinson's definition of freedom of the press was not only accurate and orthodox; it was the only definition known in Anglo-American thought and law. No libertarian theorist had offered a broader definition, and there is no known evidence proving that any American prior to 1798 — that late — thought otherwise. The *Boston Gazette*, published by Benjamin Edes and John Gill, spokesmen for Sam Adams and the radical party, replied to Hutchinson by quoting Cato's celebrated letter on "Freedom of Speech,"[108] but Cato's libertarianism had consisted of his philosophical exposition of the values of freedom of expression and his wise advice that prosecutions endangered liberty more than its abuse imperiled the state. He and all others had differed in their definitions of a free press not one bit from Hutchinson. The *Gazette* itself had offered the following statement only a few months earlier: "Political liberty consists in a freedom of speech and action, so far as the laws of a community will permit, and no farther: all beyond is criminal,

[107] *Ibid.*, pp. 244–245. Charge to the Grand Jury, August term, 1767.
[108] Schlesinger, *Prelude to Independence*, p. 96. Cato is discussed below, at pp. 115–120.

and tends to the destruction of Liberty itself. — That Society whose laws least restrain the words and actions of its members, is most free. — There is no nation on the earth, where freedom of speech is more extensive than among the English." [109]

In early 1768, the *Gazette* ran an unsigned piece, written by Dr. Joseph Warren, that scalded Governor Bernard with vituperation in an effort to hold him up to the public as a hated enemy of the province.[110] The Council unanimously agreed that the article was a seditious libel placing the governor "in the most odious light." [111] With this support Bernard appealed to the lower House, hoping for an endorsement of his plan to turn the matter over to a grand jury, but that House, in control of the radicals, simply expressed its regrets to the governor, declared itself unwilling to take any additional notice of the matter, and resolved for the first time in its history that "The Liberty of the Press is a great Bulwark of the Liberty of the People: It is, therefore, the incumbent Duty of those who are constituted the Guardians of the People's Rights to defend and maintain it." [112] Bernard, ignoring the advice of the House to go no further, turned to the courts for help.

Chief Justice Hutchinson, charging the grand jury, explained the tendency of criminal libels to disturb the peace and warned that their increased prevalence "threatens the Subversion of all Rule among us." Indeed, they came close to "high treason." Once again he defined the true meaning of freedom of the press; formerly, he recalled, no man

---

[109] *Boston Gazette*, March 9, 1767, quoted in Rossiter, *Seedtime*, p. 385.
[110] Quincy, ed., *Massachusetts Reports*, reprints the article at pp. 271–272.
[111] *Ibid.*, p. 273.
[112] *Ibid.*, p. 275. The House vote was 39 to 30.

could print his thought without a license. "When this Restraint was taken off, then was the true Liberty of the Press. Every Man who prints, prints at his Peril." He then demanded of the grand jurors indictments against those responsible for the seditious statements in the *Gazette*, but they found no bill, inspiring the newspaper, in articles written by Dr. Warren and Sam Adams, to toast the House and the grand jury for vindicating the freedom of the press. Adams also ridiculed the "absurd doctrine, *the more true, the more libellous*." Josiah Quincy, Jr., who had been present at Hutchinson's charge, added a personal note to his report of it, vaguely challenging "some Points of Law" on the authority of "Bollan on the Freedom of Speech and Writing upon Publick Affairs. . . ." [113] At a later session in 1768 the chief justice again tried and failed to get a grand jury to indict for "inflammatory, seditious Libels upon Government or the Rulers in Government, which tend to destroy all civil Peace, and strike at the Root of all Order and Government. . . ." [114] By the spring of 1769 he declared sorrowfully to a grand jury that although the "atrocious Crime" was fast multiplying, his repeated charges on the subject had been "entirely neglected," and as a result "I do not mention the Matter of Libels to you, Gentlemen — I am discouraged!" [115]

With the common-law process breaking down entirely, Governor Bernard appealed for help to the ministry in England. Edes and Gill, he recommended, should be seized and forced to identify their "treasonable and seditious" contributors; responsibility for appropriate action must, however, devolve upon the home government. But the min-

[113] *Ibid.*, pp. 263, 266, 270, 277, and 278. On Bollan, see below, at pp. 157–159.
[114] *Ibid.*, p. 305.
[115] *Ibid.*, p. 309.

istry did nothing except to pass the responsibility to the provincial government for permitting seditious libels to go unpunished. The Governor's Council, replying through William Bollan — its agent in England whom Quincy had mistaken as an authority opposed to Hutchinson's exposition of the common law — hurled a resentful "tu quoque" at the Privy Council and House of Lords for being even far more lax than Massachusetts in countenancing defamation of the government. For every seditionist in the Bay Colony "there are fifty in England," declared Bollan, alluding to the supporters of Wilkes and Junius. The Governor's Council, he asserted, simply had no power to try a case.[116] He must have known, of course, that this was not true; what he meant in all probability was that the Council under the circumstances dared not act against the lower House or bypass the jury system.

By the end of 1771 the Council could not even enforce its own authority. Its members, who were elected by the House, which had cleaned out most of the leading Tories as early as 1766, were led by James Bowdoin and were "just as much dominated by the popular or democratic party as was the House." [117] Yet in late 1771 and 1772 the Council stood foursquare with Hutchinson, now governor, in seeking to scotch incendiary writers. The explanation, perhaps, lies in the repeal of the Townshend duties, the breaking of the Nonimportation Agreement, and the up-

[116] Schlesinger, *Prelude to Independence*, pp. 310–311. The quoted material is from Duniway, *Freedom of the Press*, p. 129.

[117] Robert E. Brown, *Middle-Class Democracy and the Revolution in Massachusetts, 1691–1790* (Ithaca, 1955), p. 230. See also pp. 229 and 333. For detailed discussion of the Council's evolution toward radicalism, see Francis J. Walett, "The Massachusetts Council, 1766–1774," *William and Mary Quarterly*, 3rd ser., 6:605–627 (1949).

surge of prosperity which was accompanied by a near
collapse of the revolutionary movement until the Tea Act
of 1773 rekindled it. Whatever the reason, the Council in
late 1771 believed that Isaiah Thomas, publisher of the
Massachusetts Spy, known as "The Sedition Foundry," had
passed the threshold of tolerable limits by publishing an
article by that noble Roman, "Mucius Scaevola," who was
suspected to be Joseph Greenleaf, a justice of the peace.
Scaevola had flatly announced that Lieutenant-Governor
Oliver "stood recorded as a perjured traitor" while Governor Hutchinson "ought to be dismissed and punished as
a usurper. . . ." [118] Thomas was forthrightly summoned by
the Council to answer for this libel, but with colossal nerve
refused to comply with the order. As he related the story,
he instructed the Council's messenger to notify the governor and their honors that he could not wait upon them
since he was "busily employed in his office. . . ." [119]

In the halcyon days before the resolutionary controversy,
when the thought of mobs did not intimidate the government, the Council would have stunned such impudence by
summarily imprisoning the party. But the imperative of
acting through popular agencies forced the unanimous
Council to content itself with ordering the attorney-general
to prosecute Thomas at common law. He replied with a
piece attacking the Star Chamber doctrine of libels, called
upon Hamilton's Zenger argument to prove that truth was
a defense against seditious libel — had not Scaevola written
only the truth? — and quoted from William Bollan, the
Council's own agent in London, on the values of free dis-

[118] Quoted from the *Spy* of Nov. 14, 1771, by Buckingham,
Specimens, 1:235–236.
[119] Thomas, *History of Printing in America*, 1:380.

cussion.[120] At the following term of the Supreme Court, in February of 1772, the chief justice dwelt on the horrors of seditious libel, but the grand jury blithely refused to indict Thomas. At this point the Council took what was a daring risk in Boston at that time by ordering the attorney-general to prosecute by an information, thereby avoiding the consent of a grand jury. But this plan was so vehemently attacked by the popular party as a violation of the liberties of the subject and of freedom of the press that the prosecution was dropped. Stymied, the Council took petty revenge against Joseph Greenleaf, who had also refused to obey a summons; he was dismissed as a justice of the peace.[121] In the fall of that year, Thomas outdid himself by publishing an attack upon George III, accusing him of having corrupted the government by the appointment of "every dirty booby who was thought a convenient tool. . . ." [122] The apoplectic Hutchinson urged that Thomas be prosecuted by information, but the Council, recalling the public fury against an attempt to do that very thing earlier in the year, advised a popular but futile approach: indictment by grand jury. That body, of course, refused to return a true bill. By that time even the Ministry advised Hutchinson that "in the present temper of the times, prosecutions will be of no effect. . . ." Thomas himself was exultant but menacingly warned that if the press were ever fettered, the next step would be "padlocks on our lips." [123]

The point of course is that the press was not fettered during the revolutionary controversy, at least not the patriot

[120] Schlesinger, *Prelude to Independence*, pp. 140–141.
[121] Thomas, *History of Printing in America*, 2:380–383 and 475–476. See also Schlesinger, *Prelude to Independence*, pp. 140–142.
[122] Quoted in Schlesinger, *Prelude to Independence*, p. 148.
[123] *Ibid.*

press. If any fetters or padlocks were forged, only one body possessed the actual power as well as authority and that was the Assembly, always the most effective repressor. In Virginia where a grand jury declined to indict three publishers in 1766,[124] the House of Burgesses in 1767 demonstrated how to handle those who abused the liberty of the press. A man named James Pride, either out of naïveté or foolish courage, served a writ on a member while the House was in session, an act which that body took as an affront to its collective dignity. Summoned to explain himself, Pride hideously multiplied the affront by failing to obey the summons because of ill health; the letter which he sent by way of explanation was deemed scandalous and a high breach of privilege. The Assembly displayed its mood by commanding its sergeant-at-arms to take Pride into custody by any means necessary even if he had to break open doors and muster a posse. But a medical certificate arrived from Pride's doctor in time to prevent strong-arm measures. The suspicious House immediately commanded two physicians of its own choosing to examine Pride; they reported him without fever and able to attend on the Burgesses. This time the sergeant-at-arms brought in the malefactor, who, without even an interrogation, was delivered to the jailer on a warrant from the speaker to hold him "until discharged, by Order of the House." The prisoner was also assessed twelve pounds sixpence for the services of the Assembly's physicians and sergeant.

After nine days of imprisonment without a hearing, Pride took a drastic step. He wrote an account of his case, revealing to the public the harsh treatment he was receiving, and sent the manuscript by a friend to the Virginia *Gazette* for publication. William Rind, the printer, had the

[124] Thomas, *History of Printing in America*, 2:148.

foresight to check with the authorities before running Pride's piece. The Assembly then resolved that their prisoner's act was a seditious insult. For the first and only time he was summoned, from jail, before the bar of the house, there to receive a censure instead of a hearing. On turning him over to the jailer again, the House ordered that he be kept "in close confinement, without the Use of Pen, Ink, or Paper; and that he be fed on Bread only, and allowed no strong Liquor whatever." It was Pride's good fortune, however, that after two days of his newest punishment the House of Burgesses was prorogued by the governor, making him eligible for habeas corpus. When he was free he discovered that he had lost his post as a naval officer.[125]

The North Carolina Assembly knew how to treat licentious use of the press too. The victim was Hermon Husband, one of the leaders of the Regulators, a group of debtor farmers from the back country who elected him to the Assembly. Late in 1770 the North Carolina *Gazette*, which sympathized with the Regulators, published an article accusing a judge of having unjustly treated debtors. The members of the Assembly were chided too for not doing what was in their power to ameliorate the condition of the people. Affronted, the Assembly voted the article to be a "false, seditious, and Malicious Libel," and turned upon Husband as the suspected author. Summoned to the bar for examination, he denied responsibility for the publication. But the Assembly charged him with "prevarication." Even though he had been acquitted after trial of the charge of having incited a riot the preceding year, the Assembly condemned him as "a principal mover and promoter of the

---

[125] *Journals of the House of Burgesses of Virginia*, vol. 1766–1769, pp. 91, 97, 98–99, 100, 103, 110, 120, 121, 125. The sentence against Pride, quoted above, is at p. 121.

late riots and seditions," and on the theory that leopards
do not change their spots assumed him to be the culprit responsible for the seditious piece in the *Gazette*. When Husband declared that the people would free him if he were
jailed, the Assembly regarded him as being additionally
guilty of a bold insult and an attempt to intimidate the
members from a due discharge of their duties. A final resolution expelled him from his seat in the House.[126] He was
then arrested and held in jail for a couple of months to
await the action of a grand jury which ultimately failed
to indict.[127]

In neighboring South Carolina there was a rupture in the
relations of the upper and lower Houses of the legislature
over an issue initially involving freedom of the press.
Thomas Powell printed in his *South Carolina Gazette* a
digest of the proceedings of the Council at the request of
a member, William Henry Drayton. The Council summoned the publisher for questioning and concluded that
he had contemptuously breached its privileges. This oc-
cured in August of 1773, when the unlicensed publication
of legislative proceedings was still a crime in an America
that was committed to freedom of the press in rhetoric
only. Powell stubbornly refused to ask for pardon, provoking the Council to subject him to a formal trial at which it
was prosecutor, judge, and jury. Drayton, coming to the
publisher's defense, acknowledged that without intending
any affront to the Council he had sent him a copy of part
of the journals with a request that they be printed. Powell,
condemned anyway for a breach of privileges and contempt, was committed to the Charlestown jail. He was

[126] William L. Saunders, ed., *The Colonial Records of North
Carolina (1662–1776)* (Raleigh, 1886–1890), 8:331.
[127] See J. G. de R. Hamilton's article on Husband in the *Dictionary of American Biography*.

released two days later on a writ of habeas corpus issued
by two judges who happened also to be respectively the
speaker of the Assembly and a member of it, Rawlins
Lowndes and G. G. Powell. They accepted the arguments
of young Edmund Rutledge that the printer had a right to
publish an accurate statement of the Council's proceedings
at the request of one of its members, and, secondly, that
the Council, being an executive rather than a legislative
body, possessed no authority to commit anyone for breach
of parliamentary privilege. The publisher immediately
issued a special issue of his paper notifying the public of the
affair in such terms that the Council responded by ruling
that he was guilty of seditious libel. A committee of the
Council, including the chief justice of the province, then
reported that Speaker Lowndes and Representative Powell,
by discharging a prisoner committed by order of the Council in defense of its authority and dignity, were "guilty of
the most atrocious contempt of this house" and had "sub-
verted the constitution of this government. . . ." The
Council, accepting this report, notified the Assembly that
it expected the proper steps to be taken against the two
members for their crime.

By now freedom of the press had been completely lost
as an issue in the case. The Assembly, refusing to comply
with the Council's demands, was concerned only with
justifying the conduct of its speaker and asserting its independence against the Council, which it denied to be a
parliamentary body. Each House protested to the government in England that the other had unwarrantedly interfered in its affairs. The appeals not yet having been decided
when the war broke out, the issues were never resolved.
The point which emerges most clearly from the affair is
that the press in South Carolina was at the mercy of the

legislature. Had the *Gazette's* publication concerning the Council not been politically useful to the Assembly in its struggle of long standing against the Council, the printer would have remained in jail at the Council's pleasure.[128]

In New York the Assembly, which had intimidated a printer and his journeymen in 1766 for inadvertently publishing an address of the House with two typographical errors,[129] proved that it was capable of dealing effectively even with a radical of the patriot party. In December of 1769, the Assembly had voted to supply provisions for the king's troops in New York City, in return for Governor Colden's signature to an act authorizing the emission of needed bills of credit.[130] Three days later a handbill addressed "To the Betrayed Inhabitants of New-York," signed by a "Son of Liberty," was broadcast throughout the city. The author condemned the Assembly for abandoning the liberties of the people by passing the provisions bill, and called upon the public to rise against unjust measures. The next day another broadside appeared, over the name of "Legion," censuring the "*base inglorious* Conduct of our General Assembly" and urging the people, as had "Son of Liberty," to attend a mass protest meeting. Fourteen hundred turned out and were addressed by the radical agitator, John Lamb. The Assembly retaliated by declaring each broadside to be "a false seditious and infamous Libel" and called upon the governor to offer rewards for information leading to the discovery of the author or authors. The provision bill had passed the Assembly by a bare majority, but the resolves against the seditious writers passed unani-

[128] Thomas, *History of Printing in America*, 2:162–167, and Edward McCrady, *The History of South Carolina under the Royal Government 1719–1776* (New York, 1899), pp. 715–723.
[129] Thomas, *History of Printing in America*, 2:302–303.
[130] Becker, *Parties in New York*, pp. 77–78.

mously. Governor Colden gladly complied with the Assembly's request and issued proclamations offering one hundred and fifty pounds in reward money.[131]

Dazzled by so much money, a journeyman printer in the shop of James Parker betrayed his employer as the printer of "To the Betrayed." Parker, who in 1756 had been jailed for a week by the Assembly for printing a reflection, was now charged with having published a seditious libel, arrested, and brought before the governor and Council. All his apprentices and journeymen were taken into custody for questioning at the same time. Their testimony substantiated that of the informer and also revealed that one Alexander McDougall had corrected the proofs at the printing office. Parker himself balked at naming the author, but he could not withstand the threats of imprisonment and dismissal from his post as comptroller of the post office. He made a deal with the Council, buying immunity against prosecution and loss of his post by identifying the author and pledging to appear against him as a government witness.[132]

---

[131] E. B. O'Callaghan, ed., *Documentary History of the State of New York* (Albany, 1849–1851), 3:528–536, reproduces the broadsides and Colden's proclamations which quote the Assembly's resolutions. According to the proclamations the Assembly vote was unanimous. Isaac Q. Leake, *Memoir of the Life and Times of General John Lamb* (Albany, 1850), p. 51, claimed that one member, Philip Schuyler, voted against the resolutions. E. Wilder Spaulding, *His Excellency, George Clinton* (New York, 1938), p. 27, supports Leake. However, the diary of William Smith, a member of the Council, also supports the fact that the Assembly's vote was unanimous. See William H. W. Sabine, ed., *Historical Memoirs from 16 March 1763 to 9 July 1776 of William Smith* (New York, 1956), p. 72.

[132] "McDougall's Account," in a letter to the *New York Journal*, Feb. 15, 1770, in Thomas Jones, *History of New York During the Revolutionary War*, ed. E. F. de Lancey (New York, 1879),

The man identified by Parker was Alexander McDougall, a local merchant who with Lamb and Isaac Sears was one of the commanders of the Sons of Liberty. Later McDougall would serve in both the First and Second Continental Congresses and as a major-general during the Revolution. He died in 1786 a pillar of conservatism, the first president of the Bank of New York and founder and head of the Society of Cincinnati in New York.[133] In February of 1770, he was arrested on a charge of seditious libel against the Assembly. With Parker as a witness of his authorship, the legislature had a sure-fire case and turned the prisoner over to the common-law courts. McDougall, on examination before Chief Justice Horsmanden, remained silent except to demand a trial by jury. Bail was set at the inordinately high sum of five hundred pounds which McDougall refused to pay, although Governor Colden called him "a person of some fortune." He preferred waiting in jail as a martyr while awaiting the action of the grand jury.[134]

McDougall remained in jail for two and a half months. His imprisonment did more to publicize the cause of liberty of the press than any event since Zenger's trial. Alexander's account of that trial was republished for the first time in New York since 1736, and Parker's paper and Holt's *New York Journal* courageously plumped for McDougall and

1:432–434. See also *Historical Memoirs of William Smith*, pp. 73–75; Leake, *Lamb*, pp. 60–61; Thomas, *History of Printing in America*, 2:479–481; and Dorothy Rita Dillon, *The New York Triumvirate* (New York, 1949), pp. 106–107.

[133] *Dictionary of American Biography*.

[134] "McDougall's Account," and Colden to Lord Hillsborough, Feb. 20, 1770, in Jones, *History of New York*, 1:432–434. See also Thomas, *History of Printing in America*, 2:481; Goebel and Naughton, *Law Enforcement in New York*, p. 506 note 89.

freedom of discussion. The editor and the prisoner against whom he was to testify wrote hortatory articles urging all the colonies to enact statutes abolishing the "tyrannical Tenets" of the common law of seditious libel which was invariably associated with the infamous Star Chamber. Yet the concept of seditious libel was never attacked. There was no suggestion that government cannot be criminally assaulted by its citizens' opinions. Beneath the epithetical rhetoric was only the proposition that truth be accepted as a defense. The *New York Mercury*, however, defended the common law and backed the Assembly against McDougall.[135] The editor of conservatism's voice was Hugh Gaine, who in 1753 had been forced by the Assembly to humble himself in order to avoid prosecution for having printed its proceedings without prior license.[136]

Notwithstanding Gaine's policy, the McDougall case as managed by the Sons of Liberty became America's equivalent of Wilkes' case in England. Indeed, McDougall himself consciously posed as the American Wilkes and turned his imprisonment into a theatrical triumph, while his supporters used the free press issue as an antiadministration weapon. Forty-five, the number of the *North Briton* which had earned Wilkes his conviction for seditious libel, became the talismanic symbol of libertarianism and of the American cause against England. On the forty-fifth day of the year, for example, forty-five Liberty Boys dined in honor of McDougall on forty-five pounds of beef from a forty-five-month-old bull, drank forty-five toasts to liberty of the press and its defenders, and after dinner marched to the city

---

[135] *Historical Memoirs of William Smith*, pp. 75–76; Schlesinger, *Prelude to Independence*, pp. 115–116; Dillon, *New York Triumvirate*, p. 112.

[136] See above, p. 46.

jail to salute McDougall with forty-five cheers. On one particularly festive liberty day, forty-five songs were sung to him by forty-five virgins, every one of whom, reported a damned Tory, was forty-five years old.[137]

At the end of April McDougall, attended by a mob of his partisans on the way from prison to court, was finally brought before the grand jury which indicted him as the author of a seditious libel against the Assembly. It was the only indictment of its kind against a popular leader during the revolutionary controversy and the first of its kind in twenty-five years. Yet the unique fact that the prosecution was supported by every branch of the government, particularly the Assembly, makes the indictment understandable. So does the fact that the grand jurors were carefully picked, the "most . . . opulent & substantial gentlemen of the city." The trial was set for the next session of the court, in July, and McDougall, this time paying the huge bail assessed against him, was released from prison. On July 2, just before the trial, James Parker, the star witness of the prosecution and the only one who could testify from personal knowledge that McDougall wrote the seditious broadside, suddenly died. With his death the case against the defendant vanished. The trial was postponed till October and then again indefinitely. If McDougall gloated over the turn of events that promised him a discharge from the indictment, he failed to consider the power of a revengeful Assembly.

With the collapse of the common-law prosecution, the Assembly resolved to punish McDougall on its own author-

[137] Jones, *History of New York*, 1:27–28 & 435, citing *New-York Gazette*, Feb. 19, 1770, and *New York Journal*, March 22 and March 29, 1770; Leake, *Lamb*, p. 62; John C. Miller, *Origins of the American Revolution* (Boston, 1943), p. 306. On Wilkes, see below, pp. 145–148.

ity. Late in 1770, he was arrested on a warrant from the speaker by order of the House, and after a week in jail was brought before the bar by the sergeant-at-arms. Speaker Cruger then informed him that he was charged with having libeled the House and asked whether he was guilty or not. McDougall refused to plead to the charge until, he declared, he was informed of the identity of his accusers and the evidence against him. Cruger interrupted to threaten that he would be held in contempt for addressing the House without its prior leave, but George Clinton interceded on the prisoner's behalf with the result that McDougall was permitted to give his reasons for not pleading. He explained that he had no counsel, that the case was still pending in the courts, and that the Assembly itself had already declared the broadside to be a seditious libel and its author guilty — in other words that he feared incriminating himself. Moreover, he added, the Assembly, having initiated the prosecution against him, was now acting as his judge and jury which it had no power to do, particularly when it would be placing him under double jeopardy since he was still answerable at common law. For these reasons, McDougall declared, he would not answer the question whether he was guilty. Representative de Noyelles interjected that the House had the power to extort his answer and threatened infliction of *peine forte et dure*, a form of torture, recognized in English law, to force a suspect to plead one way or the other just so the trial might then proceed. One who stood mute, as McDougall, would be spread-eagled on the ground and have heavy metal weights placed upon his body; each day more weights would be added, while the prisoner was fed stale bread and stagnant water on alternate days. The "punishment hard and strong" continued until he either died or admitted that he was guilty or not guilty.[138] McDougall braved De Noyelles' barbaric threat, obstinately refusing to plead to the charge, thereby stymying the proceedings.

The members fell to arguing among themselves whether they might coerce a prisoner to answer an incriminating question or even take jurisdiction of a case still pending in the courts. George Clinton, though originally having voted for the resolution to prosecute McDougall's seditious libel, now supported him on technical grounds. Clinton admitted that if the Assembly were not a party to the common-law indictment it would have full power over him and, if necessary, to make him plead, might even throw him out of the window. The Assembly finally agreed to investigate the extent of its own powers in the case. McDougall was then ordered to state in writing his objections against entering a plea. His statement provoked Speaker Cruger to announce that he had reflected on the honor and dignity of the House. The members then voted that his fresh libels were in contempt of their parliamentary privilege and de-

---

[138] On *peine forte et dure*, see Sir James Fitzjames Stephen, *A History of The Criminal Law of England* (London, 1883), 1:297–299; E. M. Morgan, "The Privilege Against Self-Incrimination," *Minnesota Law Review*, 34:12–14, 20–21 (1949). England abolished this barbaric practice by a statute of 1772 which provided that a refusal to plead was equivalent to a plea of guilty which, by a statute of 1827, was changed to a plea of not guilty. The only known instance of *peine* having been inflicted in the colonies occurred in Giles Corey's case in 1692 in Salem on a charge of witchcraft; he was pressed to death. Goebel and Naughton, *Law Enforcement in Colonial New York*, p. 582, questionably assert that a "modification" of *peine* was used in 1691 when Jacob Leisler was ordered "tyed up and putt in irons" after his refusal to plead to a charge of treason. There is no record in England or America of *peine* having been used in a legislative trial; moreover at common law it might be used only in a felony case. Seditious libel was misdemeanor. Thus De Noyelles' threat was illegally based.

manded that he beg for pardon. His refusal prompted another vote sentencing him to an indeterminate period in prison. Only five members of the Assembly, including Clinton, opposed the sentence. As in Pennsylvania's Smith-Moore case, the sheriff was ordered not to honor a writ of habeas corpus. McDougall obtained a writ without avail, the sheriff notifying the court that the matter was not within its jurisdiction since the prisoner had been committed for breach of privilege. The court submitted to the legislature and McDougall remained in jail. In the meantime the Assembly accepted a committee report, based on precedents of the House of Commons, supporting the lawfulness of its authority and actions in the case. Once more an American legislature endorsed the principle that it possessed an unbounded prerogative even when personal liberty and freedom of expression were involved. McDougall finally was released when the legislative session ended, after serving nearly three months in jail. The common-law charge against him was dismissed, and America's Wilkes won his freedom.[139]

Freedom, however, did not include a right to criticize the legislature, as the cases of Pride in Virginia, Husband in North Carolina, Powell in South Carolina, and McDou-

[139] Leake, *Lamb*, pp. 71–73; Spaulding, *George Clinton*, pp. 28–29; Thomas, *History of Printing in America*, 2:482–483; Dillon, *New York Triumvirate*, pp. 119–121; Schlesinger, *Prelude to Independence*, p. 116. A microfilm copy of the *Journal of the Votes and Proceedings of the General Assembly of the Colony of New-York* for the years 1769–71, obtained from the Public Records Office in London, Doc. #953. C.O. 5/1219, located by my colleague, Lawrence Leder, after my efforts failed, indicates that a few changes are in order in this account of the McDougall case; but because the microfilm came to hand when the manuscript was in galleys, and because all the needed changes are quite trivial, I have let the original version stand, uncorrected but essentially accurate.

gall in New York amply demonstrated. Legislative proceedings could not be published without prior license; legislative measures were protected by parliamentary privilege from fault finders. Animadversion was regarded as subversion. Any verbal attack on government officials or policies which might be deemed an affront to the authority or honor of the legislature was subject to a power of repression from which not all the writs precious to the liberty of the subject could effect a rescue. If an exercise of parliamentary privilege was not the appropriate means of silencing an opponent, there were others of an extralegal nature. Vigilantism may be a necessary ingredient in the making of a revolution, and there may even have been occasions when its existence among the patriots was understandably provoked. But there is no denying that it did exist on a widespread scale, and it was always ugly, always a denial of due process, and always, before the outbreak of the war, directed not at an enemy but a fellow citizen whose opinions differed. There were even occasions when that citizen was a staunch patriot whose judgment in the opinion of extremists needed correction by drastic methods for the good of the cause. John Holt, for example, the publisher of the *New-York Gazette*, was a vigorous opponent of the Stamp Act who preferred to suspend publication of his newspaper rather than pay the tax. A letter from the Sons of Liberty notified him that he could best "promote the Cause" by continuing to publish without stamps in defiance of Parliament. Holt obeyed because the letter concluded with the threat that if he refused, "depend upon it, your House, Person and Effects, will be in imminent danger." [140] Intimidation was usually reserved, however, for those who opposed "the Cause," like John Mein,

[140] Thomas, *History of Painting in America*, 2:297.

publisher of the loyalist paper, the *Boston Chronicle*. The windows of Mein's printing office were smashed, his signs smeared with filth, his person threatened with violence, and his paper boycotted, with the result that he went out of business.[141]

The evidence forces the conclusion that Chief Justice Hutchinson had accurately summarized the situation when he acidly observed that the Adamses and their supporters were "contending for an unlimited Freedom of Thought and Action, which they would confine wholly to themselves."[142] Free speech for one side only is not free speech at all, or at best is an extraordinarily narrow concept of it. That, indeed, is the whole point: during the entire colonial period, from the time of the first settlements to the Revolutionary War and the framing of the first bills of rights, America had very little experience with freedom of speech or press as a meaningful condition of life. Nor did colonial America produce or inherit a broad concept of freedom of speech or press, as the following analysis of Anglo-American libertarian thought will demonstrate.

[141] Schlesinger, *Prelude to Independence*, pp. 107–108.
[142] Quincy, ed., *Massachusetts Reports*, p. 244.

CHAPTER THREE

❧ Early English Theory: from Milton to "Cato"

The philosophical principle of freedom of the mind had merely a slight influence on the expansion of freedom of speech and press, at least through the eighteenth century. Libertarian expositions were abundant enough, but in England until about 1776 and in America until about 1798 their libertarian quality was nearly as narrow as the common law in crucial respects. Until those late dates freedom of discussion, particularly in the realm of politics, had almost no history as a broad concept.

To be sure, one can go all the way back to the ancients, especially the Athenians and the Romans of the early Republic, and discover a few statements favoring an undefined broad liberty of expression. The plays of Euripides, for example, are a storehouse of allusions to the glories and values of free speech. The hero of *Ion*, to cite an instance, hopes that his unknown mother may be Athenian so that "by my mother may free speech be mine," else he "bears a bondman's tongue"; and a passage between Jocasta and Polyneices, in *The Pheonissae*, demonstrates the Greek understanding that unwise government results from a curb on the tongues of citizens. Demosthenes declared that no greater calamity could befall a people than "the privation of free speech." Yet there is no evidence that even the most libertarian among the Greeks suffered oral or written sedition to exist with impunity. Plato's account of the punishment of Socrates by the freedom-loving Athenians for the crime of subversive utterances is the best-known case of its kind in history.[1] Machiavelli might have been echoing the ancients as well as representing the best thought of the Renaissance when he qualified the right of every man to "think all things, speak all things, write all things," by pointing out that popular governments are aspersed because the people are free to "speak ill" of them, whereas Princes, though wise to allow the citizen a "liberty to have and sustain the opinions which please him best," must be "talked of with Reserve and Respect." [2]

Spinoza went as far as anyone up to his time in advocating that the state should permit the utmost latitude for men to speak their minds. In his neglected classic, *Theologico-Political Treatise* (1670), he presented as profound and sustained an analysis of freedom of thought and speech as had been offered, climaxing his work with a concluding chapter entitled, "That In a Free State Every Man May Think What He Likes, and Say What He Thinks." From the premise that man is "by indefeasible natural right the master of his own thoughts" and cannot abdicate his "freedom of judgment," Spinoza concluded that diverse and

[1] On Demosthenes, see Thomas Erskine May, *The Constitutional History of England* (New York, 1880), 2:102 note 1. See generally, Max Radin, "Freedom of Speech in Ancient Athens," *American Journal of Philology*, 48:215–230 (1927); and Laura Robinson, *Free Speech in the Roman Republic* (Baltimore, 1940).

[2] Quoted in [Joseph Addison?], *The Thoughts of A Tory Author Concerning the Press: With the Opinion of the Ancients and Moderns, about Freedom of* SPEECH *and* WRITING (London, 1712), pp. 7, 8.

contradictory opinions were inevitable; to compel men "to speak only according to the dictates of supreme power" would be disastrous to the state as well as to the individual. Believing, however, that "authority may be as much injured by words as by actions," he opposed an "unlimited concession" of free speech. He recognized that the individual and social interest in freedom had to be weighed against authority's competing claims: "we must, therefore, now inquire, how far such freedom can and ought to be conceded without danger to the peace of the state, or the power of the rulers." [3]

Spinoza believed in the right to speak against the state, provided that no attempt is made to introduce any change in private authority and provided that verbal opposition is grounded in reason rather than "fraud, anger, or hatred." [4] Argument that a law is unsound and deserves repeal should be permitted, as should any speculation concerning philosophy, religion, science, or "the liberal arts," even though falsehoods may proceed from unworthy motives; the possibility of abuse, contended Spinoza, ought not to warrant limiting the right. [5] That right to "freedom of speech" should be recognized by the wise ruler so that resistance to him might be legitimatized and lessened and "so that men may live together in harmony, however diverse, or even openly contradictory their opinions may be." [6] The state that punished opinions injured itself. Acts "which alone are capable of offending," rather than the "opinions of mankind," should be brought to trial; the rights of rulers, argued Spinoza, in secular and sacred matters "should merely have

[3] *Theologico-Political Treatise*, in *The Chief Works of Benedict de Spinoza*, trans. R. H. M. Elwes (London, 1883), 1:258.
[4] *Ibid.*, p. 259.
[5] *Ibid.*, p. 261.
[6] *Ibid.*, p. 263.

to do with actions, but . . . every man should think what he likes and say what he thinks." [7]

On the other hand, these libertarian notions on the scope of free expression proceeded from a premise that was shared by Machiavelli and Hobbes: the sovereign power, Spinoza wrote, has the "right to treat as enemies all men whose opinions do not, on all subjects, entirely coincide with its own"; but, he added, he was discussing the "proper" course of action for the state to follow, not its rights. Properly, it should punish only politically injurious speech as was tantamount to a seditious act. All "opinions would be seditious . . . which by their very nature nullify the compact by which the right of free action was ceded." [8] Stirring up the people against their rulers, counseling civil disobedience, advocating the enactment of laws by unconstituted authority, teaching that contracts ought not be kept or that everyone should believe as he pleases: these were, for Spinoza, criminal libels, exceptions to his rule that overt acts, rather than mere words, were alone punishable. Thus even Spinoza, for all his tolerance, drew the line at seditious utterances.

The same may be said of an equally libertarian group, the English Levellers, "who represented the first great outburst of democratic thought in history, with John Lilburne and Richard Overton leading the way." [9] Almost any Leveller tract of the 1640's contained a passage condemning censorship and the licensing system, with an argument that freedom of speech and press were essential to the establishment of free government and personal liberty. "A Remonstrance

[7] *Ibid.*, p. 265.
[8] Ibid., p. 260.
[9] Margaret Judson, *The Crisis of the Constitution* (Rutgers, 1949), p. 381.

of Many Thousand Citizens" (1646) asked Parliament to proclaim its legislative plans prior to enactment and to "heare all things that can be spoken with or against the same, and to that intent, let the imprisoned Presses at liberty, so that all mens understandings may be more conveniently informed. . . ." [10] "The Humble Petition" of 1649, Overton's work in all likelihood, argued that when men's mouths were "kept from making noise" they are "robd of their liberties," truth suppressed, and the people kept ignorant and fit only to serve the unjust ends of tyrants. A free press was "essential unto Freedom" to prevent the nation from being placed in bondage, "for what may not be done to that people who may not speak or write, but at the pleasure of Licensers." The government must "hear all voices and judgments" by removing the "least restraint upon the Press," for the people could not enjoy liberty without "speaking, writing, printing, and publishing their minds freely. . . ."[11]

Despite such principled statements, there were moments when even Levellers advocated a more systematic enforcement of the licensing system — so long as it was not aimed at them. Lilburne himself, after criticizing press restraints and unlawful search and seizure of unlicensed Leveller material, complained of the freedom allowed to royalist publications and "Malignant Books and Pamphlets tending to the ruine of the Kingdome . . . and freedome of Peo-

---

[10] "A remonstrance of Many Thousand Citizens," 1646, in Don M. Wolfe, ed., *Leveller Manifestoes of the Puritan Revolution* (New York, 1944), p. 123.

[11] "To the Right Honourable . . . The Commons of England . . . The Humble Petition . . . ," Jan. 19, 1649, *ibid.*, pp. 327–329. See also pp. 207 and 364; and William Haller and Godfrey Davies, eds. *The Leveller Tracts, 1647–1653* (New York, 1944), p. 167.

ple." [12] Samuel Chidley, in a pamphlet attacking Lilburne's opponents, requested Parliament "to silence such Babblers" and added: "I hold it one of the greatest abuses of the Commonwealth, that so many lying foolish Pamphlets have been, and are suffered to go abroad. . . ."[13]

William Walwyn, "the most consistently radical thinker among the Levellers," [14] wrote a series of magnificent tracts on behalf of "the freedome of minde," liberty of conscience, and "freedome of discourse." [15] At one point he went so far as to reject the bad-tendency test by arguing that criminal deeds alone should be punishable, but not expression.[16] Yet even Walwyn confessed, inconsistently, that words which were "scandalous, or dangerous to the State" had "upon good grounds" been prohibited by Parliament. He wrote, for example, in reference to "liberty of Con-

---

[12] "Englands Birth-Right," 1645, in William Haller, ed., *Tracts on Liberty in the Puritan Revolution, 1638–1647* (New York, 1933, 3:269.

[13] "The Dissembling Scot . . . Or a Vindication of Lieu. Col. John Lilburn and others," 1652, quoted in William C. Clyde, *The Struggle for the Freedom of the Press from Caxton to Cromwell* (London, 1934), p. 219.

[14] Joseph Frank, *The Levellers* (Cambridge, Mass., 1955), p. 30. On Walwyn, see also W. K. Jordan, *The Development of Religious Toleration in England* (Cambridge, Mass., 1934–1940), 4:176–190.

[15] "A Helpe to the Right Understanding of a Discourse Concerning Independency," 1645, in Haller, ed., *Tracts*, 3:199, 200.

[16] After defending "freedome of discourse" from the charge of tending to disturbance of the State, Walwyn added: "And as for disturbance to the State: admit any mans judgement be so misinformed, as to beleeve there is no sinne; if this man now upon this government should take away another mans goods, or commit murder or adultery; the Law is open, and he is to be punished as a malefactor, and so for all crimes that any mans judgment may mislead him unto." (*Ibid.*, 3:200.)

science," which he thought the right of every man, that no
one should be "punished or discountenanced by Authority
for his Opinion, unlesse it be dangerous to the State," and
he placed the identical restriction upon "the Presse." [17]

Several Independent tractarians went as far, but no
farther, than their Leveller contemporaries in expanding
the bounds of free expression. Roger Williams, for example,
in his celebrated defense of toleration, *The Bloudy Tenent,
of Persecution, for cause of Conscience* (1644) exempted
from the civil magistrate's jurisdiction all concernments of
conscience, even "scandalous" doctrines in opposition to
the establishment, but he broke into his argument to note
parenthetically, "(I speak not of scandal against the civil
state, which the civil magistrate ought to punish) . . ." [18]
Henry Robinson, in his superb discussion, *Liberty of Conscience*, was one of the rare writers to confront the problem
of free expression for Roman Catholics without betraying
his principles. When he contended that force or compulsion
of any kind had no place in matters of religion and that
reason and argument were the only allowable weapons,
he expressly included "Papists, Jewes, Turkes, Pagans, Here-
ticks, with all Infidels & Misbeleevers." Religious "combat"
was to be "fought out upon eaven ground, on equal terms,
neither side must expect to have greater liberty of speech,
writing, Printing, or whatsoever else, then the other [*sic*]."
All men without exception were to have the "same privilege . . . to deliver their mindes freely both in speech and

[17] "The Compassionate Samaritane," 1644, in Haller, ed., *Tracts*,
3:63, 67, 103–104.
[18] *The Bloudy Tenent, of Persecution, for cause of Conscience*,
ed. Samuel L. Caldwell (1867), in *The Writings of Roger Williams*, Publications of the Narragansett Club (Providence, 1866–
1874), 3:136. See also 3:96, 100, 110, 131, 147, 163, and 171.

writing." [19] Yet Robinson defended an equal right of speech and press only in the context of an argument for freedom of religion. There is no evidence that he differed from Roger Williams or William Walwyn, no evidence, that is, that he countenanced any expressions scandalizing the government or that his tolerance of sectarian controversy extended to exclusively secular, particularly state, matters.

John Milton, at least in his famous *Areopagitica*, had a secularist approach to the problem of liberty of inquiry and expression, when compared to Robinson, Walwyn, and Williams. Milton, of course, is traditionally regarded as a great apostle of the free mind, with Locke, Jefferson, and Mill. Unquestionably, several passages of the *Areopagitica*, which are ritualistically quoted to the exclusion of all else, carry implications of majestic breadth, but no one who reads him with care should refer to "Milton's dream of free speech for everybody." [20] He might cry out, "Give *me* liberty to know, to utter, and to argue freely according to conscience, above all liberties," [21] but his use of the personal pronoun is significant, for his well-advertised tolerance did not extend to the thought that he hated. Indeed, it extended only, as he specified, to "neighboring differences, or rather indifferences," [22] which in 1644 meant Protestantism in a variety of Puritan forms. He specifically excluded from his spectrum of neighboring opinions "Pop-

[19] "Liberty of Conscience," 1644, in Haller, ed., *Tracts*, 3:133, 134. For a discussion of Robinson's thought, see Jordan, *Religious Toleration*, 4:140–176.

[20] See, *e.g.*, Zechariah Chafee, Jr., *Three Human Rights in the Constitution of 1787* (Lawrence, Kan., 1956), p. 61.

[21] *Areopagitica*, ed. William Haller, in *The Works of John Milton* (New York, 1931–1938), Frank A. Patterson, gen. ed., p. 4:346.

[22] *Ibid.*, 4:349.

ery, and open superstition" which he thought "should be extirpat," and he banned also the "impious or evil" which "no law can possibly permit." [23]

In a recent volume of essays littered with encomiums on Milton as the father of modern intellectual liberty, two contributions stand out as the only realistic appraisals. Salvador de Madariaga noted that as late as 1673 Milton was

> still putting forward authority, and not merely authority but Bible authority, as the standard of truth. . . . I believe that it is dangerous to listen to one who claims freedom of thought in the name of an orthodoxy. . . . There is yet another standard, the willingness to grant to others that freedom of thought that you want for yourself; and from that point of view I am not certain Milton satisfies us. Indeed, I am tempted to think he did not.[24]

The Very Reverend W. R. Matthews, Dean of St. Paul's, referring to the exaggerated notion of Milton's libertarianism held by those who have not recently read his book, pointed out that he "did not support freedom of religious debate for Catholics, Anglicans, Atheists or non-Christians," and concluded, "it is clear that Milton himself would have excluded not only the overwhelming majority of Christians but the greater part of the human race from the benefit of his tolerance." [25] This Anglican statement is somewhat exaggerated, since Milton later transcended his Puritanism to encompass Anglicans in a proposed united front of all Protestants against Catholics. Yet the thrust of the exaggeration is in the right direction. Dean Matthews

---

[23] *Ibid.*

[24] Quoted in Herman Ould, ed., *Freedom of Expression. A Symposium . . . to Commemorate the Tercentenary of the Publication of Milton's "Areopagitica"* (London, 1944).

[25] Quoted *ibid.*, p. 78.

possibly had in mind the fact that the royalist writings which Milton deplored as a "court-libell against the Parlament" [26] were Anglican in character. Milton thought they should be censored, pointing out that if the licensing system had any justification, it would be in the performance of the "prime service" of preventing the circulation of such material.[27] Milton did not, in other words, even oppose the licensing system unequivocally, despite his affirmation that free and humane government results only from "free writing and free speaking. . . ." [28] Except for his criticism of royalist weeklies, he did not even interest himself in one of the chief issues in the controversy over freedom of the press at the time of the *Areopagitica:* the freedom of polemical newswriters. His silence on this issue helps explain the fact that in 1651 he was one of Cromwell's licensers or censors — despite his earlier and eloquent denunciation of such officials — since the works that came before him for his imprimatur were corontos or newsbooks, partisan sheets of current news.[29] In all likelihood Milton never intended that anything but the serious works of intellectuals, chiefly scholars and Protestant divines, should be really free. A later essay revealed the point rather explicitly when he noted that if open expression was feared because it might "unsettle the weaker sort," Latin, "which the common people understand not" would be a solution for having issues "discust among the Learned only." [30]

---

[26] *Areopagitica*, in *Works,* 4:320.
[27] *Ibid.*, 4:320–321.
[28] *Ibid.*, 4:345.
[29] For Milton as a censor, see Clyde, *Struggle for Freedom of the Press,* pp. 79–80, 172–173, and David Masson, *Life of Milton* (London, 1858–1880), 4:324–334, 432–433.
[30] *Of True Religion, Heresie, Schism, and Toleration,* 1673, in *Works,* 4:178.

In *A Treatise of Civil power in Ecclesiastical causes* (1659), Milton explicitly reserved the right of "a free and lawful debate" [31] to all Protestants, thereby allowing even Anabaptists and Socinians on the left and Anglicans on the right to enjoy a privilege formerly the prerogative of Puritanism only. But the "papist," whom Milton characterized as the "only heretic," was barred from participation,[32] though not necessarily on religious grounds. Catholicism he thought to be less a religion than "a Roman principalitie . . . justly therefore to be suspected, not tolerated by the magistrate of another countrey." [33] Although "just reason of state" may have been an understandable ground for restrictions on Catholic teaching and practice, at a time when the security of the government depended upon the maintenance of Protestant supremacy, Milton cut himself off from even this rationalization for intolerance. In 1673, in his tract on *True Religion, Heresie, Schism, and Toleration,* he wrote:

As for tolerating the exercise of their [Catholic] Religion, supposing their State activities not to be dangerous, I answer, that Toleration is either public or private; and the exercise of their Religion, as far as it is Idolatrous, can be tolerated neither way; not publicly, without grievous and unsufferable scandal giv'n to all consciencious Beholders; not privately, without great offence to God, declar'd against all Idolatry, though secret. . . .

Having shown thus, that Popery, as being Idolatrous, is not to be tolerated either in Public or in Private; it must be now thought how to remove it and hinder the growth thereof, I mean in our Natives. . . . Are we to punish them by corporal punishments, or fines in their Estates, upon

[31] *Works*, 6:13.
[32] *Ibid.*, 6:14.
[33] *Ibid.*, 6:19.

account of their Religion? I suppose it stands not with
the Clemency of the Gospel, more then what appertains to
the security of the State: But first we must remove their
Idolatry, and all the furniture thereof, whether Idols, or
the Mass wherein they adore their God under Bread and
Wine: for the Commandment forbids to adore. . . . If they
say that by removing their Idols we violate their Con-
sciences, we have no warrant to regard Conscience which
is not grounded on Scripture. . . .[34]

These constricted views on freedom of religion influenced Milton's thought on freedom of speech and press.
Writing at a time when his party was out of power and
Catholic literature was being licensed under the Restoration, he complained of having to "suffer the Idolatrous
books of Papists" and recommended against a policy of
open debate with them. "Shall we condescend to dispute
with them?" he asked, and answered emphatically, *"we
are not to dispute."* [35] He appealed to all Protestants to join
"on common ground against Popery," and to that end he
pleaded the case of civil liberty — for Protestants only.
Can one who based his religion exclusively on the Scriptures
refuse with equity "to hear or read him, who demonstrates
to have gained his knowledge by the same way? is it a fair
course to assert truth by arrogating to himself the only
freedome of speech, and stopping the mouths of others
equally gifted?" [36] In context, the question demonstrates
Milton's limited support of free speech. Perhaps his narrow
conception of intellectual liberty is best revealed by his
own recommendation for the policy to be followed on
press freedom. In the concluding section of the *Areopagitica* he endorsed a system of unlicensed printing, condi-

[34] *Ibid.*, 6:172–173.
[35] *Ibid.*, 6:174.
[36] *Ibid.*, 6:177.

tioned only upon the registration of all printers and authors; but he reserved the law of subsequent punishment for any abuse or licentiousness of the press: "Those which otherwise come forth, if they be found mischievous and libellous, the fire and the executioner will be the timeliest and the most effectuall remedy that mans prevention can use." [37]

To Americans of the Framers' generation, Milton's reputation as a libertarian was rivaled only by John Locke's. In his *Essay Concerning Human Understanding*, Locke added a new dimension to the arguments for civil liberty. His predecessors had grounded their positions on the tyranny and futility of suppression, the morality of fairness and tolerance, the self-interest of sectarianism, the dictates of the Scriptures, the needs of scholarship and of Protestantism, and the certainty that truth would best falsehood in an open encounter. Although Locke employed these arguments too, he relied mainly on the contention that the mind is so frail, its understanding so limited, its beliefs so involuntary, that truth is inaccessible to it. All men, he admonished, ought to be skeptical of the validity of their own opinions since they cannot know they are right and might very likely be in error. Opinions held with the "greatest stiffness" are more often than not the results of human incapacity — faulty judgment, prejudice, failure to examine one's own presuppositions, the inability to discover and use proofs, susceptibility to passion and irrational habits of thought. Since men are forced to operate in a "twilight zone" of knowledge, whose truth and certainty is "scanty," it would be wisest, he wrote, for all

> to maintain peace and the common offices of humanity and friendship in the diversity of opinions. . . . We should do

[37] *Areopagitica*, in *Works*, 4:353.

well to commiserate our mutual ignorance, and endeavour to remove it in all the gentle and fair ways of information, and not instantly treat others ill as obstinate and perverse because they will not renounce their own and receive our opinions, or at least those we would force upon them, when it is more probable that we are no less obstinate in not embracing some of theirs. For where is the man that has uncontestable evidence of the truth of all that he holds, or of the falsehood of all he condemns; or can say, that he has examined to the bottom all his own or other men's opinions? The necessity of believing without knowledge, nay, often upon very slight grounds, in this fleeting state of action and blindness we are in, should make us more busy and careful to inform ourselves than contain others.[38]

Despite his elaborate analysis of the formation and nature of opinion, Locke as philosopher-psychologist did no more than endorse in principle toleration for diversity of opinions. He evinced sustained interest in the problems of freedom of expression only in connection with his preoccupation for protecting liberty of conscience, the subject of his four *Letters on Toleration*. Since he addressed himself mainly to freedom for sectarian rather than secular expression, his claim of writing in behalf of "ABSOLUTE LIBERTY" [39] was overstated and even unjustifiable, considering the notable exceptions he made to principles which he supported in general. He could observe that the "opinions" of Catholics on Mass and of Jews on the New Testament, even though "false and absurd," were entitled to freedom because the business of the laws is to provide not for the truth of opinions but the safety of the Commonwealth as

[38] *An Essay Concerning Human Understanding* (London ed. of 1879, Tegg and Co.), Book IV, ch. 16, sect. 4, pp. 560–561.
[39] *A Letter concerning Toleration*, in *The Works of John Locke* (London, 1812, 11th ed.), 6:4.

well as of every individual's goods and person.[40] But he also believed that "no opinions contrary to human society, or to those moral rules which are necessary to the preservation of civil society, are to be tolerated by the magistrate." [41]

Advocating that the intolerant should not be tolerated, Locke proposed punishment of any who "will not own and teach the duty of tolerating all men in matters of mere religion." [42] In line with this view was a provision of the "Fundamental Constitutions of Carolina," which he framed, outlawing reproachful or abusive language of any religion as a disturbance of the peace.[43] In an obvious reference to Roman Catholicism, he recommended prosecution of that church which taught that "faith is not to be kept with heretics." There was no inconsistency here with his thesis that the jurisdiction of the civil magistrate did not reach religious belief or practice, since he affirmed that a right ended at the point that it prejudiced others, violated their rights, or jeopardized the peace of the state.

Locke, like Spinoza, would also punish those who taught that oaths and contracts were not binding, or that loyalty was not due to the ruler; and like Milton he regarded the opinions of atheists and the political implications of Catholic doctrine as seditious.[44] He believed that the sanctions of the law should be invoked against the members of any church who arrogated to themselves the power of deposing

[40] *Ibid.*, 6:40.
[41] *Ibid.*, 6:45.
[42] *Ibid.*, 6:46.
[43] Section 106 of "The Fundamental Constitutions of Carolina," in Francis Newton Thorpe, ed., *The Federal and State Constitutions, Colonial Charters, and Other Organic Laws* (Washington, 1909), 5:2784.
[44] *Letter concerning Toleration, Works of Locke*, 6:45–47.

kings or who professed doctrinal allegiance to another prince; for, he asked, did not their "doctrines signify, but that they may, and are ready upon any occasion to seize the government, and possess themselves of the estates and fortunes of their fellow-subjects; and that they only ask leave to be tolerated by the magistrates so long, until they find themselves strong enough to effect it?" [45] The statement, although an allusion to the relations between English Catholics and the Vatican, applied in principle to persons of any party that advocated, even by tenuous implication, the overthrow of the government or whose opinions could be suspected of disloyalty.

Locke, in other words, drew a line at seditious utterances. At no point did he, nor did any of his libertarian precursors among the Levellers or Independents, criticize the common law of seditious libel. Indeed, he went out of his way, in the midst of an argument for complete liberty of conscience, to declare that if any person under color of freely exercising his religion, might behave "seditiously, and contrary to the public peace," he was punishable "in the same manner, and not otherwise than as if it had happened in a fair or market." [46] That Locke meant mere verbal sedition, as well as overt action, is unquestionable since he distinguished between peaceable and criminal "doctrine," and he listed slanderers, as well as the seditious, with thieves, murderers, and adulterers as deserving of being "suppressed." [47] Moreover, one provision of his "Fundamental Constitutions of Carolina" stated: "No person whatsoever shall speak anything in their religious assembly irreverently or seditiously of the government or governors, or of state matters." [48]

[45] *Ibid.*, 6:45–46.
[46] *Ibid.*, 6:51.
[47] *Ibid.*, 6:52.
[48] Section 103, in Thorpe, ed., *Constitutions*, 5:2784.

The same constitution, incidentally, guaranteed freedom for "speculative opinions in religion" but was silent as to political opinions. A variety of personal rights were protected, but not speech or press.

Locke did not even defend a general freedom of expression when he lent his enormous prestige to those who successfully opposed re-enactment of the Licensing Act. In 1694 he drafted for the House of Commons a statement of eighteen reasons for ending the system of preventive censorship, not one a principled defense of liberty of the press nor a philosophical argument for the free mind. Locke argued that the lack of free competition injured the printing trades; the Licensing Act was too vague and administratively unworkable; and it was unnecessary since the common law adequately protected against licentiousness. On these grounds of expediency, prior restraints died in England.[49]

To suggest that Locke, or even Milton, was an enemy of the free mind would be absurd; they were indubitably the most eminent defenders of civil liberty in their time. But they were *of* their time, and one of its *a priori* premises, unthinkable for anyone to attack, was the state's incontestable right to proscribe sedition, a commodious concept encompassing anything from mild criticism of public policy to attempted overthrow of the government. Neither Locke, Milton, nor their contemporaries ever indicated disagreement with the common law's spacious definition of unlawful discourse nor sought to limit its application. Subsequent

[49] See Lord King, *The Life and Letters of John Locke* (London, 1858 ed.), pp. 202–209, for Locke's eighteen arguments. Maurice Cranston, *John Locke, A Biography* (London, 1957), states at p. 387, "Unlike Milton, who called for liberty in the name of liberty, Locke was content to ask for liberty in the name of trade; and unlike Milton, he achieved his end."

generations of libertarians inherited from them and passed
on to the American Framers in unaltered form an unbridled
passion for a bridled liberty of speech.

Charles Blount, Deist and republican, whose tracts were
burned by the hangman, adequately summarized seventeenth-century England's thought on the scope of permissible expression. His writings, including *Reasons Humbly
Offered for the Liberty of Unlicens'd Printing*,[50] aided
measurably in ending preventive censorship in 1694. The
following year, the introduction of a bill to re-establish
that system of restraints provoked him to write *A Just Vindication of Learning and the Liberty of the Press*.[51] The
thesis of the tract indicates that even radicals had a constricted understanding of freedom of the press. Despite his
frenetic forebodings that a new "Inquisition" might spring
from a continued requirement of imprimaturs, he complacently accepted the rigors of subsequent punishment.
Unlicensed printing presented no dangers, he argued, because if a man wrote "Scandalous Reflections upon the
Government, I presume he is by the present Laws of the
Land subject to a Fine and Imprisonment." [52] He even approved of statutory restrictions against "Popish Books,"
although he condemned censorship as a relic of popery.[53]
To Blount and the seventeenth-century libertarians, a free
press meant merely the absence of prior restraints.

The century closed without any meaningful broadening
in the definition of freedom of expression. Its defense had
enlisted some of the most acute minds in England, but their
contributions, whether polemical and sectarian or philo-
sophically magisterial, did far more to establish a rhetorical

[50] (London, 1693), 32 pp.
[51] (London, 1695), 27 pp. The title page spells his name "Blunt."
[52] *Just Vindication*, p. 23.
[53] *Ibid.*, pp. 2, 23.

rationale for unfettered discourse than to break the fetters
or even attack the common law. Indeed, neither the titans
like Roger Williams and John Locke nor the radicals like
William Walwyn and Charles Blount proposed a wider
scope for unorthodox and hated opinions than had Leonard
Busher, an obscure Baptist layman who preceded them. By
1700 no one had significantly advanced beyond Busher's
statement of 1614.[54] "Even as the chaff before the wind
cannot stand," he wrote, "so error before truth cannot
abide," [55] an expression of confidence in the open encounter
of ideas to be popularized by Milton in similar words three
decades later. Busher also believed that faith cannot be
coerced, that the magistrate had no rightful jurisdiction
over religion, and that persecution made a "shipwreck" of
conscience. He proposed, accordingly, that "all sorts of
Christians; yea, Jews, Turks, and pagans, so long as they
are peaceable, and no malefactors," should be lawfully
privileged to worship as they pleased and "to write, dispute,
confer and reason, print and publish any matter touching
religion, either for or against whomsoever," provided only
that they quoted no church fathers as proof of any point.[56]
But as Henry Burton pointed out in his introduction to a
new edition of Busher in 1646, the liberty to "speak, write,
print" was to be exercised under "wholesome and pertinent
laws" which provided penalties "to restrain all kinds of
vice or violence, all kinds of reproach, slander, or injury
either by word or deed." [57]

[54] *"Religious Peace: or A Plea for Liberty of Conscience* (London, 1614; reprinted 1646), in Edward Bean Underhill, ed., *Tracts
on Liberty of Conscience and Persecution, 1614–1661* (London,
1846), pp. 1–81.
[55] *Ibid.*, p. 53.
[56] *Ibid.*, pp. 33 and 51.
[57] *Ibid.*, p. 10.

Englishmen of the eighteenth century resolutely continued to ride the crest of an earlier consensus that the maintenance of established authority demanded the silencing of subversive discussion. Vivid memories of two revolutions fixed a steady course against any threat, whether real or imagined, to the good reputation of the government. Charles Davenant, the popular political economist, represented virtually a unanimous point of view when he granted in 1703 that it was not right in a free country to "restrain the tongues and pens of men" so as to prevent just public censure of the actions of private persons, but censure of the government and its officers would, he thought, be intolerable. "The harmony that is to make England subsist and flourish, must have its rise from a due respect, and obedience to be paid by the whole people, to that authority with which the laws have invested the different parts that compose the government." [58] A similar opinion was stated by Charles Leslie, editor of the *Rehearsal*, who praised as "wise and good" the law which prevented even true accusations against those "in post and quality. . . . For private men are not judges of their superiors. This wou'd confound all government. And the honour and dignity of our governors is to be preserv'd, without which they cou'd not govern, nor wou'd they be obey'd as they ought to be if they were render'd contemptible to their subjects; which is unavoidable if they are suffer'd to be traduc'd by every private person, and expos'd all over the nation." [59] Parliament, rather than the coffee-house or the press, was held

[58] "Essays Upon Peace at Home, and War Abroad," November 1703, Davenant's *Works*, 4:301, 302, quoted in Lawrence Hanson, *Government and the Press, 1695–1763* (Oxford, 1936), p. 1.

[59] *Rehearsal*, vol. I, no. 191, March 1707, quoted in Hanson, *Government and the Press*, pp. 1–2.

to be the only and proper place for such public criticism as was permissible.

The closest approximation to a dissenting voice on this matter was Matthew Tindal's. England's leading Deist at the turn of the century, Tindal, like every writer from Busher to Blount, was interested in an unlicensed liberty of press from the view of one with a stake in the open airing of religious controversy. But he also claimed that everyone "has a natural Right in all matters of Learning and Knowledge" to discover what can be said by speech or press on all sides of every subject, including civil and governmental matters, even if antiministerial.[60] Tindal may have been the first to elevate freedom of speech and press to the status of a natural right, a rhetorical achievement, to be sure, but a crucial step in the creation of a theory of intellectual liberty. The process by which the phrase "freedom of speech" was transformed from a description of a privilege of parliamentarians to a personal right of citizens turned, in part, on the assimilation of freedom of speech into the natural-rights theory. Tindal was also the first person on either side of the Atlantic to imply that citizens should have the same right to freedom of speech that legislators were guaranteed in the House of Commons. He made this important point somewhat obliquely by asking, "If the Honourable House of Commons have upon a solemn Debate thought fit to publish their proceedings to prevent being misrepresented, why should they deny those they Represent the same Liberty?"[61] In tracing the evolution of the concept of free speech, one might expect that numerous persons would have extrapolated a civil right from the parliamentary privilege, by simply arguing that if the repre-

---

[60] *Reasons against Restraining the Press* (London, 1704) pp. 9–10.
[61] *Ibid.* p. 10.

sentatives of the people enjoyed a broad customary or constitutional right to debate any issue concerning public
policy and the conduct of the government, then the people,
who possessed the ultimate sovereignty and to whom the
representatives were responsible, should possess the same
right of discussion. Tindal merely hinted at this idea which
seems, surprisingly, never to have received full expression
until the Sedition Act of 1798 provoked Jeffersonian thinkers to search for impregnable lines of defense.

Although Tindal was one of the earliest libertarians with
legal training, having been a law-fellow at All Soul's College, Oxford, he did not evaluate the common law's restrictions on expression, nor did he offer a solution for the legal
problems which latitudinarian views might precipitate.
His generalized opinions were woven around the single
theme that the reintroduction of licensing, as perennially
proposed, threatened Protestantism and liberty. He never
indicated disagreement with the notion that the press had
become free when removed from prior restraints. His tracts
defending himself, his printer, and his bookseller, upon
their presentment by a grand jury for publishing an attack
against the established church, rested their case on liberty
of conscience and only secondarily on liberty of the press,
without questioning the doctrine of subsequent punishment
for the "abuse" of liberty.[62]

John Asgil, politician and religious mystic, was the only
contemporary of Tindal whose literary remains class him

---

[62] *A Letter to a Friend: Occasioned by the presentment of the
grand jury for the county of Middlesex, of the author, printer and
publisher of a book entitled the rights of the christian church asserted* (London, 1708). See also a *Letter to a Member of Parliament, shewing that a restraint on the press is inconsistent with the
Protestant religion, and dangerous to the liberties of the nation*
(London, 1698).

among the libertarians. Like Tindal, his books were condemned to be burned, while he himself suffered the unenviable distinction of having been expelled from first the Irish House of Commons and later the English. With this record behind him, he wrote, in 1712, *An Essay for the Press,*[63] in which he ignored the law of seditious and blasphemous libel under which he had been censured. Although he hailed the communication of one's thoughts to others as a "natural Right of Mankind" [64] and argued, cleverly, that the abuse of this right was no more a reason for suppressing it than shutting church doors because hypocrites crowded in with the true worshippers, he confessed the necessity of maintaining restraints upon the press. But he drew the line against licensing and taxation. On the superficial notion that "licentiousness" was caused by anonymous publications, he proposed to outlaw them and require all authors to identify themselves, although his own essay was published anonymously. He gave no consideration to the possibility that the danger to the press's freedom derived largely from the necessarily vague concept of licentiousness, nor to the possibility that many discussions of public value were advanced anonymously to protect their authors from subsequent punishment.

Asgil and Tindal were libertarian by contrast to most writers of the early eighteenth century. The weight of talent and reputation was exclusively on the conservative side, as may be judged from the positions of Defoe, Swift, Addison, and Steele, as well as Leslie and Davenant. Whatever Defoe's virtues as a literary figure, he was a mercenary political journalist of the lowest kind, peddling his talents and shifty opinions to the highest party bidder. Pilloried,

[63] (London, 1712), 8 pp.
[64] *Ibid.,* p. 4.

fined, and imprisoned in 1703 for a tract on religious dissent, jailed again in 1713 for his published remarks, and convicted once more in 1715, Defoe experienced his legal difficulties firm in the conviction that the law of seditious libel was an acceptable weapon of partisan politics, justifiably used by whatever party was in power against its critics. "Governments will not be jested with, nor reflected upon," he warned, "nor is it fit that they should always lye at the mercy of every pen." [65] As a political spy he fed the ministry samples of the opposition's publications which in his opinion merited prosecution for seditious libel. On one occasion, for example, he instigated the expulsion of Richard Steele from Parliament. Defoe furnished Lord Harley, the first minister of state, with allegedly seditious excerpts from Steele's journalism and warned that his recent election by the Whigs meant that the Tory cause would be "bullied in as public a manner as possible. If, my lord, the virulent writings of this man may not be voted seditious none ever may, and if thereupon he may be expelled it would discourage the party and break all their new measures." [66] Defoe also sought to destroy the principal Whig paper, *The Flying Post*, by urging that the attorney-general bring a suit against it for sedition.[67] In 1718, he anonymously published a tract entitled *A Vindication of the Press*,[68] in which

[65] *The Review*, vol. I, no. 46, Aug. 12, 1704, quoted in Hanson, *Government and the Press*, p. 1.

[66] Defoe to Harley, Feb. 19, 1713/14, quoted by David Harrison Stevens, *Party Politics and English Journalism, 1702–1742* (Chicago, 1916), p. 27, citing Portland *MSS*, 5:384.

[67] Stevens, *Party Politics*, pp. 53–54, and Hanson, *Government and the Press*, pp. 62–63.

[68] (London, 1718), 36 pp. The copy in the New York Public Library contains a bound-in letter by Prof. William P. Trent of Columbia University, expressing certainty that Defoe was the author.

he declaimed at length on the virtues of unlicensed liberty, but kept an indiscreet silence on the subject of seditious libel — perhaps because one of the press's virtues, he said, was the maintenance of the state.

Defoe's enemy, Richard Steele, also revealed fundamental infirmities as a witness for the libertarian position. His own condemnation for criminal expression seems only to have inspired him to revenge. When his political fortunes changed for the better and he was back in favor, he complained in 1715 that "many libels are successfully dispersed under the notion of public News. . . ." [69] Jonathan Swift similarly engaged in the practice of singling out editors deserving, in his opinion, to be convicted as seditious libelers.[70]

The conservative position was most baldly and fully developed by an anonymous lawyer, "A Young Gentleman of the Temple," who in 1712 published a slim book elaborating the reasons for restraining the press.[71] He used the bold technique of stating systematically the arguments which had been advanced in favor of unlicensed liberty and then one by one ridiculing and rejecting them. No religious opinion, he thought, should be printed "but under the suffrage of those, who are proper Judges of what is Evangelical Truth, or Antichristian Error," else "all Order and Discipline" would end.[72] As for the argument that such censorship would deprive men of the means of arriving at

[69] Quoted in Hanson, *Government and the Press*, p. 85, citing George A. Aitken, *The Life of Richard Steele* (London, 1889), 2:71.

[70] Stevens, *Party Politics*, p. 78, citing Swift's *Journal to Stella*, Oct. 9, 1711.

[71] *Arguments Relating to a Restraint upon the Press in a Letter to a Bencher, from a Young Gentleman of the Temple* (London, 1712), 52 pp.

[72] *Ibid.*, p. 8.

truth by learning and weighing different opinions, he answered that the Bible itself contained all the truth there was and needed no commentary.[73] He believed that appeals to the public on political issues were quite unnecessary so long as Parliament might be petitioned directly. There was no need for the public to be involved in political controversies or to get at their truth, because enough had been said on all subjects and the Lords and Commons were capable of making decisions and of warding off arbitrary power. Indeed, the speakers of both Houses, he recommended, ought to be among the official licensers.[74] Claims that learning would be discouraged by censorship were absurd, since only "good" books merited license, and the rest were a waste of time and money. That controversy would be stifled was admitted, but silence was preferable since controversy merely made trouble; people ought to examine and reject their own novel opinions instead of obtruding them on others.[75]

Far from being a natural right, "Freedom of Speech" was a high privilege belonging only to members of Parliament; whoever else assumed that privilege by arrogating to themselves "an uncontroulable Liberty, not only of Speaking, but of Writing and Publishing what they please" were guilty of a breach of the privilege.[76] Fortunately, there were "many good Laws against the writing and publishing Seditious and Scandalous Papers," but evasion of deserved penalties was all too common because of the undetectability of anonymous authors.[77] An even "greater mischief" attended the custom of frequenting coffee-houses

[73] *Ibid.*, p. 10.
[74] *Ibid.*, pp. 14–16.
[75] *Ibid.*, p. 17.
[76] *Ibid.*, p. 21.
[77] *Ibid.*, pp. 23–24.

where men learned the art of scandal and detraction. The existing condition of unrestrained liberty bred seditious libelers, "the very Assassins of all Government," who could no longer be endured, for a "Civil War began with Ink may end in Blood." [78] The only remedy lay in the restoration of a rigorous licensing system, the details of which our anonymous lawyer worked out in a proposed statute.[79]

The moderate and more representative position was presented with considerable sophistication in another tract of 1712, ascribed uncertainly to Joseph Addison, writing under the name "Tory Author." [80] Addison, if we may assume that it was he, learnedly demonstrated that some of the most tyrannical Roman emperors, under whom libelers faced the death penalty, sometimes wisely tolerated even defamation of themselves on the theory that great people could afford to take no notice and should reply by giving as good an account of themselves as possible. Addison approved of such an attitude and even of a statement, which he quoted, from an unnamed Whig: "There never was a good Government that stood in fear of Freedom of Speech, which is the natural Liberty of Mankind; nor was ever any Administration afraid of Satyr [satire] but such as deserv'd it." [81] Private persons should have the right to criticize the government, but it would be going too far, Addison believed, to support a right for anyone to say whatever he thinks. There must be reasonable restraints, though licensing as too great a danger to liberty was not tolerable. Nor was a requirement that authors fix their names to their publications, for that would put an end to many worthwhile

[78] *Ibid.*, pp. 25, 27, 33, 45.
[79] *Ibid.*, pp. 47–51.
[80] *Thoughts of a Tory Author.*
[81] *Ibid.*, p. 13.

contributions which could only be made anonymously. Freedom of speech, as well as of press, should be confined, rather, to the limits set by truthfulness, good taste, due submission, and innocency of malice. What he was "much in love with" was "Legal Liberty," the right to speak, write, or print "whatever is not against Law."

> I believe [he stated] all we mean by Restraining the Press, is to hinder the Printing of any Seditious, Schismatical, Heretical or Antimonarchical Pamphlets. We do not intend to destroy Printing itself or to abridge any one Set of Men of the Liberties of *Englishmen;* That is, of Writing and Printing what the Law allows; what may be consistent with our Loyalty to the Q——n, and our Love to the Publick Peace; what is not against Morals or Good Manners. And surely there may be a Restraint put upon such Things without striking at the Press it self. . . ." [82]

Thus Addison complacently accepted the status quo, believing that freedom of expression had a broad scope and a high value when kept under the reasonable restraints of the common law without which true liberty would degenerate to licentiousness. No writer of the time more ably and accurately presented the prevailing notions on the subject than Addison, or "Tory Author."

The dissenting position, meanwhile, had scarcely advanced beyond the "no-prior-restraints" concept. In a score of years, the libertarian chorus had been joined only by the frail voices of Tindal and Asgil, despite the constant arrests for criminal libel. Then, in 1720, "Cato" burst upon the scene, bringing to his wide audience of readers a daring and well-developed theory of free speech. Others had been narrowly preoccupied with the problem of licensing, or

[82] *Ibid.,* pp. 1–2.

had been unable to stomach the thought of tolerating an equal liberty for those they hated, or vigorously defended liberty of expression by declamatory statements which fell short of analyzing its functions and scope, as well as its relations to governmental forms and the laws of libel. In this respect the essays of the political journalists, John Trenchard and William Gordon, collaborating under the joint pseudonym of "Cato," were unusual. They did not merely praise freedom of the press; they considered its values, meaning, and problems, and they also produced a rare discussion of freedom of *speech*. Their essays, first published in London newspapers beginning in 1720, were collected in four volumes that went through six editions between 1733 and 1755.[83] "No one," writes an historian familiar with the sources, "can spend any time in the newspapers, library inventories, and pamphlets of colonial America without realizing that *Cato's Letters* rather than Locke's *Civil Government* was the most popular, quotable, esteemed source of political ideas in the colonial period." [84]

The essay, "Of Freedom of Speech: That the same is inseparable from Publick Liberty," [85] was so popular in America, though now undeservedly forgotten, that extensive quotation of its splendid rhetoric is justifiable:

> Without Freedom of Thought, there can be no such Thing as Wisdom; and no such Thing as publick Liberty, without Freedom of Speech: Which is the Right of every Man, as far as by it he does not hurt and controul the Right of another; and this is the only Check which it ought to suffer, the only Bounds which it ought to know.

[83] [John Trenchard and William Gordon], *Cato's Letters: Or, Essays on Liberty, Civil and Religious* (London, 1733–1755).

[84] Clinton Rossiter, *Seedtime of the Republic* (New York, 1953), p. 141.

[85] No. 15, Feb. 4, 1720, in *Cato's Letters* (6th ed., 1755), 1:96–103.

This sacred Privilege is so essential to free Government, that the Security of Property; and the Freedom of Speech, always go together; and in those wretched Countries where a Man cannot call his Tongue his own, he can scarce call any Thing else his own. Whoever would overthrow the Liberty of the Nation, must begin by subduing the Freedom of Speech; a Thing terrible to publick Traytors. . . .

That Men ought to speak well of their Governors, is true, while their Governors deserve to be well spoken of; but to do publick Mischief, without hearing of it, is only the Prerogative and Felicity of Tyranny: A free People will be shewing that they are so, by their Freedom of Speech.

The Administration of Government is nothing else, but the Attendance of the Trustees of the People upon the Interest and Affairs of the People. And as it is the Part and Business of the People, for whose Sake alone all publick Matters are, or ought to be, transacted; so it is the Interest, and ought to be the Ambition, of all honest Magistrates, to have their Deeds openly examined, and publickly scanned: Only the wicked Governors of Men dread what is said of them . . .

Misrepresentation of publick Measures is easily overthrown, by representing publick Measures truly: when they are honest, they ought to be publickly known, that they may be publickly commended; but if they be knavish or pernicious, they ought to be publickly detested. . . . Freedom of Speech is the great Bulwark of Liberty; they prosper and die together: And it is the Terror of Traytors and Oppressors, and a Barrier against them. It produces excellent Writers, and encourages Men of fine Genius. . . .

All Ministers, therefore, who were Oppressors, or intended to be Oppressors, have been loud in their Complaints against Freedom of Speech, and the Licence of the Press; and always restrained, or endeavoured to restrain, both. In consequence of this, they have brow-beaten Writers, punished them violently, and against Law, and burnt their Works. By all which they shewed how much Truth alarmed them, and how much they were at Enmity with Truth. . . .

Freedom of Speech, therefore, being of such infinite Importance to the Preservation of Liberty, every one who loves Liberty ought to encourage Freedom of Speech.

In subsequent essays on the subject of libels, Cato continued his discussion. He ridiculed government officials who called "every Opposition . . . and every Attempt to preserve the People's Rights, by the odious Names of Sedition and Faction." [86] Libels, he declared, rarely fomented causeless discontent against the government; the benefits from what the law denominated libels, by keeping great men in awe and checking their behavior, outweighed their mischiefs. Libels were the inevitable result of a free press, "an Evil arising out of a much greater Good." [87] Without freedom of speech and press, there could be "neither Liberty, Property, true Religion, Arts, Sciences, Learning, or Knowledge." [88] Concededly, there was a risk in allowing liberty of expression. Let men talk freely about philosophy, religion, or government, and they may reason wrongly, irreligiously, or seditiously; but to restrain their opinions would simply result in "Injustice, Tyranny, and the most stupid Ignorance. They will know nothing of the Nature of Government beyond a Servile Submission to Power. . . ." [89]

Cato did not wish to be misunderstood as arguing for

[86] "Discourse upon Libels," No. 100, Oct. 27, 1722, *ibid.*, 3:293.
[87] "Reflections upon Libelling," No. 32, June 10, 1721, *ibid.*, 1:252.
[88] "Discourse upon Libels," 3:295.
[89] *Ibid.*, 3:296–297.

the uncontrolled liberty of men to calumniate each other or the government. Libels against the government were "always base and unlawful," [90] especially when untrue, and should be punished as an abuse of liberty so long as England's "very good laws" were "prudently and honestly executed." [91] But it was abundantly clear, notwithstanding this genuflection toward the law — keeping Cato on its safe side — that he thought the law of criminal libel was neither good nor prudently executed, indeed, that it was quite dangerous to public liberty and good government. He disapproved of prosecutions for libel except in extreme cases and even then only under a law which did not penalize criticism whose validity was demonstrable. On ground that the public had an interest in the truth about public measures and men, Cato argued that truth should be admitted as a defense against a criminal libel charge, in other words, that a defendant who could prove the accuracy of his allegedly seditious utterance should be acquitted.[92] But for a fleeting suggestion of the same point by "Tory Author" in 1712,[93] Cato was the earliest to popularize, if not originate, this idea which has usually been attributed to Andrew Hamilton in his defense of Peter Zenger in 1735. The idea was not accepted in English law until Lord Campbell's Act of 1843. Cato also opposed the practice of the courts in implying a criminal or seditious intention to defendants whose words in their "literal and natural Meaning, import nothing that is criminal; then to strain their genuine Signification to make them intend Sedition (which possibly the Author might intend too) is such a Stretch of discretionary Power,

[90] "Reflections upon Libelling," 1:252.
[91] "Discourse upon Libels," 3:299.
[92] "Reflections upon Libelling," 1:247.
[93] *Thoughts of a Tory Author*, pp. 25-26.

as must subvert all the Principles of free Government, and overturn every Species of Liberty." [94]

The best way to treat undeserved libels, thought Cato, was to "laugh at them, and despise them," rather than prosecute them.[95] He reasoned that it was not possible, in a free country, to punish libels by a general law, however much they deserved punishment, because "such a Law, consisting of so many Branches, and being of such vast Latitude, would make all Writing whatsoever, how innocent so ever, and even all Speaking, unsafe. . . . As long as there are such Things as Printing and Writing, there will be Libels: It is an Evil arising out of a much greater Good. . . . I must own, that I would rather many Libels should escape, than the Liberty of the Press should be infringed; yet no Man in *England* thinks worse of Libels than I do; especially of such as bid open Defiance to the present Protestant Establishment." [96] Clearly, Cato was the rare man who, recognizing the social utility of freedom of expression and its relationship to free government, could tolerate the thought that he hated. Others probably shared Cato's views, but did not leave a record of their argument that would influence Englishmen in the colonies. *Cato's Letters* was quoted "in every colonial newspaper from Boston to Savannah," [97] and "the most famous" [98] of his letters was the one on "Freedom of Speech." It was still being reprinted in the American press on the eve of the War for Independence.[99]

[94] "Second Discourse upon Libels," No. 101, Nov. 3, 1722, in *Cato's Letters*, 3:303.

[95] "Discourse upon Libels," 3:297–298.

[96] "Reflections upon Libelling," 1:252–253.

[97] Elizabeth Christine Cook, *Literary Influences in Colonial Newspapers* (New York, 1912), p. 81.

[98] Rossiter, *Seedtime*, p. 299.

[99] For specific citations to *Cato's Letters* in the colonial press, see Rossiter, *Seedtime*, p. 492 note 120 and p. 525 note 133. See

Cato did not, however, initiate a break-through in libertarian thought. He was a flashing star in an orthodox sky
that was occasionally but dimly lit by exponents of intellectual and political liberty. The Deist leaders of his time
who might have been expected to share his avant-garde
views on the scope of free speech were themselves only
slightly enlightened. John Toland, for example, a significant figure in the history of rationalism, was a pluperfect
liberal on the right to advance any opinions concerning religion, but followed Roger Williams in drawing limits on
political criticism. Though professing publicly to champion
liberty of the press, Toland deplored the circulation of seditious innuendoes and the licentious abuse of government
ministers. He recommended that the government defend
itself by extending the stamp tax on newspapers and even
by altogether prohibiting certain journals.[100]

Anthony Collins was another Deist leader with serious
limitations. His *Discourse of Free Thinking* argued two
propositions at great length: first, that restraints on expression resulted in cultural stagnation and ignorance; second,
that every man had a right to think and express himself
freely for the purpose of determining the meaning and
validity of any proposition in history, science, philosophy,
religion, or other realm of knowledge.[101] In another work,
Collins defended the use of ridicule, jest, and raillery in all
disputation; deploring restraints that made it impossible for
men to "speak their Minds seriously on certain subjects,"
he pleaded "for freedom of debate" in any matter of

---

especially p. 530 note 114, citing *Massachusetts Spy*, March 28,
1771, quoting Cato on freedom of the press.
[100] Frederick S. Siebert, *Freedom of the Press in England, 1476–
1776* (Urbana, 1952), citing British Museum Additional *MS* 429,
folios 49, 50.
[101] *A Discourse of Free Thinking* (London, 1723), 178 pp.

"speculation." [102] However, his thought was Miltonian in its disregard for the right to freedom of expression for any but scholars and divines. Neither the common herd nor political reporters and critics received Collins' attention. He had, moreover, a way of tacking on to a libertarian thesis a concession to orthodoxy that, innocently perhaps, bulldozed the ground out from under him. For instance, his "Apology for free Debate and Liberty of Writing" was dedicated to the following proposition: "As it is every man's natural right and duty to think, and judge for himself in matters of opinion; so he should be allow'd *freely* to *profess* his opinions, and to endeavour, when he judges proper, to *convince* others of their truth; provided those opinions do not tend to the disturbance of society." [103] Any crown prosecutor might warmly embrace that proposition, despite its natural-rights premise, because the qualifying provision accepted in principle the law of criminal libel. Mere opinions were punishable if they had the bad, though remote, tendency to disturb society.

Collins' thought was given legal expression by the anonymous author of *State Law: Or, the Doctrine of Libels, Discussed and Examined,* purportedly another defense of libertarianism.[104] This treatise of 1729 was intended to "serve as an Argument for the Liberty of the Press, as it now stands, since it shews the little necessity of any farther Restraint upon it, by demonstrating, that every one who prints any thing with a mischievous Intent, does it at his

---

[102] *A Discourse concerning Ridicule and Irony in Writing* (London, 1729), pp. 5, 24, 75–76.

[103] Page vi of the "Apology" which appears as a preface, pp. iii–lxii, to Collins' *A Discourse of the Grounds and Reasons of the Christian Religion* (London, 1724), 285 pp.

[104] (London, n.d., [1729], 2nd ed.), 136 pp.

own Peril. . . ." [105] Glowing rhetoric was vitiated by the stand-patter's conviction that Englishmen already enjoyed genuine freedom of opinion under a body of law that had but one defect: a few loopholes made it possible for cunning writers to evade the deserved penalties for crown libels and other licentious statements.[106]

Henry St. John, Viscount Bolingbroke, who achieved minor eminence as a political philosopher, was about this time the principal founder of, and a contributor to, the *Craftsman*, the organ of opposition to Walpole's administration. Bolingbroke represented himself as a zealous advocate of liberty of the press, sustaining in particular the right to animadvert on public men and measures. His conversion to libertarianism may have been more tactical than principled, since Bolingbroke in-power had been suppressive, but out-of-power was forced to take cover in the liberty of political criticism. In 1712, when secretary of state, he had been of the opinion that, "It is a melancholy consideration that the laws of our country are too weak to punish effectually those factious scribblers who presume to blacken the brightest characters and to give even scurrilous language to those who are in the first degree of honour. This, my Lord, among others, is a symptom of the decayed condition of our government, and serves to show how fatally we mistake licentiousness for liberty." [107] It was Bolingbroke who had initiated stamp taxes upon printed

[105] *Ibid.*, Preface. The identical statement appears in *A Digest of the Law Concerning Libels* (London, 1778), p. xiii, a book attributed to John Raynor, who obviously plagiarized heavily from the earlier author of *State Law.*

[106] *State Law*, p. 135.

[107] Hanson, *Government and the Press*, p. 63, quoting *Letters and Correspondence of . . . Henry St. John, Lord Viscount Bolingbroke*, ed. Gilbert Parke (London, 1798), 2:486.

matter, with the intention of driving out Whig journals, and who had masterminded an intensive campaign to crush allegedly seditious writings. When he turned to the cause of a free press, an anonymous Whig, undoubtedly with Walpole's aid, published a documentary record of Bolingbroke's former suppressions, exposing his hypocrisy and discrediting his self-interested support of open debate.[108]

Whatever his past, Bolingbroke supported *Craftsman's* energetic denunciations of the government for prosecuting Tory opinions as seditious libel. When Richard Francklin, the *Craftsman's* publisher, was indicted, one of the Bolingbroke-Francklin faction anonymously wrote a tract, in 1731, starting with the increasingly familiar generalization that in a free government, "every Man has a right to speak his Sentiments," on state matters as well as others.[109] But he did not, like most of his precursors, conclude his case with bombastic endorsements of free speech and press as if dealing with self-evident truth. His tract was distinguished by his reasoned consideration of the repressive practice of crown prosecutors and judges in wresting a seditious construction from the least innuendo of a writer who has been forced, by the penalty for outright utterance, to resort to historical analogies and circumlocution to make his point. "If this Method of Construction be allowed," demanded the *Craftsman's* defender, "what Writer can be safe? It will soon be found as effectual a Way to destroy the Liberty of the Press, and in that the Liberties of the Subject, as the appointing a Licenser previously to peruse and approve all Books, before they are admitted to be

[108] *The Craftsman's Doctrine and Practice of the Liberty of the Press* (London, 1732), 61 pp.
[109] *The Doctrine of Innuendo's Discuss'd; Or The Liberty of the Press Maintain'd* (London, 1731), 26 pp.

printed." [110] Thus, without at any time repudiating the concept of seditious libel, the author reprehended its conventional application, which is more than anyone excepting Cato had done.

[110] *Ibid.*, p. 11.

CHAPTER FOUR

❧ From the Zenger Case to the American Revolution

The American contribution to libertarian theory on freedom of speech and press, so strikingly absent prior to the Zenger case of 1735, was inconspicuous for long after. Even in the celebrated case America produced no broad concept of freedom of expression. That did not come until the very close of the eighteenth century. In pre-Zenger America, no one had ever published an essay on the subject, let alone repudiate the concept of seditious libel or condemn its conventional application by the common-law courts or by parliamentary punishment for breach of privilege. To be sure, Englishmen in America admiringly read and quoted Cato, particularly if his grandiloquence suited a momentary purpose. But the colonists gave little independent thought and even less expression to a theory of unfettered debate. Benjamin Franklin, a towering figure among colonial printers and thinkers, best illustrates the point. In 1722, when only a youth, he reprinted at length Cato's essay on "Freedom of Speech" in the *New-England Courant* after his brother, James Franklin, had been imprisoned for an article that offended the Massachusetts legislature.[1] Then, in 1731, when in England *Craftsman's* supporter was detailing an indictment of the repressive application of the law of seditious libel, Franklin's "most influential statement on freedom of the press" appeared in his *Pennsylvania Gazette,* a statement which an expert on the colonial press deemed "worth quoting at length, for it is an accurate representation of the principles of a free press which governed popular thinking in eighteenth-century America."[2] Yet Franklin simply argued that printing had to do with promoting and opposing the various opinions of men, that all opinions ought to be heard, that truth would "overmatch" error, and that vice and immorality ought not to be countenanced.[3] That Franklin practiced freedom of the press is undoubted, but his celebrated "Apology for Printers" hardly presented a definition or a philosophy of a free press. He wrote as if such things as the imprisonment of his brother had never happened. He did not, in other words, face any of the problems connected with freedom of the press. If his statement was as influential and representative as it has been reputed, it simply shows how superficial was American thinking on this subject.

If, indeed, we do not dignify as a definition of freedom of the press, or of speech, the right to say anything that the community or the law agrees with or is indifferent to, it is difficult to find a libertarian theory in America before the American Revolution — or even before the First Amendment. A statement of 1734 which easily is as representative

[1] Clinton Rossiter, *Seedtime of the Republic* (New York, 1953), pp. 298–299.

[2] *Ibid.,* p. 300.

[3] "An Apology for Printers," *Philadelphia Gazette,* June 10, 1731, quoted in Rossiter, *Seedtime;* reprinted in Albert Henry Smyth, ed., *The Writings of Benjamin Franklin* (New York, 1905–1907), 2:172–179.

as Franklin's and far more specific appeared in his competitor's newspaper, the *American Weekly Mercury*, printed by Andrew Bradford. By freedom of the press, affirmed the writer,

> I mean a Liberty, within the Bounds of Law, for any Man to communicate to the Public, his Sentiments on the Important Points of Religion and Government; of proposing any Laws, which he apprehends may be for the Good of his Countrey, and of applying for the Repeal of such, as he Judges pernicious. I mean a Liberty of detecting the wicked and destructive Measures of certain Politicians; of dragging Villany out of it's obscure lurking Holes, and exposing it in it's full Deformity to open Day; of attacking Wickedness in high Places, of disintangling the intricate Folds of a wicked and corrupt Administration, and pleading freely for a Redress of Grievances: I mean a Liberty of examining the great Articles of our Faith, by the Lights of Scripture and Reason, a Privilege derived to us in it's fullest Latitude, from our most excellent Charter. This is the Liberty of the Press, the greatest Palladium of all our other Liberties. . . .[4]

This handsome statement was predicated on a catch-clause appearing in the first line, "a Liberty, within the Bounds of Law . . . ," indicating the standard concurrence with the restraints of the common law. The statement, in fact, was prefaced by the remark that liberty did not extend to license, which the author defined as subverting religion or traducing the conduct of the government. Since "traduce" means to speak evil of or defame, the author might as well have said pithily that he favored a liberty of the press as defined by the royal judges.

The work of another American during the same decade

[4] April 25, 1734, quoted by Anna Janney DeArmond, *Andrew Bradford, Colonial Journalist* (Newark, Del., 1949), p. 92.

deserves the utmost attention. He was James Alexander, Cato's principal disciple in the colonies, the mastermind of the Zenger defense. Alexander's name has been obscured by the attention lavished upon his famed printer and client, John Peter Zenger, and upon his fellow attorney, Andrew Hamilton. A man of versatile talents, Alexander was a founder of the American Philosophical Society, surveyor-general of both New Jersey and New York, a member of the Council of both those colonies, a legal reformer, attorney-general of New Jersey, and editor of Zenger's *New York Weekly Journal*, the first politically independent newspaper in America. When Zenger, the printer and publisher, was indicted in 1735 for seditious libel, Alexander, who should have been in the prisoner's dock instead, was his counsel. It was Alexander who, when summarily disbarred in the pretrial stage of the case for accusing the presiding judge of bias, brought in Andrew Hamilton to argue the cause and provided him with a detailed brief of the argument that proved victorious. It was also Alexander who edited the famous account of the case which was reprinted so often and perpetuated the reputations of Zenger and Hamilton as heroes in the cause of freedom of the press. Finally it was Alexander who was the first colonial figure to develop a philosophy of freedom of speech-and-press, which he published in an essay after the trial.[5]

[5] On Alexander and his relationship to the Zenger case, see *Dictionary of American Biography* and Vincent Buranelli, "Peter Zenger's Editor," *American Quarterly*, 7:174–181 (Summer 1955); Buranelli, *The Trial of Peter Zenger* (New York, 1957), pp. iii, 24–25, 30–32, 68–70. *A brief Narrative of the Case and Tryal of John Peter Zenger, Printer of the New-York weekly Journal* was edited by Alexander and printed by the Zenger press in New York in 1736. Buranelli's edition of the trial is abridged and modernized. I have used the literal reprint of the first edition in Livingston Rutherfurd, *John Peter Zenger . . . Also a Reprint of the First*

The Hamilton-Alexander trial argument, despite its fame as a broad libertarian statement, was only slightly conceptual in character. The few passages constructing a rationale for freedom of the press, though not lacking in grandiloquence, were limited to the sole theme that villainy in government deserves exposure, even if the remonstrance against abuses of power be put in truth's strongest terms. In a free government, urged Hamilton, the people's mouths should not be stopped when they feel themselves oppressed. He confessed, however, that a false charge against the administration merited punishment as a seditious libel.[6] At the same time, he must be credited with having conducted the first sustained assault, even if only indirect, upon the common law of criminal utterance. *"Truth,"* he insisted, "ought to govern the whole Affair of Libels."[7] This proposition would have altered the common-law rule that the truth of a charge worsened the libel. The rule was based on the theory that truth would more likely provoke the impugned party to an act of revenge, breaching the peace, than a falsehood which he might contemptuously ignore. Hamilton ridiculed the rule, declaring it to be a "Star Chamber" inheritance meaning that truth was a greater sin than falsehood. The main point of his argument, which was derived from Cato,[8] was that the truth of a defendant's allegedly libelous statement should render him immune to punishment.[9] When the court rejected this proposition, Hamil-

Edition of the Trial (New York, 1904). Alexander's brief in the Zenger case is in Julius Goebel, Jr., and T. Raymond Naughton, *Law Enforcement in Colonial New York* (New York, 1944), pp. 782–786.

[6] *Trial of Zenger*, in Rutherfurd, *Zenger*, pp. 206, 223.
[7] *Ibid.*, p. 223.
[8] See above, p. 119.
[9] *Trial of Zenger*, in Rutherfurd, *Zenger*, pp. 198, 206, 207, 209, 212, 216, 223, 240.

ton retreated to the argument that the jury should decide the law as well as the facts in a criminal-libel case, instead of their returning a special verdict on the question whether the defendant had as a matter of fact made the statement charged and leaving the court to rule, as a matter of law, whether the words were criminal per se.

The propositions that truth should constitute an adequate defense and that the jury should decide the whole question of libel were to become the heavy cannon of the embattled libertarians of the eighteenth century. Yet, when they finally won, after many decades of contention, they might have exclaimed with the ancients, "Another such victory and we are lost!" At a time when judges were dependent instruments of the crown, a jury of one's peers and neighbors seemed to be a promising bulwark against the tyrannous enforcement of the law of seditious libel by the administration and its judges. It was an accepted article of faith that the jury, as a popular institution, would protect political critics. But juries, with the power of ruling on the guilt or innocence of alleged libels, proved to be as susceptible to prevailing prejudices as judges when they decided the fate of defendants who had expressed unpopular sentiments. Only one verdict of "not guilty" was returned in the numerous prosecutions under the Sedition Act of 1798.[10] In England, where the power of juries in libel cases was secured by Fox's Libel Act of 1792, the most repressive prosecutions were with very few exceptions successful. Jurors in America and England acted in a manner not noticeably different from Scroggs, Jeffreys, or Chase. They could be relied upon to support freedom of speech-and-press, as in the Zenger case, only if public opinion opposed the ad-

[10] J. M. Smith, *Freedom's Fetters: The Alien and Sedition Laws and American Civil Liberties* (Ithaca, 1956), p. 185.

ministration. There was a feeling that an administration might hesitate to prosecute if it had to pass the gauntlet of a jury as in all other criminal cases.

Yet the power of the jury in seditious-libel cases was a procedural safeguard that did not alter the substantive law. And even as a procedural safeguard, it was capable of creating procedural traps to the defendant's disadvantage. He could have no basis for appealing a conviction by a jury which decided the law for itself, since the law incorporated by a jury in its general verdict of "guilty" is formally unknowable even if it should have been incorrect. Fair procedure can be afforded only if the presumption can obtain that the jury took its law, though incorrectly, from the court. Moreover, the meaning and application of the law when decided by a jury can fluctuate from case to case, in effect annulling the security to which every citizen is entitled by a uniform administration of justice.[11]

More sound was the proposition that a defendant who could prove the truth of his charges should be freed. Here was a safeguard, concerning the conduct of the defense, which would have modified the substance of the law by extending the scope of permissible expression — but not by much. Where before, revelation of corruption, injustice, or incompetence in government, however documented or accurate, might be punished on the theory that truth aggravated the libel, men might, under the Cato-Hamilton-Alexander proposal, exercise the right to denounce and expose "in the strongest terms" if only they hewed to the truth. This was the bedrock of the Zenger defense: truth

[11] See Mark DeWolfe Howe, "Juries as Judges of Criminal Law," *Harvard Law Review*, 52:582-616 (February 1939), a general discussion of the subject. I have stated my own views more fully in *The Law of the Commonwealth and Chief Justice Shaw* (Cambridge, Mass., 1957), pp. 290-293.

could not be a libel; truth fixed the bounds of the right to speak, write, and publish opinions on the conduct of men in power. But to define liberty of expression as "speaking and writing truth" rooted it in shallow soil, for the very criticism that Hamilton directed at the concept of libel — that there was a "great diversity of opinions" and an even "greater uncertainty" as to what words were or were not defamatory — applied analogously to the concept of "truth." That one man's truth is another's falsehood, or that the truth of opinions is not susceptible of proof, Hamilton did not consider, nor did any of the eighteenth-century libertarians until they belatedly discovered that they had mistaken a prop of straw for brick.

Regardless of the possible limitations of Hamilton's argument as a libertarian defense of freedom of the press, it was an argument which, judging from its impact on the bench, was like the stagecoach ticket inscribed, "Good for this day only." The Zenger jury, responding to the magnificent forensics of a great lawyer engaged in a popular cause, returned a verdict of "not guilty," but the common law remained unchanged. As late as 1804, Chief Justice Morgan Lewis of New York, a Jeffersonian no less, was of the opinion that truth did not constitute a defense against a charge of seditious libel.[12]

Alexander's *A brief Narrative of the Case and Tryal of John Peter Zenger*, published by Zenger in 1736, was, with the possible exception of *Cato's Letters*, the most widely known source of libertarian thought in England and America during the eighteenth century.[13] But scant fame attended his excellent essay on freedom of speech which

[12] People v. Croswell, 3 Johnson's (N.Y.) Cases 336, 363–394 (1804).

[13] For a bibliography of the various editions of Zenger's trial, see Rutherfurd, *Zenger*, pp. 249–255.

he wrote in reply to attacks upon the ideas he had advanced, via Hamilton, at the trial. In 1737, two West Indian lawyers, one of whom was probably Jonathan Blenman, the king's attorney in Barbados, published severe strictures of a technical character against the Zenger defense, purporting to disprove on legal grounds the contention that truth was a defense against a libel charge; the thesis of both "Anglo-Americanus" and "Indus-Britannicus" was that truth not only could be libelous but necessarily exacerbated the libel.[14] Their "Remarks on the Trial of John Peter Zenger" was speedily republished in Philadelphia by the printer Andrew Bradford, who was a long-time enemy of Andrew Hamilton.[15] It was Alexander who replied in a four-part essay which was first published quite appropriately in the paper of Bradford's competitor, Franklin's *Pennsylvania Gazette*.[16]

Alexander, who used to copy selections from *Cato's Letters* for his personal edification as well as for Zenger's paper,[17] met his critics in the grand manner by sketching a history and theory of freedom of speech. Since only one other American, William Bollan, attempted the same task before the very last year of the century,[18] Alexander's essay deserves the fullest consideration. He began with

[14] "Remarks on the Trial of John Peter Zenger," signed by "Anglo-Americanus," first appeared in *Keimer's Barbadoes Gazette* between June 25 and July 23, 1737, to which "Indus-Britannicus" added a supplemental essay, with the same title, on Aug. 10, 1737. The "Remarks" of both writers were reprinted in *Caribbeana* (London, 1741), 2:198–241, and also in Howell's *State Trials*, 21: 726–764.

[15] DeArmond, *Andrew Bradford*, p. 107.

[16] Nov. 17–Dec. 8, 1737, Numbers 466–469.

[17] Buranelli, "Zenger's Editor," *American Quarterly*, 7:179.

[18] [William Bollan], *The Freedom of Speech and Writing upon Public Affairs, Considered, with an Historical View* (London, 1766), 160 pp.

first principles: "Freedom of speech is a *principal Pillar* in a free Government: when this Support is taken away, the Constitution is dissolved, and Tyranny is erected on its ruins. Republics and limited monarchies derive their strength and vigour from a *Popular Examination* into the Actions of the Magistrates." [19] Acknowledging the risks inherent in a policy of free speech, he argued that licentious expression was the price that society had to pay in return for the benefits received. "These abuses of Freedom of Speech are the excrescences of Liberty. They ought to be suppressed; but to whom dare we commit the care of doing it? An evil Magistrate, entrusted with a *power* to punish Words, is armed with a Weapon the most destructive and terrible. Under the pretense of pruning off the exuberant branches, he frequently destroys the tree." [20]

Then followed a history of prosecutions for libel, with every line radiating hatred of restraints on expression. He pictured a tyranny under the Roman Empire so great that "no man could write or open his Mouth, without being in danger of forfeiting his Head." Turning his wrath against the Tudors and Stuarts, he tersely demonstrated how each monarch aiming at despotic power had been "absolutely determined to suppress all Freedom of Speech. . . ." Quickly, effectively, he told of the martyrdoms of Sir John Elliot, William Prynn, Henry Burton, John Bastwick, and Algernon Sydney, among others, whose rightful exercise of free speech had resulted in their punishment as "disturbers of the GOVERNMENT." These tragic events Alexander ascribed to the "Star-chamber doctrine" of libel. His historical review, he explained, was an endeavor to prove "the fatal dangers that necessarily attend a Restraint on freedom

[19] *Philadelphia Gazette*, Nov. 17, 1737.
[20] *Ibid.*

of speech and the liberty of the press: upon which the following Reflection naturally occurs, viz. THAT WHOEVER ATTEMPTS TO SUPPRESS EITHER OF THOSE, *OUR NATURAL RIGHTS,* OUGHT TO BE REGARDED AS AN *ENEMY* TO LIBERTY AND THE CONSTITUTION." [21] In the end, however, the only concrete suggestion which he offered as a means of protecting these rights was truth-as-a-defense, a liberalization of the common law, to be sure, but an Achilles heel nevertheless. For nonmalicious falsehoods or mistakes, even unprovable truths, indeed, even mere opinions or conclusions from facts, might still be punishable as seditious libel. Alexander himself confessed, as had Hamilton in the Zenger defense, that "to infuse into the minds of the people an ill opinion of a just administration, is a crime that deserves no mercy. . . ." [22] The law of evidence, he failed to consider, would hardly help in any effort to prove that an administration was just or not. Opinion, derived from invisible moral standards and from seamy considerations as to whether one's ox was being gored, would be more to the point than legal proof. The fatal defect of Alexander's position was his acceptance of the principle that words giving an "ill opinion" of the government, even a "just" one, should be punished. This was the core of the concept of seditious libel, and until the libertarians attacked the core, their defense of freedom of speech or press was restricted conceptually and vulnerable to many of the very criticisms with which they lashed their opponents.

An historian who recently rediscovered Alexander's essay claims, "It presents him as the most important theorist

---

[21] *Ibid.,* Dec. 1, 1737.
[22] *Ibid.; Trial of Zenger,* in Rutherfurd, *Zenger,* p. 233.

of freedom of the press this country has ever produced." [23]
He doubtless deserves the accolade as one of our two
greatest *colonial* theorists of the rights of free expression,
for with the sole exception of William Bollan, who published in 1766, Alexander had no rivals. Other colonials
may have shared his principles, which were Cato's, but did
not develop them in print. Freedom of conscience, trial by
jury, the natural-rights theory, and popular sovereignty
were expounded by many Americans, but it would be an
exaggeration to conclude from Alexander's almost unique
essay, which was apparently forgotten shortly after its
newspaper appearance,[24] that America produced a broad
definition or a philosophy of freedom of speech.

Alexander's account of the trial went through six editions
in England in 1738, the same year in which a journal that
had joined *Craftsman* as a voice of opposition to the Whig
government of Walpole published two unsigned essays
which showed an attentive reading of Cato.[25] Both authors
were provoked to express themselves on the subject of free
political discussion because of recent punishments for seditious libel and the clamor of the administration press for
additional checks against Tory licentiousness. Both ably
discoursed on the indispensability of open political debate
to the maintenance of free government, evincing thereby
a well-conceived theory of libertarianism.

They stressed the necessity and right of the people to be
informed of the conduct of their governors so as to shape

[23] Buranelli, *The Trial of Peter Zenger*, p. 141.
[24] The essay was reprinted by Zenger's *New York Weekly Journal*, Dec. 19, 1737-Jan. 9, 1737/38; by the *Barbadoes Gazette*, Jan.
21, 1737/38; and in *Caribbeana* (London, 1741), 2:264-271.
[25] *Common Sense: or, the Englishman's Journal* (London, 1738),
pp. 331-341 and 349-354.

their own judgments on "Publick Matters" and be qualified
to chose their representatives wisely. No one before had related the electoral process to freedom of expression — a
significant advance in political and libertarian theory. The
first essayist, in depicting the wholesome influence of liberty of the press upon the formation of public opinion,
also propounded the novel thesis that the "Bulk of Mankind" were quite capable of governing themselves; the
opinion that they could not understand and decide public
issues he condemned as "the Off-spring only of Priestcraft
and Tyranny, for they alone would have the People ignorant whose desire is to deceive them." [26] Warning that a
zest for punishing libels might uproot the wheat for the
sake of a few tares, the author also recommended a policy
of tolerating most falsehoods and licentiousness as "trivial
inconveniences" arising from the liberty of the press. The
second essayist, in championing the "salutary effects" of
"Freedom of Debate," wisely suggested that the public
should be exposed to every kind of controversy, in philosophy, history, science, religion, and literature, as well as in
politics, because in the course of "examining, comparing,
forming opinions, defending them, and sometimes recanting
them," the public would acquire a "Readiness of Judgment and Passion for Truth." [27]

Despite their genuine understanding of the need for a
broad policy of political and intellectual liberty, both
writers strikingly failed to criticize the substantive law of
criminal libel. "Let Calumny and Detraction be punished
as they ought to be, in a legal manner," wrote one, while
the other supported "that Freedom of Inquiry we at
present enjoy . . . unrestrained but by equitable Laws,

[26] *Ibid.,* p. 336.
[27] *Ibid.,* p. 350.

which constitute the very essence of our Civil Liberty.
. . ." [28] The first writer, like Cato, may have been somewhat disingenuous by giving the appearance of accepting
conventional premises, but the second embraced them. The
evidence does not warrant the belief that either would have
exempted all verbal attacks on the government from subsequent punishment. Their position, in brief, was that utterances they did not consider subversive should be criminally
immune. But their party was not at the time in power.

Both writers, however, contributed more to libertarian
theory than the eminent philosopher, David Hume. He
defended the general principle of a free press as he understood it, but seems to have written in serene ignorance of
the existence and enforcement of the law of seditious libel,
not to mention the power of Parliament to punish aspersive
speech and publications as a breach of privilege. How else
could he write about "the extreme liberty, which we enjoy
in this country, of communicating whatever we please to
the public, and of openly censuring every measure, entered
into by the king or his ministers"? [29] The first sixteen editions of his essay, from 1742 to 1768, carried a passage
minimizing the dangers that might result from abuse of the
press and claiming "this liberty . . . as the common right
of mankind." But the 1770 edition omitted the passage,
while the final revised edition of 1777 added a concluding
line characterizing the "unbounded liberty of the press"
as "one of the evils" attending a mixed form of government. Any edition of Hume gave the impression that the
press was as free as it ought to be.

Henry Fielding, novelist and political journalist, revealed

[28] *Ibid.*, pp. 338 and 350.
[29] "Of the Liberty of the Press," in *Essays Moral, Political, and
Literary*, ed. T. H. Green and T. H. Grose (London, 1898), 1:94.

his sentiments more bluntly. When the Tories returned to power, after the fall of the Walpole ministry, he edited a pro-administration journal which took a dim view of Whig criticism. "In a free country," he confessed, "the people have a right to complain of any grievance which affects them, and this is the privilege of an Englishman; but surely to canvass those high and nice points, which move the finest wheels of state, matters merely belonging to the royal prerogative, in print, is in the highest degree indecent, and a gross abuse of the liberty of the press." [30]

Across the Atlantic, notwithstanding the Zenger case and Alexander's efforts, no progress was being made in libertarian thought. Indeed, it is a temptation to state that there was no libertarian thought between Alexander in 1737 and Bollan in 1766 — and none after, until 1798. Charles Chauncy, "undoubtedly the most influential clergyman of his time in Boston" and "acknowledged leader of the liberals of his generation," [31] wrote a great sermon in 1739 on liberty of conscience, but hewed to orthodoxy in banning undefined abuses of liberty or "Licentiousness." [32] A tract of 1744, ascribed to Elisha Williams, speaker of the Connecticut House, formerly president of Yale and a judge, even more brilliantly pleaded for the right of private judgment without any control from civil authority, not only as to affairs of conscience but on all issues. Williams generously supported *"the Right that every one has to speak his Sentiments openly concerning such*

[30] *Jacobite's Journal*, no. 26, May 28, 1747, quoted in Lawrence Hanson, *Government and the Press, 1695–1763* (Oxford, 1936), p. 2.

[31] *Dictionary of American Biography*.

[32] *The only Compulsion proper to be made Use of in the Affairs of Conscience and Religion* (Boston, 1739), p. 15.

Matters as affect the good of the whole." [33] But "every one" meant only Protestants; "Papists" were expressly excluded. Moreover, Williams neglected to confront any of the problems of libel law. Jonathan Mayhew, however, was more aware of such practical considerations. A radical agitator, regarded as a prophet of the American Revolution by Otis and the Adamses, this great liberal minister, in the midst of his most famous sermon of 1750 on the right of revolution and civil disobedience against wicked laws, took occasion to condemn the querulous and contemptible men in every state, "men of factious, turbulent and carping dispositions" who took hold of every trifle to justify and legitimate "seditious practices" against their rulers.[34] This superb example of unconscious irony indicated little sympathy on Mayhew's part for words *he* considered to be seditious.

In 1753, the colonial understanding of the scope of free expression was further revealed by an editorial in *The Independent Reflector*, the voice of the New York "Triumvirate," William Livingston, John Morin Scott, and William Smith, young lawyers with republican ideas and a passion to be heard. When an opposition paper refused to publish a rejoinder composed by one of them, they published a credo on liberty of the press:

> A Printer ought not to publish every Thing that is offered to him; but what is conducive of general Utility, he should not refuse, be the Author a Christian, Jew, Turk or Infidel.

[33] *A seasonable Plea for the Liberty of Conscience, and the Right of private Judgment, in Matters of Religion, without any Controul from human Authority*, By a Lover of Truth and Liberty [signing himself "Philalethes"] (Boston, 1744), pp. 6 and 40.
[34] "A Discourse Concerning Unlimited Submission," in Perry Miller and Thomas H. Johnson, eds., *The Puritans* (New York, 1938), pp. 279–280.

Such Refusal is an immediate abridgement of the Freedom of the Press. When on the other Hand, he prostitutes his Art by the Publication of any Thing injurious to his Country, it is criminal. . . . It is high Treason against the State. The usual Alarm rung in such Cases, the common Cry of an Attack upon the LIBERTY OF THE PRESS, is groundless and trifling. The Press neither has, nor can have such a Liberty, and whenever it is assumed, the Printer should be punished.[35]

The most willing tool of the crown could have applauded this definition of a free press by the republican patriots from the colony identified with Zenger and Alexander. On the other hand there could be no greater danger to open political debate than the vague crime of constructive treason, particularly if it could be committed by mere words. Even a crown lawyer knew that the law tended to rule out treason in any case where words against the government were unconnected with some treasonous project for carrying them out; such words were criminally punishable as seditious libel, a distinction of importance since the latter was a mere misdemeanor, while treason was a capital crime. That fact reveals the severity of the remarks by the New York lawyers. A few years after they had published their credo on liberty of the press, James Parker, who had been their printer and editor, wrote a broadside opposing a proposed stamp tax on newspapers that was being considered by the New York Assembly. Parker announced that in countries "where Liberty truly reigns, every one hath a Privilege of declaring his Sentiments upon all Topicks with the utmost Freedom, provided he does it with

[35] *The Independent Reflector* (New York City), Aug. 30, 1753, quoted in *The Journals of Hugh Gaine, Printer*, ed. Paul Leicester Ford (New York, 1902), 1:12–13.

proper Decency and a just Regard to the Laws." [36] It was a neat way to say that all sentiments short of seditious libel were free, an epitome of the American view of the matter.

During that decade, the 1750's, only Thomas Hayter, the Bishop of London, seems to have essayed an explanation of the meaning and compass of allowable discourse.[37] Although Hayter was most concerned with the sinfulness of personal slander, as befitted a clergyman, he generalized on secular principles in an original and startlingly libertarian manner. Freedom of speech was in his mind atop a hierarchy of nonreligious values, a right belonging and essential to the liberty of the subject. Printing being "only a more extensive and improved kind of speech," freedom of the press was to be cherished because it "derived from the Natural Right and Faculty of Speech." [38] Earlier writers had also elevated free speech to the status of a right reserved to persons in the formation of the social contract, but Hayter was the first to elaborate this notion and give it the appearance of a legal fiction by association with the talismanic symbol of English freedom, Magna Carta. He argued, at the same time, that "Liberty of Speech" was "antecedent to that great Charter of British Liberties," and concluded with the seminal proposition that speech and press were "constitutional" rights because they were "natural" rights.[39]

[36] Nov. 1759, quoted in Beverly McAnear, ed., "James Parker *versus* New York Province," *New York History*, 32:322 (July 1941).

[37] *An Essay on the Liberty of the Press, Chiefly as It Respects Personal Slander* (London, n.d.), 47 pp. From internal evidence this tract seems to have been published in the late 1750's. See, *e.g.*, at pp. 19–20, the reference to the recent posthumous publication of Bolingbroke's *Works* which appeared in 1754.

[38] *Ibid.*, pp. 6, 8.

[39] *Ibid.*, pp. 8, 18.

No one had so hallowed freedom of speech as did Hayter, and if his declaration of faith was historically and legally groundless, it had the quality of myth-making which characteristically transcends the grubbiness of fact.

Genuinely committed to natural and constitutional rights, Hayter would have permitted them a generous scope of operation. Voltaire's apocryphal aphorism, that he wholly disapproved of what Helvetius said, but would defend to the death his right to say it, described Hayter's views. He vehemently despised the opinions of Bolingbroke and of an unnamed writer for the *London Evening Post*, denouncing them uncharitably for their "pestilential" and "atrocious" abuses of the press and specifically charging them with "Libel against the Public." [40] Yet he would not punish such opinions, however noxious, for fear of abridging "the Right of Communicating our Thoughts," unless the words expressed fell into one of three categories of licentious offenses against the whole community: blasphemy, perjury, and treason. These, he thought, were the only offenses of speech and press over which the government had cognizance.[41] Since the first two were crimes against God, the good bishop's intolerance of them is understandable; his proscription of treasonable words, which he failed to define, did not, however, conform with his over-all position. By treasonable words Hayter, who was unskilled in the law, probably meant seditious libel, which no one in history had yet included within the range of legally permissible utterance. Yet Hayter must be ranked with Cato, not for the perspicacity of his analysis but as a rare representative of ultra libertarianism; for, despite the limitations he would have imposed upon speech, he cautioned against prosecu-

[40] *Ibid.*, pp. 20, 22, 29.
[41] *Ibid.*, p. 9.

tion. His emphasis was upon the conviction that the benefits of free expression outweighed its mischiefs and should not be sacrificed merely to ward off dangers to peace and security which were usually imaginary.[42] This view was particularly telling in a decade that had witnessed the jailing of one man for criticizing a Revolutionary settlement of nearly seven decades earlier, and the imprisonment of another for his acid remarks about a dead monarch.[43]

Beginning in the 1760's what had been a desultory public discussion of freedom of the press erupted into an intense debate that maintained a quick tempo throughout the remainder of the century. The celebrated Wilkes case triggered the change. Unpopular policies under George III, who meant to rule as well as reign, provoked a rash of press criticism that the king and his equally thin-skinned ministers fiercely resented. The studied insult of the king's speech of 1763 by John Wilkes in the forty-fifth issue of his journal, the *North Briton,* was unendurable. Upon an information for libel filed by the attorney-general, general search warrants were issued by one of the secretaries of state leading to the arrest of no less than forty nine persons, including Wilkes, his printer, and his publisher. Within a short time, about two hundred informations were filed, more than the number of prosecutions in the whole reign of George II, lasting thirty-three years.[44] The vast majority of cases never came to the trial stage, but the mass arrests,

[42] *Ibid.,* pp. 1, 36.

[43] The reference here is to the trials of Richard Nutt in 1754 and of John Shebbeare in 1758, both unreported cases. See James Paterson, *The Liberty of the Press, Speech, and Public Worship* (London, 1880), p. 97. Chief Justice Mansfield cited Nutt's case in Rex v. Dean of St. Asaph, Howell's *State Trials,* 21:1038 (1783).

[44] Thomas Erskine May, *The Constitutional History of England* (New York, 1880), 1:112 note 2, relying on the *Memoirs of Horace Walpole.*

harassments, and imposition of costs upon the persons concerned stimulated a widespread and growing suspicion that the government's administration of the law in crown-libel cases fell short of minimum standards of justice.

In the treatment and prosecution of Wilkes himself, the government found that it had mounted a tiger. No one since the days of John Lilburne, more than a century earlier, proved to be such a resourceful and pugnacious antagonist against the combined forces of all branches of the government. Capitalizing on the stupid and relentless persecution against him, Wilkes made his cause the symbol of constitutional liberty. His private study had been ransacked on a general warrant and all his papers seized for incriminating evidence; his *North Briton* No. 45 was voted to be a seditious libel by Commons, ordered to be burned, and he himself was expelled as an M.P. He fled across the Channel to escape street gangs and certain conviction in the courts. Convicted in absentia of seditious libel and of obscene libel, as well, for an unpublished manuscript obtained by the government through bribery, Wilkes was sentenced to outlawry when he failed to appear for sentence. His letters and tracts from Paris won him so sympathetic a response at home that he returned to clear his name. The sentence of outlawry was reversed on a technicality by Lord Chief Justice Mansfield, but the popular idol was jailed for twenty-two months to serve his conviction for criminal libels. His fine of £1,000 was raised twenty times over by public subscription under the auspices of the newly formed and well-organized "Society for Supporting the Bill of Rights," which was also instrumental in his being thrice elected to Commons while still in prison. He emerged as the most popular political figure in England and served constructively in Parliament where, it is not irrelevant to add, he ably defended the American cause, justifying his inflated reputation among the colonists, to whom the name Wilkes personified liberty.[45] They associated Wilkes with freedom of press with the same fervor as they did Zenger.[46]

The irony is that Wilkes himself held rather orthodox opinions on the subject of freedom of the press. He was, to be sure, one of its most staunch practitioners, but he gave little thought to the subject despite his grueling experiences with the law of criminal libel. The famous *North Briton* papers ignore all theory about freedom of the press, with the slight exception of No. 1, which passingly hailed the Englishman's birthright as a means of terrorizing evil ministers by exposing their designs and duplicity.[47] In the course of Wilkes's intensive defense of himself over a four-year period, nothing in his private correspondence, public letters, speeches, or pamphlets indicates disagreement with the substantive law of seditious libel.[48] At one point he asserted that truth could not constitute a libel, but his principal defense was a flat denial that his words were libelous, a defense which somehow implies a criticism of the existing law.[49] He admitted, however, that the expression of opinion should not give "any open public offense" to any establishment or individual. "The crime," declared Wilkes, "commences from thence, and the magistrate has

---

[45] My summary of the Wilkes case is based chiefly on the narrative in Raymond Postgate, *That Devil Wilkes* (New York, 1929). See also George Nobbe, *The North Briton* (New York, 1939), particularly ch. 16.

[46] Rossiter, *Seedtime*, p. 527 note 158.

[47] *The North Briton* (Dublin, 1766), 1:1, June 5, 1762.

[48] See [John Wilkes], *English Liberty . . . containing the Private Correspondence, Public Letters, Speeches, and Addresses, of John Wilkes* (London, n.d. [1769], 391 pp.

[49] *Ibid.*, p. 128.

a right to interpose and even to punish outrageous and indecent attacks on what any community has decreed to be sacred; not only the rules of good breeding, but the laws of society are then infringed." [50] This was a good formulation of the conservative position which no libertarian could possibly endorse. When Wilkes defined the "two important questions of public Liberty" that were involved in his case, he did not even mention freedom of the press; the danger of general warrants and of the seizure of private papers were what interested him, and when he added a third question of public liberty it had to do with outlawry.[51]

While Wilkes himself did nothing whatever to advance freedom of the press, his case stirred up an unflagging controversy about it. Outraged conservatives, who repeated their stale views in support of the government, united behind the conviction that the Wilkes case demonstrated that there were instances "in which the Hangman may be properly employed to correct the political Errata of the Press, without injuring its Liberty. . . ." [52] "Candor," who identified himself only as a Gray's Inn lawyer, wrote the ablest conservative tract; it went through three editions between 1764 and 1770.[53] Although he excoriated the government for its "inquisitorial" policies of search and seizure in the hope of ferreting out evidence of seditious

[50] *Ibid.*, p. 132.
[51] *Ibid.*, pp. 156, 192.
[52] Anon., *The Liberty of the Press* (London, n.d., [ca. 1763]). See also John Brown [Vicar of Newcastle], *Thoughts on Civil Liberty, on Licentiousness, and Faction* (London, 1765), pp. 153–155.
[53] *A Letter from Candor to the Public Advertiser* (London, 1764). I have used the third edition, of 1770, available in *A Collection of Interesting Political Tracts*, edited, probably, by J. Almon (London, 1773), 1:1–40.

libel,[54] Candor confessed his admiration of the law as laid down by Lord Mansfield in Wilkes's case. Liberty of the press meant simply freedom from prior restraint, subject to the penalties of the common law for abuse of that liberty. The truth, far from being a defense, aggravated a libel. The function of the jury was limited to deciding whether the defendant had in fact made the statement charged, while the court reserved exclusively to itself as a matter of law the question whether the statement was criminally libelous. The law was clear and just to Candor, and he wrote in the hope that

> unlearned men will acquiesce in the respectable authorities which I have quoted, and cease to reflect upon government, or the ways of administration and public justice. In God's name, what business have private men to write or to speak about public matters? Such kind of liberty leads to all sorts of license and obloquy, the very reverse of politeness; and the greatest man, be he ever so cautious, if such things are endured, may be traduced. . . .
>
> The advantage of inoffensive speech or writing, and absolute submission to government is so great, that I am sure every man ought to rejoice in such wholesome regulations. . . . It seems to me to be really an excellent device for keeping the scribbling race from meddling with political questions, at least from ever drawing their pens a second time upon such subjects.[55]

The reply to Candor came in a small book which went through seven editions between 1764 and 1771.[56] The

---

[54] *Ibid.*, pp. 22–23.
[55] *Ibid.*, pp. 8, 9–10.
[56] The first edition bears the title *An Enquiry into the Doctrine, Lately Propagated, concerning Libels, Warrants, and the Seizure of Papers . . . in a Letter to Mr. Almon from the Father of Can-*

author, identifying himself only as "Father of Candor," was, from the internal evidence, an eminent public figure with a legal background. Whoever he was, he was the first in England to assail, even indirectly, the common law of seditious libel. He did so in the same manner as had Alexander and Hamilton in the Zenger case, twenty-nine years earlier, speaking thunderously but sometimes thrashing about with a frail stick. "The whole doctrine of libels," he proclaimed, "and the criminal mode of prosecuting them by information, grew with that accursed court the star-chamber" which had relied upon "that slavish imperial law, usually denominated the civil law. You will find nothing of it in our books higher than the time of Q. Elizabeth and Sir Edward Coke." [57] None could guess what might or might not be considered a seditious libel by some judge or attorney-general. The crime was dangerously undefinable, the name libel an "arbitrary brand." [58] The public had a vital stake in continuance of so-called "libels." Had it not been for such speeches and writings that had been prosecuted as libels, declared Father of Candor, there never would have been a Glorious Revolution nor would England be enjoying either a Protestant religion "or one jot of civil liberty." [59] The liberty of "exposing and opposing a bad Administration" he thought was a necessary right

---

dor (London, 1764), 135 pp. Although I have used the rare first edition, my citations are to the more easily obtainable seventh edition, which was reprinted in volume 1 of the same *Collection of Interesting Political Tracts* in which Candor's essay appeared. The works are separately paginated. The seventh edition of Father of Candor bears the title, *A Letter Concerning Libels, Warrants, the Seizure of Papers, and Sureties for the Peace of Behaviour . . . With the Postscript and Appendix* (London, 1771), 164 pp.

[57] *Ibid.*, p. 23.
[58] *Ibid.*, pp. 40–41.
[59] *Ibid.*, p. 49.

of a free people and the foremost benefit that could be derived from an unrestrained press.

Should a critic be charged with crime, however, he had a right to be tried by a jury of his peers, not by a royally appointed judge. There was a "constitutional reason of infinite moment to a free people" why jurors should always decide whether an accused's words were libelous: ninety-nine times out of a hundred, prosecutions for public libels were a dispute between the ministers and the people. If the jury could not decide the question of libel, England, he warned, would lose not only the liberty of the press but every other liberty besides. No man that disapproved of the measures of a court would venture to discuss their propriety. No man would dare utter a syllable in print against any power of office, much less against any royal prerogative, however illegally usurped. He would be sure to be charged with a libel by the attorney-general and end in prison.[60] "I will venture to prophecy," wrote Father of Candor, "that if the reigning notions concerning libels be pushed a little farther, no man will dare to open his mouth, much less to use his pen, against the worst administration that can take place, however much it may behoove the people to be apprised of the condition they are likely to be in. In short, I do not see what can be the issue of such law, but an universal acquiescence to any man or measures, that is, a downright passive obedience."[61]

The saving way lay in an encouragement of animadversions upon the conduct of ministers to check their bad actions and give them incentive for doing what is praiseworthy. But if criticism was deemed libelous whether true or false, if the truth could be a libel, then England was a

[60] *Ibid.*, p. 17.
[61] *Ibid.*, p. 46.

short step from "complete despotism" which would be
reached when the same doctrine was applied to oral utterances. "And then what a blessed condition should we all
be in! when neither the liberty of free writing or free
speech, about every body's concern, about the management of public money, public law and public affairs was
permitted; and every body was afraid to utter what every
body however could not help thinking." [62] The only
remedy that would avert the evil was to make truth, as
judged by a jury, "an absolute defence" in the case of state
libels.[63] Of course, granted Father of Candor, a "wilfully
false" publication was certainly damnable and seditious,
but the question of willfulness or malicious intent should
also be left to the jury.[64]

The reforms suggested by Father of Candor, though
widening the threshold of permissible discussion, would
have made jurors the virtual *ex post facto* censors of publications. But in theory at least, the threshold would have
been widened even more than proposed by the Zenger
defense, if, as a condition of being judged seditious, a falsehood had to be wilfully or maliciously made. Assuming
that a jury could accurately judge an accused's state of
mind at the time of his composition, his publication, however wrong or false, if not maliciously inspired, would not
be criminal unless tending in the opinion of the jury to
breach the peace or cause crime. On the other hand the
notion that mere words were punishable because of their

[62] *Ibid.*, p. 47.
[63] The same position was adopted by Joseph Towers in his tract,
which also appeared in 1764, *An Enquiry into the Question,
Whether Juries are, or are not, Judges of Law, as well as of Fact;
With a particular Reference to the case of Libels* (London, 1764),
31 pp.
[64] Father of Candor, pp. 48 and 160.

bad tendency held the most repressive implications; and malice or criminal intent, which had always been held an essential element of the crime of seditious libel,[65] was usually presumed from the publication's bad tendency, itself a presumption. Were truth an "absolute defence" as Father of Candor demanded, malice and bad tendency would be irrelevant considerations. They would be highly relevant, however, if the defendant could not prove the truth of his statements, which would be the case if they were in fact false, or if they were opinions neither true nor false, or if they were factually correct but unprovably so. In either of these three instances, none of which was considered by Father of Candor, truth as a defense, his main prop, was useless; it was also irrelevant since the defendant's fate would then depend on whether or not the jury found his intent to be malicious, a judgment which they would form from their subjective evaluation of the harmless or harmful tendency of his words, an evaluation which later practice showed to be dependent upon their approval of his character and opinions. The history of sedition trials in the United States, under the federal sedition acts of 1798, 1918, and 1940, demonstrates that a requirement that criminal intent be proved to a jury's satisfaction is a *pro forma* one, an empty protection of the accused.

Father of Candor intended, however, that jurors be guided by the general principle that the bad tendency of words should not warrant their punishment. This was his

[65] Sir James F. Stephen argued, however, that a criminal intention in the writer was either not part of the common-law definition or else mere surplusage which need not be proved, since the crime itself was simply the publication of censure, the intention therefore being only the intention to publish censure and not the intention to produce by the publication some evil effect. Stephen, *A History of the Criminal Law of England* (London, 1883), 2:344, 350–353.

most significant contribution by far to libertarian theory, for with the exception of the idea that words per se should not be deemed criminal, Father of Candor's repudiation of the bad-tendency test promised the most far-reaching protection for freedom of discourse and criticism. At one point, it seemed as if he might go all the way by endorsing the principle that only overt acts should be subject to the criminal law, for he declared that "sedition cannot be committed by words, but by public and violent action." [66] The notion was an aberration, however, since he regarded willfully false publications against a just administration to be seditious. Although his repudiation of the bad-tendency test cannot be taken at face value, the principle that he laid down, being of far greater importance than his own exceptions to it, implied a tremendous expansion in the scope of allowable expression. He grounded his position on the premise that libel was not an "actual breach of the peace." [67] That crime, he declared, "seems to express, *ex vi termini*, some positive bodily injury, or some immediate dread thereof at least; and that, whatever a challenge, in writing, to any particular might be, a general libel upon public measures, could never be construed to be so." [68] This, he claimed, was a point of the utmost importance since libels were held to be criminal because of their tendency to breach of the peace. But, he argued, "what only tends to, cannot be itself, a breach of the peace, as the thing tending to cannot be one and the same with the thing tended to; and consequently such tendency cannot by any possibility be an *actual* breach of the peace." [69]

Only four theorists had ventured as far as Father of

[66] Father of Candor, p. 34.
[67] *Ibid.*, p. 71.
[68] *Ibid.*, p. 20.
[69] *Ibid.*, p. 161.

Candor in explicitly suggesting as much free play for the expression of opinion, and all, like Father of Candor, inconsistently qualified their presentations so as to acknowledge the criminality of utterances which they considered malicious, scandalous, seditious, or dangerous to the state. As early as 1644 Roger Williams had vaguely implied that opinions should be exempt from punishment unless directly causing the commission of some criminal deed,[70] but he was referring only to the realm of religion. He not only supported punishment of scandal against the state; he believed that if anyone under color of conscience "should preach or write that there ought to be no commanders or officers, because all are equal in Christ, therefore no masters nor officers, no laws nor orders, nor corrections nor punishments;—I say, I never denied, but in such cases, whatever is pretended, the commander or commanders may judge, resist, compel and punish such transgressors. . . ."[71] William Walwyn, in 1645, more clearly proposed an overt-acts test. In the course of rebutting an antagonist's charge that "freedom of discourse" would "tend to the encreasing of erronious [sic] opinions, and disturbance to the State," he concluded: "And as for disturbance to the State; admit any mans judgment be so misinformed, as to beleeve there is no sinne; if this man now upon this government should take away another mans goods, or commit murder or

[70] "Secondly a false religion and worship will not hurt the civil state in case the worshipper breaks no civil law. . . . The civil laws not being broken, the civil peace is not broken: and this only is the point in question." *The Bloudy Tenent, of Persecution, for cause of Conscience*, in *The Writings of Roger Williams*, Publications of the Narragansett Club (Providence, 1866–1874), 3:198. See also at pp. 78–79, 96, 100, 147, 163, 171.

[71] "To the Town of Providence," January 1654/55, in *Letters of Roger Williams*, ed. John Russell Bartlett (vol. 6 of *Writings of Williams*), p. 279.

adultery; the Law is open, and he is to be punished as a malefactor, and so for all crimes that any mans judgment may mislead him unto [sic]." [72] Spinoza was the next to advocate that "only the acts which alone are capable of offending" should be punished, but that every man should think what he likes and say what he thinks.[73] Yet Spinoza and Walwyn both accepted the validity of punishing seditious libel.

The overt-acts test had also been broached by Baron Montesquieu in 1748, in his *Esprit des Lois*. At one point he told the story of the execution of Marsyas for having dreamed of murdering Dionysius. Dionysius' retaliation was tyrannical, declared Montesquieu, for though murder had been the subject of Marsyas' thought, "yet he had made no attempt towards it. The laws do not take upon them to punish any other than overt acts." In a footnote he added, "The Thought must be joined with some sort of action." [74] Discussing unlawful speech, Montesquieu observed that malicious words were punishable as were certain words whose specific nature had been defined and outlawed, but words generally "do not constitute an overt act; they remain only an idea." Carried into action, however, they assumed the nature of that action. He gave, as an example, the case of a man who went into the market place with the intention of inciting the subjects to revolt. His words became treasonous when "annexed to a criminal

[72] "A Helpe to the Right Understanding of a Discourse Concerning Independency," 1645, in William Haller, ed., *Tracts on Liberty in the Puritan Revolution 1638–1647* (New York, 1933), 3:200. See the discussion of Walwyn above, pp. 93–94.

[73] *Theologico-Political Treatise*, 1670, in *The Chief Works of Benedict de Spinoza*, trans. R. H. M. Elwes (London, 1883), 1:265. See the discussion of Spinoza above, pp. 89–91.

[74] Book XII, "Of Thoughts," section 11, var. eds.

action." [75] But for Walwyn, Spinoza, Montesquieu, and possibly Williams, no one before Father of Candor had proposed, however inconsistently, a repudiation of the bad-tendency test or an acceptance of the test of overt acts.[76] Until someone worked out a formulation of this position, supported by a consistent body of thought analyzing the tough problems which it presented and suggesting workable guide-lines of application, libertarian discussion on the meaning and scope of free speech would be surrounded by a haze of rhetoric that obscured inchoate, contradictory, and illusory principles.

In 1766, William Bollan, once the agent in England for

[75] Book XII, "Of Indiscreet Speeches," section 12.

[76] In Theodore Schroeder's little-known, extremely useful, and often unreliable book, *Constitutional Free Speech Defined and Defended in an Unfinished Argument in a Case of Blasphemy* (New York, 1919), there is a long chapter, "Overt Act and Actual Injury *versus* Evil Psychological Tendency," pp. 391–427, that purports to be a history of the overt-acts test to 1800. Schroeder ignores Walwyn, Williams, and Spinoza, but does include Montesquieu in his discussion of the precedents prior to Father of Candor's book. In his eagerness to adduce precedents, Schroeder includes the writings of Martin Luther, John Milton, Jeremy Taylor, Edward Bagshaw, John Owen, John Locke, Thomas Delaune, Hubert Languet, [Edward?] Hitchin, Joshua Toulmin, John Hoadley, John Wickliffe, John Jones, and Anthony Ellys. I have examined their writings which Schoeder cites to prove their endorsement of the overt-acts test and can state that neither those writings nor the extracts from them reproduced by Schroeder warrant his inclusion of any of the named individuals as supporters of that test. In many cases Schroeder's own evidence disproves his point. His chapter is a combination of prodigious research and wishful thinking. Endowed with a vivid imagination he read into most passages meanings which they simply do not have and often contradict. I am nevertheless indebted to Schroeder's book and in particular to his *Free Speech Bibliography* (New York, 1922), an invaluable guide to the sources which historians of First Amendment freedoms have grossly neglected.

the Massachusetts upper House, formerly advocate-general of the colony, published what was surely the most learned work in English on the subject of free speech. *The Freedom of Speech and Writing upon Public Affairs, Considered, with an Historical View*,[77] while a first-rate, elaborately detailed legal history of the subject from the time of the ancients, was essentially a restatement of the ideas earlier presented by Cato and Alexander. Yet it is significant as being the only work by an American besides Alexander's until the very close of the century; indeed, it was the last restatement in English of the theory and function of free expression until 1793 when the Reverend Robert Hall published his address on the subject.[78] The many tracts which appeared in England between Bollan's work and Hall's passed lightly over or ignored the relation of free speech to responsible government, the preservation of personal liberty, the formation of enlightened public opinion, the discovery of new knowledge, and, generally, the advancement of the public welfare. Bollan's explanation of the rationale for a policy of broad freedom was imbedded in an interminable rehearsal of tyranny under the Stuarts, with the Court of Star Chamber cast as the villainous body responsible for having introduced unconstitutional doctrines of criminal libel. Although he was an Anglican himself, Bollan movingly related the stories of Prynn, Leighton, Lilburne, and other Puritans persecuted for their political and religious opinions; in the course of his narrative he sought to demonstrate how the repression of "free inquiry" led to arbitrary searches and seizures, cruel punish-

[77] (London, 1766). The volume is 160 folio-sized pages of small print. On Bollan, see also above, pp. 70–71.
[78] See below, pp. 254–256, for a discussion of Hall.

ments, compulsory self-incrimination, and trial by judge instead of by jury.

But Bollan's recommendations lacked originality and breadth, for the theme of the book was that the accused in a criminal-libel case should have the right to plead truth as a defense, while the jury should have the power of deciding questions of falsity and malice. But for these reforms, which were partly procedural in character, he left the law of seditious libel uncriticized, no doubt because he thought the power of the press was so great it might be used by the wrong people to "divide and destroy us." Lamenting abuses of freedom, he cautioned that railing was not reasoning; moreover, criminations might injure and inflame but never inform or reform. There must be "just and proper bounds," he observed;[79] and Sir William Blackstone, in his fourth volume of *Commentaries on the Laws of England*, published in 1769, agreed in principle.[80]

In that latter year, when crowds were still clustering about the gates of Wilkes's prison, shouting huzzas in his honor, the government was given cause to prove that the "proper bounds" of a free press prevented criticism of the king. A letter under the pseudonym of "Junius," first appearing in the *London Evening Post* and republished in most of the city's newspapers, blamed George III for a series of stupid blunders, advised a change of policy, and demanded a new ministry. It was a daring performance, sarcastically castigating the government and cautioning the king to bear in mind the fate of the Stuart despots. Efforts to discover the identity of "Junius" failing, the government turned its wrath upon the many publishers of the notorious

[79] Bollan, *Freedom of Speech and Writing*, p. 137.
[80] Vol. 4, ch. 11, sect. 12, pp. 150–153.

letter, which had become a best-seller when reprinted in *The London Museum*, a monthly journal published and distributed by John Almon. Almon already enjoyed a reputation among government officials as a sedition-monger; not the least of his infamy was his publication of Father of Candor in 1764, followed the next year by a new edition of the Zenger trial. The most logical scapegoat, Almon was prosecuted and convicted for seditious libel, Lord Chief Justice Mansfield himself deciding that the accused's publication and sale of the "Junius" letter constituted the crime charge.[81] In the next trial, that of Henry Woodfall, in whose paper the "Junius" letter first appeared, the jury balked by returning a verdict of guilty of publishing "only," suggesting that they did not believe the accused to be a seditious libeller.[82] While Mansfield took the uncertain verdict under advisement — he finally ruled on the necessity of a new trial — the government grimly proceeded with the prosecutions of two more of Junius' publishers, despite the mounting criticism in the London press against Mansfield's exposition of trial procedure in state libels. In two new trials, staged the same day, the juries stunningly returned general verdicts of not guilty, in spite of Mansfield's instructions that they possessed no power to do so unless convinced that the defendants had not in fact published the letter, which they positively had.[83] Mansfield had done all that he could to avert another Woodfall verdict, yet ended by getting a Zenger verdict. Confronted by popular acclamation of the acquittals, the government quietly dropped the prosecutions of the other publishers against whom informations had been filed, but

[81] Rex v. Almon, Howell's *State Trials*, 20:803 (1770).
[82] Rex v. Woodfall, Howell's *State Trials*, 20:895 (1770).
[83] Rex v. Miller, Howell's *State Trials*, 20:870 (1770).

it could not quash the public alarm that crown-libel doctrines menaced the Englishman's beloved institution, trial by one's peers.

The alarm, spreading to Parliament, provoked a debate on the legitimacy of Mansfield's rulings. Lords Camden and Chatham, the elder Pitt, led Mansfield's censurers, but in the end the House of Lords inconclusively dropped the subject. In the Commons, Edmund Burke and John Glynn, the sergeant-at-law who had represented the Junius defendants, also assailed the doctrine that the criminality of an alleged libel was not within the cognizance of a jury; but a bill supporting jury powers failed to be enacted. Thus Parliament impliedly endorsed Mansfield's interpretation of the law of the land in cases of seditious libel.[84] Most significantly of all, not even his critics had questioned his narrow definition of a free press. In Woodfall's case, he had declared: "As for the freedom of the press, I will tell you what it is; the liberty of the press is, that a man may print what he pleases without license; as long as it remains so, the liberty of the press is not restrained." [85]

Their efforts unavailing in Parliament, the reformers appealed to the court of public opinion. A succession of letters, tracts, and books appeared in the next several years, purporting, in the words of one subtitle, to be *A Full Refutation of Lord Mansfield's lawless opinion in Crown Libels*.[86] What turned out to be "lawless," however, was Mansfield's supposed subversion of the rights of jurors and the related right of the accused to be tried by his peers when charged with crime. Most of the writers were much more concerned with criminal procedure in libel trials

[84] May, *Constitutional History of England*, 2:116–118.
[85] Howell's *State Trials*, 20:903 (1770).
[86] *The Juryman's Touchstone; or, A Full Refutation* . . . By The Censor General (London, 1771), 93 pp.

than with the substantive problem of libels or freedom of the press. Robert Morris, a barrister and secretary of the Society for Supporters of the Bill of Rights, might blast Mansfield's "Star-chamber law" of libels as "the most pernicious and abominable doctrine," but he was speaking about the denial of the jury's right to accept truth as a defense and judge for themselves whether the words charged were libelous.[87]

Henry Woodfall, himself a publisher and a defendant in the Junius trials, writing as "Phileleutherus Anglicanus," admitted that false or malicious vilification of the government was criminal. He simply wanted an accused's intent to be judged by a jury. That he cared about freedom of the press is unquestionable, but his attack was not directed at Mansfield's definition of it. Although he ran on about the "gag" imposed by the "inquisition" of the judges, he confidently relied on juries to secure for the press its proper freedom.[88] So, too, the anonymous author who viewed "with pleasure" the recent prosecutions of those who had circulated "such dangerous productions" as the Junius letter,[89] yet could characterize the law of crown libels as "the great canker-worm of the state."[90] It was the minimizing of the jury's function that galled him. While he thought

[87] *A Letter to Sir Richard Aston, . . . Containing . . . some Thought on the Modern Doctrine of Libels* (London, 1770), 20, 38-39.

[88] *A Summary of the Law of Libel. In Four Letters* (1770), reprinted in *A Collection of Scarce and Interesting Tracts* (London, 1788, editor unnamed), 4:197-221.

[89] *Another Letter to Mr. Almon, in Matter of Libel* (1770), reprinted in *A Collection of Scarce and Interesting Tracts*, 4:7. The *Letter* covers pp. 5-157.

[90] *A Second Postscript to a Late Pamphlet, Entitled, A Letter to Mr. Almon, in Matter of Libel,* in *A Collection of Scarce and Interesting Tracts*, 4:196. The *Second Postscript* is at pp. 158-196.

an attack on the constitution or government to be criminal, he could tolerate public censure of ministers if a writer's intent as judged by a jury was not malicious. Another anonymous author believed England to be menaced by a "Rebellion of the Press . . . which has made the pen of prostituted scribblers more destructive than the sword." He asked Parliament to legislate additional restrictions on "intellectual licentiousness" by making truth and temperance of criticism an adequate defense against a charge of libel.[91] "Censor General's" condemnation of the government's practice of prosecuting by information in cases of seditious libel, thereby evading the necessity of securing a grand jury's assent,[92] represented a widespread sentiment that was part of the concentrated concern for securing accused libelers a trial by their peers similar in every respect to trials for other crimes. Francis Maseres best summarized this view, as the American Revolution foreclosed the debate for a time, when he noted that prosecutions for seditious libel were attended with so much danger to "the right of animadverting freely and publicly (but with a strict adherence to truth) on the pernicious tendency of public measures, that one would wish them entirely under the controul of the people themselves. . . ."[93]

[91] *Literary Liberty Considered; in a Letter to Henry Sampson Woodfall* (London, 1774), pp. 6–7, 12, 16, 22.
[92] *The Juryman's Touchstone*, pp. 85–86.
[93] *An Enquiry Into the Extent of the Power of Juries, on Trials of Indictments or Informations, for Publishing Seditious, or other Criminal Writings, or Libels. Extracted from a Miscellaneous Collection of Papers that were Published in 1776, Intitled, Additional Papers Concerning the Province of Quebec* (Dublin, 1792), p. 4. See also William Bollan, *Essay on the Right of Every Man in a free State to Speak and Write Freely* (London, 1772), an abridgment of Bollan's large book of 1766; and [James Burgh], *Political Disquisitions* (London, 1775), 3:246–247.

Amidst this concern for preserving trial by jury and making it the security of freedom of the press, a dissenting minister, preoccupied with the rights of conscience, carried libertarian theory as far as it could go. He was the Reverend Philip Furneaux, who in 1770 published a volume criticizing Blackstone's exposition of the laws of toleration.[94] In the course of a masterful analysis, Furneaux challenged the common law's imposition of restraints on the expression of religious and irreligious opinions. The profession of atheistic beliefs, denial of God or the Trinity, railing against the ordinances of the established church, exposing the Scriptures to contempt, and in general any opinion allegedly tending to produce in the minds of the people a bad opinion of religion were deemed criminally libelous. The crime of blasphemous libel was analogous to that of seditious libel, the main difference being that the sanctions of the law were thought necessary to protect the good reputation of God or religion instead of the government. While Furneaux never addressed himself to the problem of political speech, the principles which he supported were as applicable to the law of seditious libel as to libels on religion. It was Furneaux who advocated the ultralibertarian thesis that the expression of opinions, religious opinions to be sure, should be entirely free. He flatly rejected the bad-tendency test of words, proposing in its place punishment of overt acts only.

Furneaux was not the first to advocate this view. His predecessors as noted earlier, had been Walwyn, Spinoza, Montesquieu, and Father of Candor. In their cases, however, the principle of punishing deeds instead of words had

[94] *Letters to the Honourable Mr. Justice Blackstone, Concerning His Exposition of the Act of Toleration . . . in His Celebrated Commentaries on the Laws of England* (London, 1770; 2nd ed., 1771).

been incidentally mentioned in the midst of a body of doctrine to which it was foreign. They had acknowledged
the principle, to their vast credit, but left it unused as if it
were a round hole into which the square pegs of their
thought would not fit. By contrast, Furneaux built his
whole structure around that principle, thereby avoiding
the inconsistencies and exceptions to it that his precursors
had made foundational. Furneaux alone smashed through
the heavy crust of conventional limitations on expression
in which other libertarians had acquiesced. Whether out
of innocence or an imperious scorn for the unimportant,
he ignored the controversial issues of trial procedure, jurors'
rights, malice, and truth versus falsity which had so gripped
their attention. Where they bowed before the concept of
licentiousness as a bound, and with it, the rightfulness of
punishing supposed abuses of the liberty of expression, he
condemned the concept as worthless on the ground that
it could have only a personal definition. Where they sanc-
tioned the punishment of hateful sentiment whose tendency
they or a jury might admit to be dangerous or subversive,
he utterly cast aside the bad tendency test as a subjective
rationale for repression. For these reasons and because his
work was republished in at least two editions in America
before the Revolution,[95] extracts from his elaborate formulation are warranted, even though he focused almost exclusively on freedom of religious speech.

"Are we," he asked, "to leave every man at liberty to
propagate what sentiments he pleases?" His affirmative

[95] *An interesting appendix to Sir William Blackstone's Commentaries on the laws of England* (Philadelphia, 1773); and *The Palladium of Conscience* (Philadelphia, 1773). Both American editions
were reprintings of the second English edition of Furneaux, published in London, 1771. My citations are to the latter edition; see
the preceding note.

answer was categorical, based on the premise that the laws of society should have nothing to do with mere principles, opinions, or sentiments, "but only with those overt acts arising from them, which are contrary to the peace and good order of society." [96] Some might object that this policy would give free rein to even views "which have a *tendency* to introduce immorality and licentiousness," which the magistrates ought to check. But, Furneaux rejoined, the magistrate had no business checking any religious opinions:

> For if the magistrate be possessed of a power to restrain and punish any principles relating to religion because of their tendency, as he be the judge of that tendency; as he must be, if he be vested with authority to punish on that account; religious liberty is entirely at an end; or, which is the same thing, is under the countroul, and at the mercy of the magistrate, according as he shall think the tenets in question affect the foundation of moral obligation, or are favourable or unfavourable to religion and morality. But, if the line be drawn between mere religious principle and the tendency of it, on the one hand; and those overt acts which affect the publick peace and order, on the other; and if the latter alone be assigned to the jurisdiction of the magistrate, as being guardian of the peace of society . . . the boundaries between civil power and liberty, in religious matters, are clearly marked and determined; and the latter will not be wider or narrower, or just nothing at all, according to the magistrate's opinion of the good or bad tendency of principles.

> If it be objected, that when the tendency of principles is unfavourable to the peace and good order of society, as it may be, it is the magistrate's duty then, and for that reason to restrain them by penal laws: I reply, that the tendency of

[96] *Ibid.*, p. 59.

principles, tho' it be *unfavourable*, is not *prejudicial* to society, till it issues in some overt acts against the public peace
and order; and when it does, *then* the magistrate's authority
to punish commences; that is, he may punish the *overt acts*,
but not the *tendency*, which is not actually hurtful; and
therefore his penal laws should be directed against *overt acts
only*, which are detrimental to the peace and good order of
society, let them spring from what principles they will; and
not against *principles*, or the *tendency* of principles.

The distinction between the tendency of principles, and
the overt acts arising from them is, and cannot but be, observed in many cases of a civil nature, in order to determine
the bounds of the magistrate's power, or at least to limit the
exercise of it, in such cases. It would not be difficult to mention customs and manners, as well as principles, which have
a tendency unfavourable to society; and which, nevertheless,
cannot be restrained by penal laws, except with the total
destruction of civil liberty. And here the magistrate must be
contented with pointing his penal laws against the overt acts
resulting from them. In the same manner he should act in
regard to mens professing, or rejecting, religious principles
or systems. Punishing a man for the tendency of his principles is punishing him *before* he is guilty, for fear he *should
be* guilty.[97]

Furneaux had proposed the ultimate freedom for words,
at least for words about religion. His reference to civil as
distinguished from religious cases, in the quotation above,
and his thesis that "religious and *civil* liberty have a recip-
rocal influence in producing and supporting one another," [98]
indicate, although dubiously, that his overt-acts test of
criminality may have been intended to refer to words of
any nature, political as well as religious. His test was as

[97] *Ibid.*, pp. 61–63.
[98] *Ibid.*, p. 202.

applicable to the one as to the other, and the common law was basically the same for both. In either case, Furneaux may have gone too far, for he would have left society defenseless against verbal crimes of any nature, be they public obscenities, solicitations to crime, or incitements to crime. Montesquieu's case of the man who goes into the market place with the intention of provoking the subjects to revolt cannot be ignored. If the subjects are actually incited to violence, the speaker deserves punishment. Should he fail, if his audience, for example, listens with derisive amusement, there might still be a justification for locking him up had he knowingly and expressly counseled the commission of some crime. The authorities might even be warranted in taking steps to silence him in the midst of his speech, if, in the phrase of Father of Candor, there was "some immediate dread" of an actual breach of peace.[99] A test of criminality that weighs the danger of a criminal deed being immediately provoked is particularly relevant in the case of a publication, when the writer, unlike the speaker, cannot be interrupted.

To his credit, Furneaux erred on the side of freedom, but his margin of error was so great as to render his formulation intolerable even to a society which conscientiously strives to maintain the uttermost freedom of discussion consonant with its own safety. Repudiation of the bad-tendency test, on the ground that it condemns words which might theoretically at some future time cause some imaginary harm, does not require that the overt-acts test of criminality must be embraced as the only valid libertarian position. If political change of a radical character is pos-

[99] *A Letter Concerning Libels*, in *Collection of Interesting Political Tracts*, 1:20.

sible by peaceable means through representative institutions that are responsive to public opinion, there is no reason to extend the protection of the laws to utterances that directly and intentionally incite to imminent overt acts which Furneaux himself would punish.

The idea that he had thrown into the debate on the scope of permissible expression took only shallow root. As a century earlier when freedom of speech and press had been championed primarily by those who sought an open debate on religion, so, now, the new and ultralibertarian view seemed at first to appeal chiefly to the dissenters and others devoted to the cause of liberty of conscience. One of Furneaux' followers, the Reverend Ebenezer Ratcliffe, regarded the risk of danger from opinions as "no great price to pay for truth and the privilege of expressing our sentiments without controul." [100] Though Ratcliffe distinguished deeds, which were punishable, from words, which were not, he formulated the principle, perhaps innocently, in a way that acknowledged a power in the government to reach the utterance as well as the criminal conduct which it inspired; for his contention was "that the magistracy has no right to take cognizance of sentiments and opinions, till they have produced criminal overt acts, evidently injurious to society." [101]

In the same year, 1773, the Reverend Andrew Kippis restated the Furneaux thesis in its pristine purity. Observing that penal statutes extended only to such offenses as endangered the safety of the state or were injurious to persons and property, Kippis concluded that only overt acts were

---

[100] *Two Letters Addressed to the Right Rev. Prelates* (London, 1773), p. 50.
[101] *Ibid.*, p. 100.

punishable. "The true and proper notion of an overt act," he contended, "is an act done with malicious intention, an act criminally injurious to the public, and which can be proved to be such by just and legal evidence." [102] That neither preaching nor publication could constitute an overt act, according to Kippis, was clear from his insistence that physical injury alone could override the claims of conscience. If the state interfered at any point before the actual injury occurred, under the pretext of the evil tendency of the words, "it will be impossible to know where to stop. Speculations and fancies about the tendencies of opinions may be carried on to the entire destruction of liberty. . . ." [103]

Among secular writers, Francis Maseres, in 1776, came close to the Furneaux-Kippis position when he insisted that the "dangerous tendency" must be proved "real and manifest" to the jury's satisfaction; at one point, Maseres seemed to adopt the view that unless witnesses testified that the supposedly seditious statement "actually occasioned that disturbance which it seemed to be intended to create," its tendency would not warrant a verdict of guilty. [104] The only other secularist to adopt an ultralibertarian position before Jefferson did so was the great Jeremy Bentham, in 1776. In a critique of Blackstone's ideas on government, Bentham blithely declared without any explanation that the existence of a free government depended in part upon the freedom with which "malcontents may communicate their sentiments, concert their plans, and practice every mode of opposition short of actual revolt, before the execu-

[102] *A Vindication of the Protestant Dissenting Ministers* (London, 1773), p. 98.
[103] *Ibid.*, p. 99.
[104] *An Enquiry Into the Extent of the Power of Juries*, pp. 6 and 24; see also pp. 13, 18, 22, and 28.

tive power can be legally justified in disturbing them." [105]
This was the broadest statement on the scope of political
expression that anyone had ever or could ever make. Perhaps Bentham did not intend his undeveloped thought to
be taken literally or did not understand that it condoned
seditious conspiracy and successful incitement to breach of
the peace, riot, and other crimes short of actual revolt. Not
even the Jeffersonians at the height of their libertarian
theorizing, between 1798 and 1801, went that far.

The history of Anglo-American thought on freedom of
speech and press from the early seventeenth century to the
American Revolution had been remarkably uniform until
the eve of the Revolution when a few aberrant writers
broke away from a fixed pattern. No one had ever explicitly disavowed the concept of seditious libel even to the
point of supporting a right to advocate the peaceable overthrow of the monarchy, the House of Lords, or the constitution. Bentham to be sure clearly implied as much, but
his fugitive thought had no support whatever from earlier
writers, not even the most radical of them. All, expressly
or by clear and necessary implication, had accepted in
principle the notion that the state might be criminally
assaulted merely by words, even by words which had no
consequence other than producing disesteem or contempt
in the minds of the people. Some of them insisted on a
showing of good evidence that such was the effect of the
words; many demanded that the speaker's words be maliciously intended to have that effect and/or be false. Others
would invoke the sanctions of the law against mere words
in extreme cases only, a formula usually covering liars in
the opposing party rather than the purveyors of crafty

[105] *A Fragment on Government* (London, 1776), ch. IV, sect.
xxiv, at p. 154 of the 1st edition.

innuendo or unvarnished truth on their own side. Thus
their criticism was aimed against a promiscuous or wrong
application of the law of seditious libel rather than against
the substance of that law. The same may be said of their
extraordinary stress on the functions of juries in libel prosecutions. If a jury, having judged the whole of the law and
fact, returned a verdict of guilty upon an indictment for
utterances tending toward sedition, no secularist libertarian,
again excepting Bentham, could or would protest. Con-
ceivably Bentham might be joined by the Reverends Furneaux, Ratcliffe, and Kippis, advocates of the overt-acts
test, but none of them had taken a stand on the problem of
seditious libel. They had defended religious rather than
political speech. Libertarian thought over the course of a
century and a half conformed to the belief that seditious
libel, as well as seditious acts, was a crime. It conformed
also, and unquestioningly, to Parliament's power to punish
critical utterances as a breach of privilege. Not one of the
libertarians, whether for want of courage or want of disagreement, even ventured to discuss the subject. Yet freedom of expression was every bit as severely restrained by
Parliament as by the legal officers of the crown in the
cabinet and in the courts.

An elaborate rationale for a broad policy of free speech
and press had been worked out — no inconsiderable
achievement; but from Milton to Maseres, libertarian theorists balked at applying the principle of their own arguments. They either retreated to vitiating exceptions or
stopped short of following the principle to its logical conclusion. Despite all their grand reasoning that should have
brought them to an outright rejection of the concept of
seditious libel, they not only acquiesced in it, but acquiesced
also in the law's definition of the scope of permissible

political expression. Milton, Roger Williams, Locke, and the seventeenth-century writers could conceive of no freedom for political expression greater than that existing in the absence of prior restraints. The utmost of their demands was the end of the licensing system of previous censorship. By 1776, the libertarians had progressed little farther. They had named as a legitimate object of animadversion all public men, measures, and institutions, and they had enlarged on the benefits to be derived from the most critical and candid discussions; but always they conditioned the exercise of free speech and press on subservience to the laws of the land. A patriot newspaper in Boston put the thought quite neatly in 1767 when declaring that "Man, in a state of nature, has undoubtedly a right to speak and act without controul. In a state of civil society, that right is limited by the law — Political liberty consists in a freedom of speech and action, so far as the laws of a community will permit, and no farther; all beyond is criminal, and tends to the destruction of Liberty itself." [106] The universal acceptance of this theory resulted in an acceptance, too, of a definition of freedom of the press as a freedom from prior restraints, or, what amounts to the same thing, a freedom circumscribed by the penalties for criminal libel. On this definition the seventeenth-century libertarians from Busher to Blount had made their stand, and the eighteenth-century libertarians — Cato, Alexander, Bishop, Hayter, Father of Candor, Bollan, and Maseres — concurred, and by concurring they accepted in substance the Blackstone-Mansfield definition: freedom, under law, from prior restraint.

Speech, of course, unlike publications, had never and could not have been subject to the licensing system, there

[106] *Boston Gazette*, March 9, 1767, quoted in Rossiter, *Seedtime*, p. 385.

being no requirements of permits for speakers, so that the "no prior restraints" definition was, technically, not relevant to oral utterances. What is important, however, is that freedom of speech was always limited by the barricade against criminal utterances. When the press was freed from prior restraints it simply became directly amenable to the law of libel as speech had always been. Thus, freedom of speech and freedom of the press, being subject to the same restraints of subsequent punishment, were rarely distinguished. Most writers, including Addison, Cato, and Alexander, who employed the term "freedom of speech" with great frequency, used it synonymously with freedom of the press. Even in the seventeenth century when the licensing system was still operative, Walwyn, Robinson, and Milton used "freedome of speech," "liberty of speaking," or some such reference to oral statement when they were inveighing against prior restraints and therefore must have meant freedom of the press. Father of Candor and William Bollan were the only authors who did not refer to the two rights interchangeably, for both noted that speech was free so long as it was truthful, while truth was not a defense to a charge of libelous publication. In this respect, speech was freer than the press, but not by much, for truth, as has been pointed out, has its limitations as a defense, particularly when opinion is prosecuted. At best, the libertarians dissented from Blackstone and Mansfield when defining the outermost bounds of the press only by claiming that a true publication could not be libelous. But for this difference Father of Candor and Bollan were at one with Blackstone and Mansfield in agreeing on the criminality of utterances, spoken or printed, which defamed the government.

Those who were dissatisfied with the common law aimed their strictures at prosecutions by information, at the doctrine that truth aggravated a libel, and at the limited function of juries. But the critics failed to suggest that the prosecutions against alleged seditious libelers should never have been instituted in the first place. They failed, that is, to repudiate the concept of seditious libel. Bentham, had he descended from Olympus and dealt with real problems, might have done so; Furneaux and his followers among the religious libertarians might have done so also, had they addressed themselves to secular problems like the Junius prosecutions. As for the civil libertarians, however, their flaming bolts of denunciation against the "Star Chamber law of libel" fizzled out when they could agree with their martyred leader, John Wilkes, that no one who publicly offended a community by outrageous attacks on whatever it had deemed "sacred" should be tolerated. Wilkes was pure of heart, as he was the first to affirm, but genuine malefactors would do well to beware the penalties awaiting them for verbal disobedience to a just government whose proscription against seditious discourse suffered only from certain remedial defects not affecting the fundamental soundness of the law.

Commitment to this view of the matter, side by side with a rhetorical tradition that should have implied the contrary but addressed itself only to transcendant propositions uncontaminated by reality, constituted the American inheritance from libertarian thought. It was the only inheritance the colonists knew, and if, with the exceptions of Alexander and Bollan, it was English rather than American — though the two can scarcely be distinguished — all that is revealed thereby is the impoverished condition of American thinking on the subject. The one word best summarizing that thinking was acquiescence.

CHAPTER FIVE

✑ From the Revolution to the First Amendment

Speech and press were not free anywhere during the Revolution. A long war for independence is scarcely a propitious time for the birth and nurturing of freedom of expression or any civil liberties. Everywhere there was unlimited liberty to praise the American cause; criticism of it brought the zealots of patriotism with tar and feathers. Even on the rare occasion when some revolutionist might ritualistically reaffirm devotion to freedom of expression, there was a tacit understanding that "liberty of speech," as Professor Schlesinger has so aptly said, "belonged solely to those who spoke the speech of liberty." [1]

The Continental Congress offered an illuminating example. In presenting its case before the inhabitants of Quebec, Congress on the eve of the Revolution had made a great statement on the function of a free press:

The last right we shall mention regards the freedom of the press. The importance of this consists, besides the advancement of truth, science, morality and arts in general, in its diffusion of liberal sentiments on the administration of gov-

[1] *Prelude to Independence* (New York, 1958), p. 189.

ernment, its ready communication of thoughts between subjects, and its consequential promotion of union among them,
whereby oppressive officials are shamed or intimidated into
more honorable and just modes of conducting affairs.[2]

This was one of the rare American declarations that comprehended so broad a concept of the public affairs which
might be openly discussed; comparable statements were
usually limited to matters of government and perhaps religion, but here were included "truth, science, morality and
arts." But the noble libertarianism of the Quebec declaration of 1774 was not for home consumption, since its most
significant phrase stressed the diffusion of "liberal sentiments." Illiberal, that is, loyalist sentiments were simply
suppressed.

The Committee of Inspection for Newport, Rhode
Island, which included the censorship and intimidation of
printers among its duties, showed the American understanding of Congress' Quebec declaration by invoking it
as justification for boycotting a Tory publisher, James
Rivington. Following the old common-law distinction between liberty and licentiousness, the Newport Committee
argued that freedom of the press meant diffusion of "liberal
sentiments" but not "wrong sentiments respecting the
measures now carrying on for the recovery and establishment of our rights. . . ."[3] Late in 1775 Rivington's press
was smashed by a band of armed men led by America's
Wilkes — Alexander McDougall — and Isaac Sears, one of
his most steadfast supporters back in those trying days of

[2] "To the Inhabitants of the Province of Quebec," Oct. 24, 1774,
in Worthington Chauncey Ford, *et al.*, eds., *Journals of the Continental Congress, 1774-1789* (Washington, 1904-1937), 1:108.
[3] Peter Force, ed., *American Archives Consisting of a Collection
of Authentic Records* (Washington, 1837 ff.), 4th ser., 2:12-13.

1770 when McDougall had been martyred for the liberty of the press.[4]

Daniel Fowle, who had fled to New Hampshire after his imprisonment in Massachusetts back in 1754, was, like all editors, kept under close supervision by patriot committees. When his *New Hampshire Gazette* published a piece in January of 1776 against the trend toward independence, he was reported to the provincial Assembly, summoned before its bar, and censured for statements "Derogatory to the Honour of this Assembly, as well as of the Honble Continental Congress and Injurious to the cause of Liberty Now Contending for." Fowle took a sharp warning to heart and promptly suspended his paper.[5]

Four months before independence was declared, Samuel Loudon, patriot editor of the *New York Packet,* permitted remuneration rather than republicanism to influence his judgment when he accepted the job of printing a loyalist reply to Tom Paine's *Common Sense.* His dedication to the principle that both sides should have a hearing impelled him to advertise the forthcoming pamphlet. For Loudon's pains, McDougall, his attorney John Morin Scott, Sears, and Lamb, at the head of a gang of vigilantes, broke down the door of his house, hauled him from bed, and forced him to lead them to the plates of the loyalist tract. They destroyed the plates and burned 1,500 impressions along with

---

[4] The Rivington story is related in Thomas Jones, *History of New York During the Revolutionary War,* ed. E. F. de Lancey (New York, 1879), 1:65–66 and 561–568, 2:341; Schlesinger, *Prelude to Independence,* p. 240; and Sidney I. Pomerantz, "The Patriot Newspaper and the American Revolution," in Richard B. Morris, ed., *The Era of the American Revolution* (New York, 1939), pp. 316–318.

[5] Philip Davidson, *Propaganda and the American Revolution, 1763–1783* (Chapel Hill, N.C., 1941), p. 172.

the manuscript. The night's events were boasted of the next day as an act of patriotism and liberty, while every printer in New York City read a copy of the following communique: "Sir, if you print, or suffer to be printed in your press anything against the rights and liberties of America, or in favor of our inveterate foes, the King, Ministry, and Parliament of Great Britain, death and destruction, ruin and perdition, shall be your portion. Signed, by order of the Committee of tarring and feathering. Legion." Thereafter no loyalist publication was ever printed in New York.[6]

John Adams' writings suggest the manner in which the patriots did somersaults with the common law of seditious libel. Back in 1765, when the British were in control, Adams had written an essay for the *Boston Gazette* in which he addressed his publishers, Edes and Gill, in the following brave words:

The stale, impudent insinuations of slander and sedition, with which the gormandizers of power have endeavored to discredit your paper, are so much the more to your honor; for the jaws of power are always stretched out, if possible, to destroy the freedom of thinking, speaking, and writing. . . . Be not intimidated, therefore, by any terrors, from publishing with the utmost freedom *whatever* can be warranted by the laws of your country. . . .[7]

By 1774, when the "jaws of power" were beginning to grow American incisors, Adams began to sound more like Chief Justice Hutchinson. In his most widely circulated

[6] Jones, *History of New York*, 1:63–64, 566–567. See also *American Archives*, 4th ser., 5:439–440, 1389, 1441–1442, and the sketch of Loudon in the *Dictionary of American Biography*.

[7] "A Dissertation on the Canon and Feudal Law," in John Adams, *Works; with a Life of the Author*, ed. Charles Francis Adams (Boston, 1850–1856), 3:457.

contribution to the literature of the Revolution, the "No-
vanglus" letters, he censured "the scandalous license of the
tory presses." [8] Hutchinson had naturally regarded defiance
of crown authority as scandalous license, but he and Adams
were in agreement on the fundamental principle that abuse
of the press, as each respectively understood it, was a thing
apart from the true liberty of the press. By early 1776
Adams evinced the spirit of the Newport Committee of Inspection when he proposed that making adherence to the
independence movement the legal test of loyalty would
have the beneficial result of stopping "unfriendly" papers.
Then, "the presses will produce no more seditious or trai-
torous speculations. Slanders upon public men and measures
will be lessened." [9]

Similar sentiments were expressed during the same year
by Francis Hopkinson of the Continental Congress, a signer
of the Declaration of Independence. The liberty of the
press, in his opinion, had been justly esteemed as one of
the most important privileges in a free government. Indeed,
no man held that privilege in more sacred esteem than he.
The channels of information must be kept open and un-
corrupted. "But when this privilege is manifestly abused,
and the press becomes an engine for sowing the most dangerous dissensions, for spreading false alarms, and undermining the very foundations of government, ought not that
government upon the plain principles of self-preservation
to silence by its own authority, such a daring violator of its
peace, and tear from its bosom the serpent that would sting
it to death?" He concluded that the council of safety would
be justified in "silencing a press, whose weekly productions
insult the feelings of the people, and are so openly inimical

[8] *Works*, 4:32.
[9] Letter to John Winthrop, June 23, 1776, *ibid.*, 9:409.

to the American cause." [10] Clearly, when power had passed to the Americans it presented the opportunity of legal repression by the newly constituted state governments, and "the ghost of John Peter Zenger quietly sank back into its grave." [11]

Congress itself, in 1776, urged the states to enact legislation to prevent people from being "deceived and drawn into erroneous opinion." [12] Connecticut anticipated this recommendation by its statute of 1775 providing for the prosecution of any person who wrote or spoke a libel against Congress or the acts of the state legislature.[13] By 1778 all the states had acted.[14] The mass of legislation, which included loyalty oaths for all male citizens, went far beyond the needs of military security. Punishment for revealing troop movements or discouraging enlistments was one thing; punishment for derogatory comments about the Continental currency or misconduct of the war effort passed the abyss between legitimate war measures and tyrannous repression. Open denunciation of the patriot cause was in several states a crime even worse than sedition. As Professor Willard Hurst says in his study of "Treason in the United States," during the Revolution the concept of treasonable adherence to the enemy "was certainly given an extremely sweeping application in the legislation which imposed pen-

[10] The first lines quoted are from Schlesinger, *Prelude to Independence*, p. 298, citing Hopkinson's article in the *Pennsylvania Evening Post*, Nov. 16, 1776. The last line quoted is from the same article, slightly revised, in *The Miscellaneous Essays and Occasional Writings of Francis Hopkinson* (Philadelphia, 1792), 1:136.

[11] The phrase is Schlesinger's, *Prelude to Independence*, p. 189.

[12] *Journals of Continental Congress*, 4:18, Jan. 2, 1776.

[13] Claude H. Van Tyne, *The Loyalists in the American Revolution* (New York, 1902), p. 199.

[14] See Van Tyne, *Loyalists*, Appendix C, pp. 327–329, for a state-by-state list of "Laws Against Freedom of Speech and Action."

alties ranging from heavy fines or jail sentences to the death sentence and complete forfeiture of property *for the mere utterance of opinions* denying the independent authority of the new states and asserting the continued sovereignty of the King." [15] Professor Van Tyne summed up the matter when he declared, "The freedom of speech was suppressed, the liberty of the press destroyed. . . ." [16]

In the decade between the cessation of hostilities and the ratification of the First Amendment (1781–1791), independence and peace brought America its first opportunity to develop a legal system and a society in which all men were free to express their opinions, however unpopular, on any subject, short of direct and immediate incitement to crime. No doubt America during this period, as earlier, was as free as, and probably freer than, any other place in the world. But a comparative statement of this sort does not indicate how free free speech was. What is significant is the fact that the American states, with the possible exceptions of Virginia and Pennsylvania, did not take the opportunity of abandoning or seriously limiting the oppressive common law of seditious libel.

Yet some of our best constitutional authorities have argued that one object of the Revolution was "to get rid of the English common law on liberty of speech and of the press." [17] It is closer to the truth to say that the Revolution almost got rid of freedom of speech and press, instead of the common law on the subject. Apart from that fact, the

[15] Willard Hurst, "Treason in the United States," *Harvard Law Review*, 58:266 (1944). Italics added.
[16] Van Tyne, *Loyalists*, p. 66.
[17] Henry Schofield, *Essays on Constitutional Law and Equity* (Boston, 1921), 2:521–522; Zechariah Chafee, Jr., *Free Speech in the United States* (Cambridge, Mass., 1948), p. 20.

thesis that the Revolution had a libertarian objective as to speech and press is open to the criticism that its supporting evidence is frail. It consists chiefly of, first, a declaration that the states constitutionally protected freedom of speech and press, and, second, an assumption that such protection superseded the common law.

The world's first instance of freedom of speech being elevated to a constitutional right came in 1776 when Pennsylvania, in its first constitution, provided, "That the people have a right to freedom of speech, and of writing, and publishing their sentiments; therefore the freedom of the press ought not to be restrained."[18] There are no sources for 1776 that indicate what was understood in Pennsylvania by "freedom of speech" or press, or how broadly its protection was intended. But Pennsylvania's suppression of loyalist speech during the Revolution suggests that speech was no freer in that state than in the others. Peaceable Quaker meetings were harassed and intimidated, homes were broken into, scores imprisoned and even exiled from the state. Those persecuted included not only individuals *suspected* of overt acts against the war effort, but also those "who talked too freely about the mistakes of Congress, or the virtues of the British government; in fact, often their only offense was a refusal of the [test] oath."[19] As will be seen, Pennsylvania sources from 1787 to the end of the century indicate acceptance of the common law's restraints upon free speech and press.

The 1777 constitution of the independent republic of

[18] Article XII, Declaration of Rights, Pennsylvania Constitution of 1776, in Francis Newton Thorpe, ed., *The Federal and State Constitutions, Colonial Charters, and Other Organic Laws* (Washington, 1909), 5:3083.

[19] Van Tyne, *Loyalists*, p. 232. See also pp. 132, 210, 217, and 227.

Vermont,[20] admitted to the Union in 1791, copied Pennsylvania's free-speech provision, but the same provision, in a draft of a constitution drawn by John Adams, was rejected by the Massachusetts legislature in 1778.[21] When Massachusetts finally adopted its constitution, in 1780, it protected the press only,[22] despite formal statements from several towns demanding protection for speech too. The statement of the Boston committee, which is representative of the others, demonstrates that freedom of speech was desired to protect open political discussion: "The Liberty of Speech & of the press with respect to publick Men & their publick Conduct & publick measures, is essential to the Security of freedom in a State, & shall not therefore be restrained in this Common Wealth." [23] The desire of the town of Milton to protect political speech seems to reflect a purpose to modify the common law of seditious utterances to the extent of making truth a defense: "For unless *this* Liberty of Speech is granted, we are apprehensive it may be dangerous in some future time, even in Publick Town meetings, to speak the truth of weak, or wicked Rulers. . . ." [24] Massachusetts did not, however, constitutionally protect speech nor did any other state except Pennsylvania and independent Vermont.

Not only were there twelve states which left speech

[20] Article XIV, Declaration of Rights, Vermont Constitution of 1777, in Thorpe, *Constitutions*, 7:3741.
[21] Clyde A. Duniway, *The Development of Freedom of the Press in Massachusetts* (New York, 1906), pp. 133–134; Adams, *Works*, 4:227.
[22] "The liberty of the press is essential to the security of freedom in a state; it ought not, therefore, to be restricted in this commonwealth." Article XVI, Declaration of Rights, Massachusetts Constitution of 1780, in Thorpe, *Constitutions*, 3:1892.
[23] Quoted in Duniway, *Freedom of the Press*, p. 135.
[24] *Ibid.*

wholly unprotected: four states — Connecticut and Rhode Island, which did not frame constitutions, and New York and New Jersey, which did — provided no constitutional protection to freedom of the press. If, as has been assumed by a host of distinguished historians,[25] a generalized and undefined constitutional declaration in favor of freedom of speech or freedom of the press superseded the common law of criminal utterances, then it is equally legitimate to assume from the silence of twelve states that there it was the intention to preserve intact the common law as to speech and in four states to preserve it as to the press. Indeed the latter assumption is far more supportable than the former. The history of Pennsylvania, for example, shows that the only one of the original states to protect constitutionally both speech and press did not intend to abandon the common law of seditious libel. Why should we infer that the other eight states which constitutionally protected freedom of the press intended a departure from the common law? The phrase "freedom of the press" as used in their state constitutions possessed no magical supersessionary powers, nor was it self-defining. There is no evidence to show that it was not used in its prevailing common-law or Blackstonian sense to mean a guarantee against previous restraints and a subjection to subsequent restraints for licentious or seditious abuse. The evidence, in fact, shows that the Blackstonian definition was the intended one, just as it was the traditional and the taught one.

If, however, we assume that in the nine original states, plus Vermont, which constitutionally provided for freedom of the press, there was a broader concept of that freedom than merely the Blackstonian one, the question is, how much broader? It has been claimed that freedom of the

[25] See above, pp. 1–3.

press "in a general way" was understood to mean "the right of unrestricted discussion of public affairs." [26] An eighteenth-century constitution-maker would have agreed, but only because he was committed to the common-law notion that discussion was "unrestricted" if there was a guarantee against previous restraints. He did not regard the fear or actual imposition of subsequent punishment for scandalizing the government as a restraint upon the true or proper liberty of the press, particularly if the utterance was "false" and "malicious." The word "unrestricted" surely did not mean, to the eighteenth-century libertarian, the absence of subsequent punishment for the expression of any opinions not criminally inciting. A vague but supportable statement of the eighteenth-century general understanding of freedom of the press, or of speech, would exclude the ambiguous word "unrestricted" and would grope with terms that convey the idea of a freedom to write, print, or utter anything that was temperate, accurate, well-intentioned, and that fell short of what a court or the community might deem seditious or libelous.

Beyond the assumption that a simple constitutional affirmation, "the freedom of the press ought not to be restrained," *ex vi termini* superseded the common law, what evidence can be adduced on behalf of the thesis that the Revolution repudiated Blackstone on seditious libel? The resolutions of the committees of Boston and Milton, quoted earlier, indicate no abandonment of the common law beyond making truth a defense to the charge of criminal libel. To the same effect are the remarks by Benjamin Franklin in 1789. If freedom of the press, he declared, meant the liberty to calumniate one another, it ought to be limited by a civil libel statute, but if it meant "the Lib-

[26] Chafee, *Free Speech*, p. 19.

erty of discussing the Propriety of Public Measures and Political opinions, let us have as much of it as you please." Franklin clearly preferred a remedy in the form of a civil suit for damages, instead of indictment for seditious libel, when public men were calumniated. He did not express himself, however, on the legal remedy for calumny against the government, except to remark, in the same article, that as to writers who affront the government's reputation, "we should, in moderation, content ourselves with tarring and feathering and tossing them in a blanket." [27] This last recommendation may have been facetiously intended; perhaps it was no more than a nostalgic reminiscence of the time, not long before, when seditious libelers were effectively dispatched without the interminable delays of the law. Whatever Franklin intended by the remark, it had ugly overtones. More than likely his endorsement of unlimited discussion was understood to be hedged by the qualification that verbal criticisms of the government must be

[27] "An Account of the Supremest Court of Judicature in Pennsylvania, Viz, The Court of the Press," published as a newspaper essay, 1789, and reprinted in Albert Henry Smyth, ed., *The Writings of Benjamin Franklin* (New York, 1905–1907), 10:38, 40. J. M. Smith, *Freedom's Fetters: The Alien and Sedition Laws and American Civil Liberties* (Ithaca, 1956), p. 137, interprets the tar-and-feathers remark as "horseplay." But the piece was written throughout with a satirically bitter touch, with the licentiousness of the press as its theme. The title indicated that one whose reputation had been scandalized in the press had no appeal. Franklin recommended the "cudgel" and tar and feathers until the legislature enacted a statute explicitly marking the "extent and limits" of freedom of the press. (*Writings*, 10:40.) In 1782 he wrote that a publisher should regard himself as a "Guardian of his Country's Reputation, and refuse to insert such Writings as may hurt it." (Letter to Francis Hopkinson, Dec. 24, 1782, in *Writings*, 8:648.) In his *Autobiography* he stated that newspapers printing scurrilous reflections on government were an infamous disgrace. (*Ibid.*, 1:344).

guided by moderation, truth, and good motives. During a long lifetime in politics and publishing, Franklin never went on record as criticizing the concept of seditious libel. Neither he nor his contemporaries abandoned the concept that a republican state can be criminally assailed by mere words.

The thesis that the Revolution had as one of its objectives the elimination of the common law on freedom of speech and press also includes among its evidence the declaration to the inhabitants of Quebec by the Continental Congress in 1774.[28] But that document, which specifically endorsed only the diffusion of "liberal sentiments on the administration of government," has been misread.[29] Its true meaning, as indicated above, was revealed by Congress itself just fifteen months later in a recommendation to the states that they take appropriate measures against "erroneous opinions." Two items of evidence are, however, more persuasive. They are the Virginia Statute of Religious Freedom of 1785 and the Cushing-Adams correspondence of 1789.

The preamble to the great statute which was written by Jefferson indicates his indebtedness to Philip Furneaux, for the bad-tendency test of criminality was explicitly rejected and a new test defined in its place:

> that to suffer the civil magistrate to intrude his powers into the field of opinion and to restrain the profession or propa-

[28] See Smith, *Freedom's Fetters*, p. 427; Chafee, *Free Speech*, p. 17; Schofield, *Essays*, 2:522; John Kelly, "Criminal Libel and Free Speech," *Kansas Law Review*, 6:307 (1958).

[29] This judgment excludes only Schlesinger, who alone among recent writers on the subject manages to keep his personal preferences separated from the evidence. In his *Prelude to Independence*, at p. 189, he realistically observes that as far as freedom of the press was concerned, the declaration to Quebec was intended "purely for export."

gation of principles *on supposition of their ill tendency* is a
dangerous falacy [*sic*], which at once destroys all *religious*
liberty, because he being of course judge of that tendency,
will make his opinions the rule of judgment, and approve
or condemn the sentiments of others only as they shall
square with or differ from his own; that it is time enough for
the rightful purposes of civil government for its officers to
interfere when principles break out into overt acts against
peace and good order; and finally, that truth is great and
will prevail if left to herself; that she is the proper antagonist
to error, and has nothing to fear from the conflict unless
by human interposition disarmed of her natural weapons,
free argument and debate; errors ceasing to be dangerous
when it is permitted freely to contradict them.[30]

This statement does refer to "the field of opinion" generally, although in context only freedom of religion is provided for and explicitly named. Yet the principles of the
statement could, theoretically, apply with equal vigor to
speech and press which are related and linked together
with freedom of religion in the First Amendment. The
new test of criminality adopted by the Statute of Religious
Freedom substitutes for the bad-tendency test, which was
at the heart of the law of criminal libel, the test of direct,
immediate, and actual incitement to crime resulting from
utterance: prosecution is proper only when "principles
break out into *overt acts.*"

In Virginia, therefore, there is a basis for the presumption
that the common law of criminal libel was meant to be
superseded by the protection afforded to the freedoms of
religion and press. That presumption, however, as evidence
to be introduced later will indicate, may be an extremely
shaky one, since the overt-acts test was not applied in

[30] *The Papers of Thomas Jefferson,* ed. Julian P. Boyd, *et al.,*
(Princeton, 1950 ff., series in progress), 2:546. Italics added.

Virginia to certain political utterances proscribed by the state legislature. Moreover, there is a certain illogic in assuming that the principle of the Statute of Religious Freedom revealed the intention behind Virginia's constitutional protection of the press, which *preceded* the statute by nine years. In any case it was not the intention of any of the other states to get rid of the common-law concept of seditious libel. None of them gave statutory or constitutional recognition to the principle embodied in the preamble of Virginia's 1785 statute. If it was an object of the Revolution to repudiate *in toto* the well-known and infamous Blackstone-Mansfield exposition of the common law's restrictions on freedom of expression, how very strange it is that Americans of the revolutionary generation did not say so. The closest statements to that effect always accepted the justice of punishing false opinions or scandals against the government. Furthermore, excepting the Virginia Statute of Religious Freedom, all the evidence which may be submitted to prove an intention to supersede the common law and provide for an unrestricted freedom of discussion is logically and legally reconcilable with Blackstone's view that opinions are free but subject to prosecution for falsity, malice, bad tendency, and the like.

Data on the reception of the common law during the Revolution tend to establish the acceptance of the Blackstonian definition of liberty of press and speech. Twelve states, including all nine guaranteeing a free press, provided by constitution or statute that the common law of England before the Revolution was to operate with full force unless inconsistent with or repugnant to some other constitutional or statutory provision.[31] In the states where no protection

---

[31] See, generally, Ford W. Hall, "The Common Law: An Account of Its Reception in the United States," *Vanderbilt Law Review*, 4:797–800 (June 1951).

to freedom of speech and/or press was afforded, there is not even the basis of an implication that it was the intention to get rid of the idea that a republican form of government may be criminally libeled by the opinions of its citizens. As for the states that constitutionally protected freedom of speech and/or press, it can of course be argued that the law of criminal utterances was inconsistent with or repugnant to the constitutional guarantee, a simple declaration on behalf of free expression. But such an argument must be based on inferences from current libertarian premises and would lack the support of evidence from the 1776-1791 period. The evidence goes the other way.

If, for example, Virginia can be considered to have rejected the bad-tendency test of political speech in the context of a statute protecting only the free exercise of religion, then consideration must be given to the context of the guarantees of freedom of religion in other states. Two states, in the midst of affording a constitutional guarantee to that freedom, provided that its exercise could not justify libeling the government. North Carolina's article on religious liberty (1776) contained this qualification: "Provided, that nothing herein contained shall be construed to exempt preachers of treasonable or *seditious discourses,* from legal trial and punishment." [32] If preachers were not exempt from the law of seditious libel, others were not either. South Carolina's equivalent clause (1778) stated: "No person whatever shall speak anything in their religious assembly irreverently or *seditiously* of the government of this State." [33] If one could not in church speak seditiously of the state, he could not do so elsewhere. To the same effect, though not as

[32] Section XXXIV, North Carolina Constitution of 1776, in Thorpe, *Constitutions,* 5:2793. Italics added.
[33] Section XXXVIII, South Carolina Constitution of 1778, in Thorpe, *Constitutions,* 6:3257. Italics added.

explicitly, are the qualifying clauses of the religious-freedom provisions in the first constitutions of New York,[34] New Hampshire,[35] Massachusetts,[36] Georgia,[37] and Maryland.[38] The last, for example, provided (1776) that no one "under colour of religion . . . shall disturb the good order, peace or safety of the State, or shall infringe the laws of morality. . . ." At common law, an utterance tending to disturb the peace of the state was seditious. New York, New Hampshire, Massachusetts, and Georgia used similar language, prohibiting exercises of religion repugnant to the public peace or safety.

Thus, if it is a legitimate inference on the part of some scholars[39] that the Virginia Statute of Religious Freedom laid down a new test of criminality which applied to speech and press as well as religion, then by analogous implication, seven other states, five of which constitutionally protected "the freedom of the press," preserved as to speech and press, as well as religion, the common law of criminal libel.

One final body of evidence, the Cushing-Adams correspondence of 1789, seemingly points to a broad understanding of freedom of speech and press, although not to an abandonment of the concept of seditious libel. William Cushing, who had been an influential member of the con-

[34] Section XXXVIII, New York Constitution of 1777, in Thorpe, *Constitutions*, 5:2637.

[35] Article V, Bill of Rights, New Hampshire Constitution of 1784, in Thorpe, *Constitutions*, 4:2454.

[36] Article II, Declaration of Rights, Massachusetts Constitution of 1780, in Thorpe, *Constitutions*, 3:1889.

[37] Article LVI, Georgia Constitution of 1777, in Thorpe, *Constitutions*, 2:784.

[38] Article XXXIII, Declaration of Rights, Maryland Constitution of 1776, in Thorpe, *Constitutions*, 3:1689.

[39] See, *e.g.*, Schofield, *Essays*, 2:522; Smith, *Freedom's Fetters*, p. 428; Kelly, "Criminal Libel," *Kansas Law Review*, 6:307.

vention which framed the Massachusetts constitution, was
in 1789 serving his twelfth year as chief justice of his state.
He addressed a long, thoughtful letter to John Adams,
giving his interpretation of their state constitution's free-
press clause which had been originally drafted by Adams.
The clause affirmed, "The liberty of the press is essential
to the security of freedom in a state; it ought not, therefore, to be restrained in this commonwealth." Cushing was
deeply concerned with the question whether a publication
aspersing the conduct of officeholders could be punished
under the free-press clause, "when such charges are supportable by the truth of fact?" [40] That clause "being very
general and unlimited," Cushing asked, "what guard or
limitation can be put upon it?" He was certain it did not
protect libels upon private reputations, nor did it render
immune from prosecution "*injuring* the public or individuals by propagating falsehoods." But he wanted Adams'
opinion on his belief that the clause did guarantee a freedom to discuss all subjects and characters "within the
bounds of truth. . . ." Blackstone, he admitted, had defined
the liberty of the press as a freedom from previous restraints and not as a freedom from punishment for the
publication of criminal matter.

But the words of our article understood according to
plain English, make no such distinction, and must exclude
subsequent restraints, as much as *previous restraints*. In other
words, if all men are restrained by the fear of jails, scourges

[40] [Frank W. Grinnell, ed.], "Hitherto Unpublished Correspondence Between Chief Justice Cushing and John Adams in 1789,"
Cushing to Adams, Feb. 18, 1789, in *Massachusetts Law Quarterly,*
27:12 (October 1942). Cushing's letter covers pp. 12–15; Adams
reply of March 7 is at p. 16. All quotations which follow are from
this source. The original manuscripts are in the Cushing Papers,
Massachusetts Historical Society.

and loss of ears from examining the conduct of persons in administration and where their conduct is illegal, tyrannical and tending to overthrow the Constitution and introduce slavery, are so restrained from declaring it to the public *that* will be as effectual a restraint as any *previous* restraint whatever.

The question upon the article, is this — What is that liberty of the press, which is essential to the security of freedom? The propagating literature and knowledge by printing or otherwise tends to illuminate men's minds and to establish them in principles of freedom. But it cannot be denied also, that a free scanning of the conduct of administration and shewing the tendency of it, and where truth will warrant, making it manifest that it is subversive of all law, liberty and the Constitution; it can't be denied. I think that the liberty tends to the *security of freedom in a State;* even more directly and essentially than the liberty of printing upon literary and speculative subjects in general. Without this liberty of the press could we have supported our liberties against british administration? or could our revolution have taken place? Pretty certainly it could not, at the time it did. Under a sense and impression of this sort, I conceive, this article was adopted. This liberty of publishing truth can never effectually injure a good government, or honest administrators; but it may save a state from the necessity of a revolution, as well as bring one about, when it is necessary. It may be objected that a public prosecution is the safe and regular course, in case of malefeasance. But what single person would venture himself upon so invidious and dangerous a task against a man high in interest, influence and power?

But this liberty of the press having truth for its basis who can stand before it? Besides it may facilitate a legal prosecution, which might not, otherwise, have been dared to be attempted. When the press is made the vehicle of falsehood and scandal, let the authors be punished with becoming rigour.

But why need any honest man be afraid of truth? The guilty only fear it; and I am inclined to think with Gordon (Vol. 3 No. 20 of Cato's Letters) that truth sacredly adhered to, can never upon the whole prejudice, right religion, equal government or a government founded upon proper balances and checks, or the happiness of society in any respect, but must be favorable to them all.

Suppressing this liberty by penal laws will it not more endanger freedom than do good to government? The weight of government is sufficient to prevent any very dangerous consequences occasioned by *provocations* resulting from charges founded in truth; whether such charges are made in *a legal course or otherwise*. In either case, the *provocation* (which Judge Blackstone says is the sole foundation of the law against libels) being much the same.

But not to trouble you with a multiplying of words; If I am wrong I should be glad to be set right, &c., &c.

Adams replied as follows:

The difficult and important question is whether the truth of words can be admitted by the court to be given in evidence to the jury, upon a plea of not guilty? In England I suppose it is settled. But it is a serious Question whether our Constitution is not at present so different as to render the innovation necessary? Our chief magistrates and Senators &c are annually eligible by the people. How are their characters and conduct to be known to their constituents but by the press? If the press is stopped and the people kept in Ignorance we had much better have the first magistrate and Senators hereditary. I therefore, am very clear that under the Articles of our Constitution which you have quoted, it would be safest to admit evidence to the jury of the Truth of accusations, and if the jury found them true and that they were published for the Public good, they would readily acquit.⌋

The Cushing-Adams correspondence has been quoted at length because it is one of the very rare American expositions of the meaning of freedom of the press before the Sedition Act controversy beginning in 1798; because it is the most detailed and libertarian of those expositions; and because it is scarcely known.[41] What observations will that correspondence yield? First, it is clear that even though Cushing partially repudiated Blackstone when arguing that a guarantee of freedom of the press meant an exclusion of subsequent as well as previous restraints, the chief justice was only going as far as Cato, Alexander, Andrew Hamilton, Bollan, Father of Candor, and a new generation of English writers who were active in the 1780's.[42] Each had a bow with two strings to it: truth should be a defense against a charge of criminal utterance; the jury should decide whether the defendant's words were criminal. As noted earlier, truth as a defense meant a modification of the common law in substance as well as procedure. It would unquestionably have liberalized the common law by expanding the scope of permissible expression to include even derogatory and scandalous publications if they were true and presumably written for the public good, or at least, without malice.

But truth is a mischievous, often an illusory, standard

---

[41] I believe that the only writer concerned with the original understanding of freedom of speech and press who has used the Cushing-Adams correspondence is Kelly, "Criminal Libel," *Kansas Law Review*, 6:309 (1958), and he neglected to mention the source. See note 39 above. But see Justice Frankfurter's opinion in Beauharnais v. Ill., 343 U.S. 250, 255 note 4.

[42] The postrevolutionary English writers will be discussed in the final chapter, below.

that defies knowledge and understanding. It cannot, that is, always be proved. What is not a fact on an order that can be substantiated by the law of evidence is an untruth or a nontruth, an opinion at the very best, and the political opinions of men notoriously differ. The other fellow's are usually false, and "falsity," as Cushing and Adams agreed, was evidence of libel. They did not allow for freedom of *opinion* or for the mistakes in facts or reasoning which are so prevalent in political give-and-take. They set a nearly impossible standard, truth, which they would have had jurors judge. A jury is a court of public opinion, often synonymous with public prejudice, and is not an adequate measure of truth, nor are judges. The fault lies in giving fallible men judgment of truth rather than asking them to determine whether the words charged actually led to criminal deeds or whether under the circumstances of time and place the words would have caused the crime but for the effective intervention of the government. Jurors can judge whether the evidence proves the truth of a charge that some official has taken a bribe, but their fallibility is too great to entrust to them a judgment on the truth of an accusation that the government, or one of its policies, or a member of its administration is unjust, tyrannical, or repugnant to the public interest. Accusations of the latter order, not charges of bribes, were almost without exception the subject of prosecutions, the very fact that made the doctrine of seditious libel such an oppressive fetter on freedom of expression. The best and most relevant illustration is the entire corpus of prosecutions for seditious libel under the Sedition Act of 1798.

That statute which nearly abolished freedom of speech and press embodied the reforms proposed by Cushing and Adams. As Professor Chafee pointed out, the Sedition Act entrusted criminality to the jury and admitted truth as a defense. On the other hand, freedom of speech might exist without these two technical safeguards.

The essential question is not, who is judge of the criminality of an utterance, but what is the test of its criminality. The common law and the Sedition Act of 1798 made the test blame of the government and its officials, because to bring them into disrepute tended to overthrow the state. The real question in every free speech controversy is this: whether the state can punish all words which have some tendency, however remote, to bring about acts in violation of law, or only words which directly incite to acts in violation of law.[43]

President Adams willingly signed the Sedition Act and eagerly urged its enforcement, while Cushing, then an associate justice of the Supreme Court of the United States, presided over some of the trials and charged juries on the constitutionality of the statute.[44] The actions of both men were fully consistent with the opinions expressed in their correspondence of 1789, for they accepted then, as in 1798–1799, the concept of seditious libel. They believed then, as Cushing said, that falsehoods and scandals against the government should be punished "with becoming rigour." Their libertarianism was founded upon a brave acceptance of truth as they understood it. Why, asked Cushing, need an honest man "be afraid of truth? The guilty only fear it. . . ." Neither he nor Adams believed that falsehoods or wrong opinions of a bad tendency warranted free circulation.

They asserted that the publication of truth could not effectually injure a good government or an honest adminis-

[43] Chafee, *Free Speech*, p. 23.
[44] Smith, *Freedom's Fetters*, pp. 97–98, 152, 242, 267, 268, 271, 284, 311, 363, and 371.

trator, but they would not take the crucial step of asserting that error of opinion may be tolerated where reason is left free to combat it, even as to those who wished to dissolve the Union or change its form of government. Had Cushing written that a good government or an honest administrator could not be injured by error of opinion or even by malicious falsehood, he would have evinced a libertarian understanding that was incompatible with the concept of seditious libel. When President Adams wrote that United States Attorney William Rawle was unfit for his job if he did not think that *Aurora's* criticism was libelous and subject to prosecution; when he wrote of Thomas Cooper's criticism that he had "no doubt it is a libel against the whole government, and as such ought to be prosecuted";[45] he was revealing an attitude that he displayed in the 1770's when fulminating against the seditious character of unpatriotic talk. Even in 1765, when he had urged Edes and Gill to publish their sentiments freely, he counseled that they should go only as far as "can be warranted by the laws of your country. . . ." He always embraced the opinion that antigovernment talk which he believed to be unjustified was seditious. That he supported truth as a defense and would give a free hand to juries showed a libertarianism constricted by an unquestioned premise that words of a bad tendency were criminal.

The frail protection offered to freedom of the press by the Cushing-Adams proposals of 1789 was manifested when only one Sedition Act jury returned a verdict of acquittal. But neither the juries, the judges, nor the president should be condemned for not believing the truth of the defendents' opinions, for those who were on the side of the pros-

[45] Letters from Adams to T. Pickering, Aug. 1, 1799, and Aug. 13, 1799, in *Works*, 9:5 and 13-14.

ecution reacted to those opinions in a manner that was par
for the human animal, identifying their own politics with
truth. They shared, moreover, a belief in the predominant
doctrine that government can be criminally assaulted by
opinions. To be sure, those opinions had to be malicious
and false, but the doctrine of seditious libel, even modified,
implied an extremely narrow concept of freedom of the
press.

A final observation must be made on the Cushing-Adams
correspondence. It is not a dependable revelation of the
intention underlying constitutional guarantees of freedom
of the press or speech. Cushing and Adams were proposing,
not disposing; moreover they were not representing the
constitutional law of Massachusetts as of 1789 or for many
years later.[46] From Cushing's bewilderment as to the meaning of the state's free-press clause and his comment that
the questions he raised had never been decided, it is clear
that his ideas were not exposing the general understanding
of that clause's meaning in the minds of the 1780 convention that framed it. Cushing had been at that convention;
Adams actually wrote the first draft. The latter agreed in
1789 that it "would be" better to construe the clause as
Cushing suggested. The two were engaged in a reform, not
a declaration of the thinking of 1780. At that date, when
the constitution was adopted, freedom of the press meant
what it had always meant. In some respects, such as the
validity of truth as a defense or the function of juries in
criminal-libel cases, its meaning was not clear. As Franklin
wrote in 1789, "few of us, I believe, have distinct Ideas of
Its Nature and Extent." [47] Similarly, Hamilton wrote that

[46] See below, pp. 207–213, for a discussion of the law of criminal
libels in Massachusetts.
[47] "The Court of the Press" (1789), *Writings of Franklin*, 10:37.

freedom of the press defied precise definition.[48] But there was an unquestioned consensus that its freedom did not extend to an immunity against punishment for seditious libel, although the evidence is difficult to dig out because the most deeply rooted assumptions are often not articulated.

One of the few public men of the time who did articulate his assumptions was James Wilson of Pennsylvania. Excepting James Madison, Wilson was probably the most influential framer of the United States Constitution and as great a legal expert as any one in the new nation. At the Pennsylvania ratifying convention of 1787 Wilson had occasion, like his fellow Framers in other state ratifying conventions, to deny an Anti-Federalist accusation that the failure to guarantee freedom of the press meant that oppression of opinion was constitutionally possible. Wilson, like so many of his fellow Framers, expressly stated on the subject of the press that "there is given to the general government no power whatsoever concerning it: and no law, in pursuance of the constitution, can possibly be enacted, to destroy that liberty." [49] But Wilson, unlike his fellow Framers, discussed the subject further. In answer to the charge that federal judges might proceed under federal statutes punishing libels, he replied:

> I presume it was not in the view of the honorable gentleman to say that there is no such thing as a libel, or that the writers of such ought not to be punished. The idea of the liberty of the press is not carried so far as this in any country—*what is meant by the liberty of the press is that there*

[48] *The Federalist*, No. 84, p. 560 of The Modern Library edition, ed. Edward Mead Earle (New York, n.d.).

[49] John Bach McMaster and Frederick D. Stone, eds., *Pennsylvania and the Federal Constitution, 1787–1788* (Philadelphia, 1888), p. 308.

should be no antecedent restraint upon it; but that every author is responsible when he attacks the security or welfare of the *government,* or the safety, character and property of the individual.

With regard to attacks upon the public, the mode of proceeding is by a prosecution. . . . Now, Sir, if this libel is to be tried, it must be tried where the offence was committed . . . the trial must be held in the State; therefore on this occasion it must be tried where it was published, if the indictment is for publishing; and it must be tried likewise by a jury of that State.[50]

Here, in the most explicit language, is James Wilson, a major figure, restating the English or Blackstonian definition of freedom of the press. His statement leaves no doubt that he believed the law of seditious libel to be in force, for he spoke of the legal responsibility of writers who attacked the security or welfare of the government, and he added that for such attacks the remedy was prosecution. It should be noted, however, that he believed that the United States was devoid of jurisdiction over seditious libel. That verbal crime against the federal government was to be prosecuted in the state where the offense was committed and under state law. No one at the Pennsylvania convention essayed to deny Wilson's exposition of the law. Thus, in the only state among the original thirteen to guarantee both freedom of speech and press in a constitution drawn before the federal Bill of Rights, those guarantees were not considered to have implied an abandonment of the common law's injunction against libels on the government.

Pennsylvania adopted a new state constitution in 1790, shortly after ratifying the First Amendment. The new state constitution was drafted, significantly, by James

[50] *Ibid.,* pp. 308–309. Italics added.

Wilson. The section on speech and press was elaborate, by comparison to the parallel provision of the constitution of 1776. The new section anticipated Fox's Libel Act by two years, by allowing the jury to decide whether the accused's statement was libelous as a matter of law, and anticipated Lord Campbell's Act of 1843 by making truth a defense in a prosecution for criminal libel. Previously, of course, the law of criminal libel allowed the jury to decide only whether the accused had in fact made the statement alleged, leaving to the judge the right to decide as a matter of law whether the statement was libelous. And, previously, truth was not a defense on ground that the greater the truth, the greater the provocation and therefore the greater the libel. Pennsylvania's constitution of 1790 was the first to embody these reforms which unquestionably altered the common law of libel as it had been known previously.

The provision of 1790 began by guaranteeing the printing presses to anyone examining government proceedings, "and no law shall ever be made to restrain the right thereof." In context, this is Blackstone: no prior censorship. Consider the next clause which uses the Blackstonian language of "free but responsible": "The free communication of thoughts and opinions is one of the invaluable rights of man; and every citizen may freely speak, write, and print on any subject, *being responsible for the abuse of that liberty*. In prosecution for the publication of papers investigating the official conduct of officers or men in a public capacity, or where the matter published is proper for public information, the truth thereof may be given in evidence . . . ," etc.[51] Clearly, Pennsylvania, and Delaware too by a

[51] Article IX, section 7, Pennsylvania Constitution of 1790, in Thorpe, *Constitutions*, 5:3100. Italics added.

similar provision in its constitution of 1792,[52] accepted the concept that a republican form of government can be politically libeled and that the offender should be criminally prosecuted.

Respublica v. *Oswald*, 1788,[53] is a Pennsylvania case in point, as are the charges to the grand jury by Chief Justice Thomas McKean in 1797[54] and by Alexander Addison, presiding judge of the state Court of Common Pleas, in 1798,[55] and the 1805 case of *Respublica* v. *Dennie*.[56] The last-named case ended in an acquittal, but the state's indictment of the Federalist defendant for seditious libel against both Pennsylvania and the United States because of his essay denouncing democracy and President Jefferson hardly bespeaks a repudiation of the common law or a broad understanding of freedom of the press. Addison, Pennsylvania's counterpart of Justice Samuel Chase, was an arrogant political judge who deserved his removal from the bench by impeachment. But McKean cannot be written off. He was successively a leading figure in the revolutionary movement in Delaware, a signer of the Declaration of Independence, governor of Delaware, president of the Continental Congress, second only to Wilson in securing Pennsylvania's ratification of the Constitution, chief justice of Pennsylvania for twenty-two years, and Jeffersonian governor for eight.

[52] Article I, section 5, Delaware Constitution of 1792, in Thorpe, *Constitutions*, 1:569.

[53] 1 Dallas (Penn. Reports) 319 (1788).

[54] "Trial of William Cobbett," November 1797, in Francis Wharton, ed., *State Trials of the United States during the Administrations of Washington and Adams* (Philadelphia, 1849), pp. 323–324.

[55] Selections from Addison's charges are reprinted in Mark Howe, ed., *Readings in American Legal History* (Cambridge, Mass., 1949), pp. 348–358.

[56] 4 Yeates' (Penn.) Reports 267 (1805).

In Oswald's case, two years before the reforms of the 1790 constitution, the chief justice announced unequivocally that freedom of the press meant just what it meant in England. The defendant's argument to the contrary received short shrift. Oswald had been indicted first for a gross libel, breaching the peace, against a private person. He defended himself in his newspaper, the *Independent Gazetteer*, in an address to the public that alleged the prosecution against him to have been politically inspired by his enemies, including the brother of a member of the state Supreme Court in which the action had been instituted. Alluding to "prejudices . . . against me on the bench," he appealed to his jury for a fair trial. Chief Justice McKean promptly tried him without a jury and convicted him for contempt in the form of a libel upon the court. Oswald, in his address to the public, had declared, more out of hope than accuracy, "The doctrine of libel being a doctrine incompatible with law and liberty, and at once destructive of the privileges of a free country, in the communication of our thoughts, has not hitherto gained any footing in *Pennsylvania*. . . ." He added that he supposed his fellow citizens would not allow the freedom of the press to be violated "upon any refined pretence which oppressive ingenuity or courtly study can invent." [57] McKean, joined by Judge George Bryan, a stanch Anti-Federalist and libertarian, ruled that "there is nothing in the constitution of this state, respecting the liberty of the press, that has not been authorized by the constitution of that kingdom [England] for near a century past." He also observed that although every man might publish his opinions, the peace and dignity of society required an inquiry into a writer's motives in order to distinguish between publications "which

[57] Respublica v. Oswald, 1 Dallas 319, 320 (1788).

are meant for use and reformation, and with an eye solely to the public good, and those merely intended to delude and defame. To the latter description, it is impossible that any good government should afford protection and impunity." [58] As an aftermath to the conviction, impeachment charges were preferred against McKean and Bryan for procedural irregularities and for violating the liberty of the press. William Lewis, who had prosecuted Oswald, defended the judges before the Assembly in a speech endorsing Blackstone's definition of a free press, concluding that the "dawn of true freedom" arose in England with the expiration of the licensing system. The Assembly sustained McKean and Bryan. [59]

Even after the constitutional reform of 1790 McKean observed that the constitutional guarantee of a free press was merely declaratory of the common law. Charging the grand jury in the trial of William Cobbett for criminal libel, in 1797, the Jeffersonian chief justice declared:

> The liberty of the press is, indeed, essential to the nature of a free State, but this consists in laying no previous restraints upon public actions, and not in freedom from censure for criminal matter, when published. Every freeman has an undoubted right to lay what sentiments he pleases before the public; to forbid this, is to destroy the freedom of the press; but if he publishes what is improper, mischievous or illegal, he must take the consequences of his temerity. To punish dangerous or offensive writings, which, when published, shall, on a fair and impartial trial, be adjudged of a pernicious tendency, is necessary for the preservation of peace and good order, of government and religion, the only solid foundation of civil liberty. Thus the will of individuals is

[58] *Ibid.*, at pp. 322 and 325.
[59] The record of the impeachment proceedings is in Respublica v. Oswald, 1 Dallas 319, at pp. 330–337.

still left free; the abuse only of that free will is the object of punishment. Our presses in Pennsylvania are thus free. The common law, with respect to this, is confirmed and established by the Constitution.[60]

Thus, in Pennsylvania, whose constitutional provisions in 1776 and 1790 were the most libertarian in the Union as to freedom of speech and press, the common law had not been superseded. McKean's 1797 exposition of the free-press clause might have been issued under the name of Hutchinson, Blackstone, or Mansfield.

Massachusetts, like Pennsylvania, also provided constitutional protection to the freedom of the press, but also recognized the law of criminal libel including seditious utterances. Under the rule of the royal governors during the period of the verbal war with England prior to the battle of Lexington, no restraints upon the Massachusetts press had actually been imposed. The governors and their Councils sought to initiate prosecutions for sedition against several patriot editors, but no grand jury would indict them; public opinion against the government had been so strong that the governors did not even dare to circumvent the grand jury by directing the attorney-general to proceed by information rather than indictment. Yet, in the free state of Massachusetts, with its constitutional guarantee of liberty of the press, grand juries returned criminal-libel indictments in 1787, 1791, 1798, and 1802, as well as later.

In 1787 George Brock and Gideon Pond, who had published articles in sympathy with Shays's Rebellion, were indicted for libeling the government, but their cases never came to trial.[61] In 1791, Edmund Freeman, an editor, for

[60] "Trial of Cobbett," Wharton, ed., *State Trials*, 323–324.
[61] Duniway, *Freedom of the Press*, p. 142 note 1, citing *Suffolk Court (Mass.) Files*, Nos. 104616, 104618, 106011.

having grossly libeled a member of the legislature, was criminally prosecuted on the theory that his words tended to breach the public peace of the Commonwealth. The prosecutor, Attorney-General James Sullivan, later Jeffersonian governor of the state, maintained that the constitutional guarantee of a free press meant only the absence of a licensing act; he quoted Blackstone at interminable length to prove the point and urged that in this first trial for criminal libel under the state constitution, licentiousness must be distinguished from liberty. The defendant's attorneys, Harrison Gray Otis and R. G. Amory, did not challenge Sullivan's principles. Although not asking for a ruling that truth was a defense, they denied licentiousness or breach of peace on the part of Freeman and sought to prove the accuracy of his publication. Three judges presided at the trial. Judge Sergeant stressed the unlawfulness of words tending to breach the public peace. Judge Sumner offered the jury his opinion that truth was no defense and that the guarantee of a free press notwithstanding, licentiousness, falsehood, and verbal injury to the public were answerable to the law. Chief Justice Dana, and Judge Sumner too, charged the jury in full accordance with prosecutor Sullivan's argument on the definition of liberty of the press, although Dana apprised the jury of the fact that he sympathized with truth as a defense even as he noted that he reserved a ruling on the question.[62] The jury's verdict was not guilty, but as the historian of *The Development of*

---

[62] The case is reported in the Boston *Independent Chronicle*. The indictment, the allegedly libelous publication, and Sullivan's introductory address are reprinted in the issue of Feb. 24, 1791. The arguments of defense counsel appear in the issues of March 3 and 10; the trial testimony is not reproduced. Sullivan's closing is in the issue of March 17 with Sumner's charge. Dana's charge appears in the issue of March 24 as does Sergeant's.

Freedom of the Press in Massachusetts concludes: "a judicial construction of liberty of the press in the state had been announced, differing in no wise from the opinions of Chief Justice Hutchinson in 1768 or of the Superior Court of Judicature in 1724. In effect it was affirmed that the constitutional provision of 1780 was merely declaratory of the law as it had existed for nearly sixty years, with an added prohibition of any possible reestablishment of censorship." [63]

This observation is substantiated by the indictments for seditious libel against Thomas Adams, editor of the Boston *Independent Chronicle,* and his brother Abijah, the paper's clerk and bookkeeper. Thomas already had the honor of being the first important editor indicted by the United States under the Sedition Act. Released on bail, pending trial, he continued his candid blasts against the Adams administration and the Sedition Act itself. [64] In February of 1799 he added a new target, the Massachusetts legislature. The legislature, in repudiating the Virginia Resolutions that condemned the Sedition Act, had declared that seditiousness of speech and press was punishable on the principles of the common law; moreover, that the state and federal constitutional protections to freedom of expression had "generally but one construction": the right to "utter and publish the truth" by a "rational use and not the abuse" of liberty. [65] Abijah Adams, managing the *Chronicle* during

[63] Duniway, p. 143.

[64] See Smith, *Freedom's Fetters,* pp. 247–253, for a discussion of the background of the indictment against Thomas Adams under the Sedition Act.

[65] "Answers of the Several State Legislatures . . . Massachusetts," in Jonathan Elliot, ed., *The Debates in the Several State Conventions . . . and Other Illustrations of the Constitution* (Philadelphia, 1941, 2nd ed., rev.), 4:535, 536.

the illness of brother Thomas, publicly demanded that some Federalist explain how the members of the state legislature could be faithful to their oaths to support the sovereignty of the Commonwealth if they had rejected the resolutions of Virginia that claimed a state's right to decide on the constitutionality of the Sedition Act.[66] This remark was regarded as a charge that the state legislators had willfully perjured themselves in taking their oaths of office. The Adams brothers, at the request of the majority of the legislators, were then indicted at common law for seditiously libeling the General Court.

The illness of Thomas Adams made it possible for only Abijah to be tried. He was represented by George Blake, who became a United States attorney under Jefferson. Blake admitted that "wanton, flagrant abuses of the press" were not protected by the guarantee of a free press, but he argued that no indictment could be maintained for a libel against the state. The law of seditious libel, he contended, not being suited to the spirit and genius of a republican form of government founded by consent of the governed, must have been superseded as repugnant to the protection afforded to freedom of the press.[67] Acceptance of the Blackstonian definition would make that protection merely "nominal . . . vague, empty, and delusive," since it would lead the unwary citizen into a wide field of political disquisition only to "abandon him to infamy and destruction." If Adams could be convicted for his remark, then any offensive publication would be punishable in the same manner and degree as if no guarantee of liberty of the

[66] *Independent Chronicle* (Boston), issue of Feb. 14-Feb. 18, 1799.
[67] *Ibid.*, issue of March 4-7, 1799, and April 8-11, 1799. The point on "wanton, flagrant abuses" appears in the issue of April 11-15. The report of Blake's argument, which has been ascribed to Blake himself, continues through the issue of April 29-May 2.

press existed, rendering the constitutional clause merely declaratory of the common law. The purpose of that clause, insisted Blake, was to render immunity to the strongest censure of the government. A degree of licentiousness, he concluded, was inseparable from genuine freedom of the press, "and the nicest operation of *mental chemistry* could not dissipate the one, without losing in the process some valuable portion of the other." [68]

Attorney-General Sullivan, with whom Blake had studied law, set his former pupil right on the subject of seditious libel and liberty of the press, arguing that the latter did not imply freedom for the former. Relying on Blackstone, Sullivan advanced the usual argument that the clause on freedom of the press was merely declaratory of the common law. He apparently regarded this view as not inconsistent with permitting truth as a defense, a small advantage enjoyed by the defendant with the court's consent. [69] Chief Justice Dana of the Supreme Judicial Court, in charging the jury, began with the assertion that the common law of England was the glorious birthright of every American, endorsed Sullivan's argument without reservation, and concluded: "however censurable the libel might be in itself, it could not be more dangerous to the public tranquility, than the propagation of principles which were advanced by the *counsel* in the defense, and through the channel of the

[68] *Ibid.*, issue of April 11–15.

[69] My statement summarizing Sullivan's argument is based on Blake's references to it. The *Independent Chronicle*, which is the only newspaper I used, did not report the prosecutor's argument separately. On the permission to Blake to argue truth as a defense, see the *Chronicle* for April 29-May 2. One of the few errors in Duniway's superb study, *The Development of Freedom of the Press in Massachusetts*, is his implication at p. 146 that the first trial at which truth was permitted as a defense in that state occurred in 1803.

same press, as well as before as since the indictment was founded." [70] The records of the court show the following verdict of the jury: "The jury find that the Paper described in the Indictment is a Libel, they do not find the said Abijah guilty of printing, but they find him guilty of publishing the same in manner and form as set forth in the Indictment." [71] Abijah was sentenced to a month in jail, was forced to pay the costs of prosecution, and had to post a bond for subsequent good behavior. In 1802 another publisher, J. S. Lillie, was convicted and sentenced to three months for a libel on Chief Justice Dana himself.[72]

[70] The *Independent Chronicle* did not report Dana's charge to the Jury except for snatches that are interspersed between and in the report of Blake's argument. The lines quoted from Dana appear in the issue of April 25–29.

[71] The *Chronicle* reported the verdict as "guilty of publishing only," issue of March 4–7, but noted in the issue of March 7–11 that it had been criticized for its report of the verdict, yet stuck to its original statement. I have relied upon Duniway, *Freedom of the Press*, p. 145, for a statement of the verdict as quoted from the manuscript records of the court, citing Records of the Supreme Judicial Court, February, 1798–August, 1799, pp. 183–186, and *Suffolk Court Files*, No. 108191 (1). I have not personally checked these primary sources.

[72] Duniway, *Freedom of the Press*, p. 146. As late as 1826 the Supreme Judicial Court, in an opinion by Chief Justice Parker, observed: "The general principle decided is, that it is immaterial to the character of a libel *as a public* offence, whether the matter of it be true or false. . . . Nor does our constitution or declaration of rights abrogate the common law in this respect, as some have insisted. . . . The *liberty* of the press, not its *licentiousness;* this is the construction which a just regard to the other parts of that instrument, and to the wisdom of those who formed it requires. . . . Besides, it is well understood, and received as a commentary on this provision for the liberty of the press, that it was intended to prevent all such *previous restraints* upon publications as had been practised by other governments, and in early times here, to stifle the efforts of patriots towards enlightening their fellow subjects upon

Unfortunately historians have so neglected the subject of criminal law and freedom of speech-and-press that Duniway's study of Massachusetts is the only work of its kind, leaving us with no systematic body of knowledge about trials for seditious libel in other states. But the Pennsylvania evidence which has been reviewed above proves that Massachusetts is not the only state whose history between 1776 and 1800 gives reason to be skeptical about unsubstantiated declarations that the English law of sedition "was repudiated by every American" or that the First Amendment was written by men "who intended to wipe out the common law of sedition, and make further prosecutions for criticism of the government, without any incite-

their rights and the duties of rulers. The liberty of the press was to be unrestrained, but he who used it was to be responsible in case of its abuse. . . . The common law therefore is left unimpaired by the constitution . . ." except that truth was admissable as a defense in certain cases involving animadversion upon elected officials and candidates for office. (Commonwealth v. Blanding, 3 Pickering [Mass.] 304, 312-314 *passim.*) In 1827 the legislature of Massachusetts enacted a statute making truth a defense in all criminal libels when published with "good motives and for justifiable ends." (Laws of Massachusetts, 1827, ch. CVII, printed in Duniway, p. 159.) In 1838 when the Supreme Judicial Court sustained the conviction of Kneeland for blasphemy, the guarantee of a free press was construed as follows: "The obvious intent of this provision was to prevent the enactment of license laws, or other direct restraints upon publication, leaving individuals at liberty to print, without the previous permission of any officer of government, subject to responsibility for the matter printed." The Court, speaking through Chief Justice Shaw, added that freedom of the press did not mean "a general license for scandal, calumny and falsehood against individuals, institutions, and governments. . . ." (Commonwealth v. Kneeland, 20 Pickering [Mass.] 206, 219 [1838].) For a discussion of Kneeland's case, see Leonard W. Levy, *The Law of the Commonwealth and Chief Justice Shaw* (Cambridge, Mass., 1957), pp. 43-58.

ment to law-breaking, forever impossible in the United States of America." [73] With the exception of Oswald's remark in 1788 that the doctrine of libels was incompatible with liberty, no statement to this effect by any American can be found from the time of the revolutionary controversy through the ratification of the First Amendment. What can be found indicates the contrary proposition.

The immediate history of the drafting and adoption of the First Amendment's freedom of speech and press clause does not suggest an intent to institute broad reform. At the Constitutional Convention a motion to preface the new Constitution with a bill of rights was defeated ten to zero, the delegates voting as state units.[74] Another motion to insert a declaration "that the liberty of the Press should be inviolably preserved," was also defeated, after Sherman of Connecticut observed tersely, "It is unnecessary. The power of Congress does not extend to the Press." [75] From late 1787 through the following year the political attention of the country was engrossed by the proposed Constitution. Excepting the generalized reluctance to yield too much state sovereignty, the most important single objection to ratification was the failure of the Constitution to provide for a bill of rights. Yet it is astonishing to discover that the debate on a bill of rights, during the ratification controversy, was conducted at a level of abstraction so vague as to convey the impression that Americans of 1787–1788 had only the most nebulous conception of the meaning of the particular rights they sought to insure; indeed, many of the principal advocates of a bill of rights had only a nebulous idea of what it ought to contain. Freedom of the press

[73] Chafee, *Free Speech*, p. 21.

[74] Charles C. Tansill, ed., *Documents Illustrative of the Formation of the Union of the American States* (Washington, 1927), p. 716.

[75] *Ibid.*, p. 726.

was everywhere a grand topic for declamation, but the insistent demand for its protection on parchment was not accompanied by a reasoned analysis of what it meant, how far it extended, and under what circumstances it might be limited. One suspects that some opponents of ratification, including some of the most distinguished Anti-Federalists, callously resorted to alarming the people. It was easier than informing them, and the provocation of an emotional climate of fear made the definition of freedom of the press, and other liberties, unnecessary. Merely to denounce the omission of freedom of the press was superbly effective and even useful as a mask for less elevating, perhaps sordid, objections to the Constitution concerning such matters as tax and commerce powers. One searches in vain for a definition of any of the First Amendment freedoms in the rhetorical effusions of George Clinton, Elbridge Gerry, Patrick Henry, Thomas Jefferson, Richard Henry Lee, Luther Martin, George Mason, Spencer Roane, Melancthon Smith, and other advocates of a Bill of Rights. Nor do the newspapers, pamphlets, or debates of the state ratifying conventions offer illumination.

The only individuals who revealed what they were talking about when mentioning freedom of the press were Hugh Williamson, George Nicholas, and James Wilson. Ben Franklin at this time, although not in the context of the ratification controversy, also spoke with clarity in an essay which has been reviewed above. He favored as much discussion as possible of "public measures and political opinions," but recommended harsh treatment for anyone calumniating the government or affronting its reputation. During the same period, John Adams and William Cushing in their private correspondence, agreeing that the press was free "within the bounds of truth," relegated falsehood,

216 LEGACY OF SUPPRESSION

scandal, and bad motives to the realm of criminal publications. In Pennsylvania, where Oswald's trial occurred during this time, Thomas McKean and George Bryan revealed that the key toward understanding a constitutional guarantee of the liberty of the press was to be found in Blackstone; while in Massachusetts a few years later, but before the ratification of the First Amendment, James Sullivan and Francis Dana evidenced their agreement with McKean and Bryan.

Excepting Franklin, James Wilson and Hugh Williamson were the only Framers, members of the federal Convention, who troubled to explain their understanding of freedom of the press. Wilson's views, which have already been discussed, aligned him with Blackstone and refuted any notion that a free-press clause might supersede the common law of seditious libel. Williamson of North Carolina, in an essay, "Remarks in the New Plan of Government," declared in 1788: "There was a time in England when neither book, pamphlet, nor paper could be published without a license from government. That restraint was finally removed in the year 1694; and, by such removal, the press became perfectly free, for it is not under the restraint of any license. Certainly the new government can have no power to impose restraints." [76] Obviously, freedom of the press meant to Williamson what it had meant to Blackstone.

The only other statements of the period implying a definition were by two Virginians who, while not participating in the Federal Convention or in the Congress which framed the Bill of Rights, were closely associated with the Framers. George Nicholas was one of the leading supporters of Jefferson and Madison in the Virginia legislature,

[76] Paul L. Ford, ed., *Essays on the Constitution of the United States* (Brooklyn, 1892), p. 394.

fought for the Statute of Religious Freedom, and later, as attorney-general of Kentucky, would help Jefferson frame the Kentucky Resolutions of 1798 against the Sedition Act. In 1788, at the Virginia ratifying convention, he declared: "The liberty of the press is secured. . . . In the time of King William, there passed an act for licensing the press. That was repealed. Since that time it has been looked upon as safe." [77] While less explicit than Williamson's statement, Nicholas' also accepted Blackstone. John Marshall, the future chief justice, also speaking as a member of the Virginia ratifying convention, asked, "Is it presumable that they [Congress] will make a law to punish men who are of different opinions in politics from themselves? Is it presumable that they will do it in one single case, *unless it be such a case as must satisfy the people at large?*" [78] Marshall's rhetorical question clearly implied his view that minority critics might be suppressed or "punished" if public opinion demanded or if the people went along with Congress. It is noteworthy that Nicholas and Marshall were from the one state which presumably had rejected the bad-tendency test upon which the common law of seditious libel rested. Amid the torrent of words spoken about liberty of the press or free speech before the final ratification of the First Amendment in 1791, there are no other statements by public men even implying a definition or a position on the question whether the law of seditious libel was operative.

State as distinguished from individual pronouncements were no more illuminating. Ratification by the first nine states, the requisite number to adopt the constitution, was in no case accompanied by a recommendation for a federal

[77] Elliot, ed., *Debates*, 3:247.
[78] *Ibid.*, 3:560. Italics added.

amendment guaranteeing freedom of speech or press. Indeed, the Pennsylvania ratifying convention, led by Wilson and McKean, rejected a proposal for such an amendment phrased in the language of the Pennsylvania constitution of 1776.[79] The Maryland convention took no action on any of the amendments recommended by its committee on amendments; one of these declared, "That the freedom of the press be inviolably preserved." To which was added this explanation by the committee: "In prosecutions in the federal courts for libels, the constitutional preservation of this great and fundamental right may prove invaluable." [80] The necessary implication of this statement by Maryland's Anti-Federalist libertarians, is that prosecutions for criminal libel might be maintained in the federal courts under common if not statutory law.

Of the twelve states to ratify the Constitution before the First Amendment was drafted in Congress in 1789, only the last three, Virginia, North Carolina, and New York, sought to safeguard the expression of opinion from violation by the new national government. Although neither Virginia nor North Carolina protected speech in its own constitution, they both proposed a federal bill of rights that included a provision, modeled on the Pennsylvania language of 1776, which began, "That the people have a right to freedom of speech. . . ." [81] In the preamble to her proposed bill of rights, Virginia also declared that "among other essential rights the liberty of Conscience and of the Press cannot be cancelled abridged restrained or modified by any authority

---

[79] McMaster and Stone, eds., *Pennsylvania and the Federal Constitution*, pp. 422, 424, 462, 464.

[80] Elliot, ed., *Debates*, 2:552.

[81] Tansill, ed., *Documents Illustrative of the Formation of the Union*, pp. 1030 and 1047.

of the United States." [82] Virginia's concern for protecting
freedom of speech and press against national invasion was
probably genuine, though hardly as intense as her desire to
secure state authority against a concurrent jurisdiction in
the national government on the subject of criminal libels.
State sovereignty, that is, was probably the dominant Virginian concern. In any event, Virginia's recommendation
for an amendment to the United States Constitution in
1788, as in the case of her presumed rejection of the bad-
tendency test in 1785, ought not to be construed too liber-
ally. Consider not only the comments by Nicholas and
Marshall, quoted above, but also the Virginia statute of
1785, re-enacted in 1792. That statute, which aimed at
prohibiting the creation of any government within the
state's boundaries without the legislature's consent, provided that, "EVERY person . . . who shall by *writing* or
advised *speaking*, endeavour to instigate the people of this
commonwealth to erect or establish such government without such assent aforesaid, shall be adjudged guilty of a high
crime and misdemeanor. . . ." [83] The statute did not be-
speak a broad understanding in Virginia that freedom of
political speech and press included a right to express any
principle that did not "break out into overt acts." On the
contrary, Virginia's failure to distinguish mere words from
the overt criminal deed of attempting by unconstitutional
means to erect a new government, embodied the bad-tendency test of utterances.

[82] *Ibid.*, p. 1027.
[83] Virginia Code, 1803, ch. CXXXVI, quoted in Dennis v. U.S.
341 U.S. 494, 521 note 3. Italics added. See also Thomas F. Carroll,
"Freedom of Speech and of the Press in the Federalist Period: The
Sedition Act," *Michigan Law Review*, 18:633 (May 1920), citing
the same statute in Hening, *Laws of Virginia*, 12:41–43 and Shep-
herd, *Laws of Virginia*, 1:187.

New York's ratification of the Constitution in 1788 was accompanied by the recommendation for an amendment worded, "That the Freedom of the Press ought not to be violated or restrained," [84] although no comparable provision existed in that state's constitution. As in the case of the other states recommending a guarantee of First Amendment freedoms, no explanatory statement defining the meaning or compass of any of those freedoms accompanied New York's recommendation. Her expressed solicitude for freedom of the press in 1788 cannot be considered as proof of her faithfulness to the principles of the great Zenger case. In New York freedom of the press meant what Blackstone had defined it to be, although popular understanding may have assumed that truth was a defense against a charge of criminal libel and that jurors possessed a power which Blackstone denied. In 1799 a state court imprisoned a printer for four months and fined him too for the crime of having copied from another newspaper the innuendo that Alexander Hamilton was hostile to the republican form of government and worked with the British government to undermine it by trying to buy out the Philadelphia *Aurora*. The indictment was instigated by Hamilton himself on the theory that the calumny against him had the "dangerous tendency," he said, of destroying the confidence of the people in the leading defenders of the administration. At the trial the court refused to allow evidence to prove the truth of the defendant's accusation, even though the prosecution consented to permit truth as a defense. Hamilton, the star witness for the state, testified that the Philadelphia *Aurora*, the source from which the seditious libel was derived and the country's foremost organ of the Jeffer-

[84] Tansill, ed., *Documents Illustrative of the Formation of the Union*, p. 1037.

sonian party, was hostile to the government of the United States.[85]

If the controversy in the states over the ratification of the Constitution without a bill of rights revealed little about the meaning and scope of freedom of speech-and-press, the debates by the First Congress, which framed the First Amendment, are even less illuminating. Congress debated the clauses on religion, but on the remainder of the First Amendment considered only whether the right of peaceable assembly vested the people with the power to instruct their representatives how to vote. In the course of that discussion, Madison made the only recorded statement on the subject of speech or press. If by peaceable assembly, he said, "we mean nothing more than this, that the people have a right to express and communicate their sentiments and wishes, we have provided for it already. The right of freedom of speech is secured; the liberty of the press is expressly declared to be beyond the reach of this Government. . . ."[86] Any interpretation of the meaning and compass of freedom of speech-and-press drawn from this vague statement would strain credulity. That the United States government could not abridge liberty of expression did not necessarily imply that expression was illimitable, for the states were definitely left in possession of their restrictive powers.

The original intention of the House, however, was to guarantee the freedoms protected by the First Amendment against state violation. An amendment proposed to the

[85] "Trial of David Frothingham, for a Libel on General Hamilton," New York, 1799, in Wharton, ed., *State Trials*, pp. 649–651. Frothingham's case is narrated at length in Smith, *Freedom's Fetters*, pp. 400–414, on the basis of much new research.

[86] *The Debates and Proceedings in the Congress of the United States* (Washington, 1834 ff.) 1:766, 1st Cong., 1st Sess. Cited hereafter as *Annals of Congress*, the bookbinder's title.

House by Madison, along with his other recommendations for what became the Bill of Rights, provided that, "No State shall violate the equal rights of conscience, or the freedom of the press, or the trial by jury in criminal cases." [87] Madison offered no explanation for having omitted freedom of speech from this amendment, nor did he explain what he meant by freedom of the press. He did declare, in defense of his proposed restrictions on the states, that they were "of equal, if not greater importance" than the prohibitions against the state enactment of *ex post facto* laws, bills of attainder, or laws impairing the obligations of contracts. He argued that the powers of the states were more likely to be abused than those of the national government "if not controlled by the general principle, that laws are unconstitutional which infringe the rights of the community." He thought it proper that "every Government should be disarmed of powers which trench upon those particular rights" of press, conscience, and jury trial. The amendment was all the more needed, he asserted, because some of the states did not protect these rights in their own constitutions. As for those that did, a "double security" could not reasonably be opposed.[88]

Madison's proposal for a restriction on the states was assigned, with his other recommended amendments, to a select committee of the House to frame a bill of rights. The committee adopted the proposal but expanded it to include "the freedom of speech." The recommendation of the committee to the House was: "no State shall infringe the equal rights of conscience, nor the freedom of speech or of the press, nor of the right of trial by jury in criminal cases." [89]

[87] *Ibid.*, 1:452.
[88] *Ibid.*, 1:458.
[89] *Ibid.*, 1:783.

When this proposal was debated by the House, only one member declared his opposition. Tucker of South Carolina, stating simply that it would be "better . . . to leave the State Governments to themselves, and not to interfere with them more than we already do . . . ," moved to strike out the amendment.[90] Madison, in reply, declared that he "conceived this to be the most valuable amendment in the whole list. If there was any reason to restrain the Government of the United States from infringing upon these essential rights, it was equally necessary that they should be secured against the State Governments." He thought the people would support the amendment for that reason.[91] Livermore of New Hampshire, the only other speaker, agreed with Madison and suggested a slight stylistic change. The House then rejected Tucker's motion and by a two-thirds majority passed the amendment.[92] But it met its demise in the Senate. That body included many, like Tucker in the House, who were jealous of state prerogatives and believed that the Constitution already imposed too many limitations upon the states. All we know about the Senate's deliberations is that a motion to adopt did not receive the necessary two-thirds vote, though by what margin is unrecorded.[93] As a result of the failure of the Senate to pass the amendment, assuming that it would have been ratified, the Constitution of the United States offered against state violation no protection whatever to speech and press, or to religion.[94]

[90] *Ibid.*, 1:783–784.
[91] *Ibid.*, 1:784.
[92] *Ibid.* The exact vote is not recorded.
[93] *Ibid.*, 1:78. *The Journal of the First Session of the Senate of the United States of America* (New York, 1789), p. 121, reveals no more.
[94] Beginning in 1925 the word "liberty" of the Fourteenth Amendment's due process clause was construed by the Supreme Court to incorporate the freedoms of the First Amendment. Git-

The First Amendment imposed limitations upon only the national government. The limitations seemed clear enough, but the meanings of the subjects protected were not. The Congressional debate on the amendment, even as to its clause on establishments of religion as well as the free speech-and-press clause, was unclear and apathetic; ambiguity, brevity, and imprecision in thought and expression characterize the comments of the few members who spoke. It is doubtful that the House understood the debate, cared deeply about its outcome, or shared a common understanding of the finished amendment. The meager records of the Senate tell us only that a motion was voted down to alter the amendment so that freedom of the press should be protected "in as ample a manner as hath at any time been secured by the common law." [95] There is no way of knowing whether the motion was defeated on the ground that it was too narrow, too broad, or simply unnecessary. But its phraseology reflects a belief in the mind of its proposer that the common law adequately protected freedom of the press.

State action on the proposed Bill of Rights apparently occasioned slight comment either in or out of the legislatures, except in Virginia.[96] Nine states perfunctorily approved the Bill of Rights by mid-June of 1790.[97] Since records of legislative debates are nonexistent, there is no

---

low v. N.Y., 268 U.S. 652 (1925); Near v. Minn., 283 U.S. 697 (1931); Cantwell v. Conn., 310 U.S. 296 (1940); and Everson v. Bd. of Ed., 330 U.S. 1 (1947).

[95] *Journal of the First Session of the Senate*, p. 117.

[96] David M. Matteson, "The Organization of the Government under the Constitution," in Sol Bloom, Director General, *History of the Formation of the Union under the Constitution* (Washington, 1943), pp. 316, 317.

[97] *Ibid.*, pp. 317–319.

way of expressly knowing what the First Amendment freedoms were understood to mean. Private correspondence, newspapers, and tracts are unilluminating. Many may have cared about protecting freedom of speech-and-press, but no one seems to have cared enough to clarify what he meant by the subject upon which he lavished praise. If definition were unnecessary because of the existence of a tacit and widespread understanding of "liberty of the press," only the received or traditional understanding could have been possible. To assume the existence of a general, latitudinarian understanding that veered substantially from the common-law definition is incredible, given the total absence of argumentive analysis of the meaning of the clause on speech and press. Any novel definition expanding the scope of free expression or repudiating, even altering, the concept of seditious libel would have been the subject of public debate or comment. Not even the Anti-Federalists offered the argument that the clause on speech and press was unsatisfactory because insufficiently protective.

The Anti-Federalists, those opposed to the Constitution, had originally raised the objection that a bill of rights protecting personal liberties was a *sine qua non* of ratification, while supporters of the new frame of government regarded a bill of rights as superfluous. The Federalists who expressed themselves on the subject unanimously concurred in stating that Congress, or the "general government," had no power whatever to legislate in a manner violative of personal liberties, no power, for example, to legislate on matters respecting speech or press unless to protect literary property by enacting copyright laws. A bill of rights, as Hamilton argued, would be a bill of restraints on national powers, but "why declare that things shall not be done which there is no power to do? Why, for instance, should it be said that the liberty of the press shall not be restrained, when no power is given by which restrictions may be imposed." [98] The Framers intended a federal system of government with the central government to exercise only such powers as were specifically enumerated or were necessary and proper to carry out those enumerated. It followed that the power to punish for criminal libels was denied to the United States in the minds of the Framers. They had vested no such power and intended that none be exercised or abused. In other words, the Framers believed that even without an express limitation such as that later imposed by the First Amendment, Congress was bereft of authority to restrict freedom of speech or press in any manner. The Framers tended also to be rather skeptical of the value of "parchment barriers" against "overbearing majorities," as Madison put it. [99] Many of them during the controversy over the ratification of the Constitution shared Hamilton's opinion that the Anti-Federalist cry for a bill of rights was more than unwarranted; it was part of a plan "to frighten the people with ideal bugbears, in order to mould them to their own purposes." [100]

After leading Federalists, Madison pre-eminent among them, finally though reluctantly assented to the necessity of allaying popular fears by pledging themselves to frame amendments guaranteeing individual rights as soon as the

[98] *The Federalist*, no. 84, p. 559 of The Modern Library Edition. See also the statement of James Wilson in Elliot, ed., *Debates*, 4:435 ff. and 453 ff.

[99] Madison to Jefferson, Oct. 17, 1788, in Gaillard Hunt, ed., *The Writings of James Madison* (New York, 1900–1910), 5:272. For an illustration of a similar sentiment being expressed by Virginians alone, see Elliot, ed., *Debates*, 3:70 (Randolph), 298 (Pendleton), and 561 (Marshall).

[100] Hamilton's "Caesar" letters, October 1788, in Ford, ed., *Essays*, p. 289.

new government went into operation, the Anti-Federalists began to play down their propaganda on behalf of individual rights. That they sincerely believed in the desirability of some sonorous declaration constituting a bill of rights is not questionable. But they used the issue of a bill of rights as a smokescreen for those objections to the Constitution that could not be dramatically popularized. When Madison persistently pushed the framing of protections to personal liberty, they sought to scuttle a bill of rights by delaying tactics and by annexing amendments that would aggrandize state powers. Hugh Williamson, a signer of the Constitution, informed Madison that the North Carolina Anti-Federalists did not really want a bill of rights; while William R. Davie, who had been Williamson's colleague in the Federal Convention, exultantly wrote that Madison's introduction in Congress of the amendments that were to become the Bill of Rights had "confounded the Anties exceedingly. . . ." [101] To Madison, Davie explained that the "Anties" preferred additional restrictions on the substantive powers of Congress rather than an enumeration of personal freedoms.[102] Similarly, Pendleton of Virginia wrote of Madison's amendments that "nothing was further from the wish of some, who covered their Opposition to the Government under the masque of uncommon zeal for amendments . . .";[103] and Tench Coxe of Pennsylvania

[101] Williamson to Madison, May 24, 1789, quoted in Elizabeth G. McPherson, ed., "Unpublished Letters from North Carolinians to James Madison and James Monroe," *North Carolina Historical Review*, 14:162–163 (1937); Davie to Iredell, June 4, 1789, quoted in Griffith J. McRee, *Life and Correspondence of James Iredell* (New York, 1857–1858), 2:260.

[102] Davie to Madison, June 10, 1789, in "Unpublished Letters," *North Carolina Hist. Rev.*, 14:167.

[103] Quoted in Matteson, "Organization of the Government," p. 301.

praised Madison for stripping the Constitution's opponents "of every rational [*sic*], and most of the popular arguments they have heretofore used." [104]

As for the Anti-Federalists themselves, their leaders in the House, including Burke, Gerry, Sumter, and Tucker, first stalled against taking up Madison's amendments for consideration,[105] then resorted to moving fresh amendments that would cripple the national government,[106] and finally ended by depreciating the importance of the very protections of individual liberty that they once demanded as a guarantee against impending tyranny. Burke of South Carolina, for instance, in the course of the debate on the free speech-and-press clause, rose to declare that Madison's amendments, which had been approved by a select committee that had included Burke himself, were "not those solid and substantial amendments which the people expect; they are little better than whip-syllabub, frothy and full of wind, formed only to please the palate; . . . . Upon the whole, I think it will be found that we have done nothing but lose our time, and that it will be better to drop the subject. . . ." [107] Madison himself believed that Burke and his allies were attempting "to defeat by delaying a plan short of their wishes. . . ." [108] The private correspondence of Senators William Grayson and Richard Henry Lee of

[104] Coxe to Madison, June 18, 1789, quoted in *Documentary History of the Constitution of the United States of America, 1786–1870. Derived from Records, Manuscripts, and Rolls Deposited in the Bureau of Rolls and Library of the Department of State* (Washington, 1894–1905), 5:178.

[105] See *Annals of Congress*, 1:443, 462, 466, and 774.

[106] See *Annals of Congress*, 1:776, 786-787, 790–791, 797, 800–801, 803, 805–807.

[107] *Annals of Congress*, 1:774.

[108] Madison to Randolph, Aug. 21, 1789, in Madison's *Writings*, 5:471.

Virginia, both Anti-Federalists, reveals the explanation for the attitude of their party toward a bill of rights. A few days after Madison had introduced his guarantees, Grayson complained to his mentor, Patrick Henry, that the Federalists meant to enact "amendments which shall effect [*sic*] personal liberty alone, leaving the great points of the Judiciary, direct taxation, &c, to stand as they are. . . ." [109] After Lee and Grayson failed in their effort to have the Senate amend the House's proposals by adopting the recommendations of the Virginia ratifying convention on direct taxation, the treaty power, navigation laws, and other subjects, Lee regretted the original Anti-Federalist strategy of opposing the Constitution unless revised by the addition of a bill of rights and other amendments. He sorrowfully informed Henry that "the idea of subsequent amendments, was little better than putting oneself to death first, in expectation that the doctor, who wished our destruction, would afterwards restore us to life." [110] After the Senate approved the amendments that became the Bill of Rights, Grayson reported, "they are good for nothing, and I believe, as many others do, that they will do more harm than benefit." [111]

Within six months of the time it was submitted to the states for approval, the Bill of Rights was ratified by nine of them; Virginia, Massachusetts, Connecticut, and Georgia were the four recalcitrants by mid-1790. The last three did not ratify until 1939, when on the sesquicentennial anniversary of the Constitution they belatedly assented. Of the three, Georgia had taken the position that amendments

[109] Grayson to Henry, June 12, 1789, quoted in William Wirt Henry, *Patrick Henry: Life, Correspondence and Speeches* (New York, 1891), 3:391.

[110] Lee to Henry, Sept. 14, 1789, *ibid.*, 3:399.

[111] Grayson to Henry, Sept. 29, 1789, *ibid.*, 3:406.

were unnecessary until experience under the Constitution showed a need for them; the Connecticut Yankees seemed to have thought that any suggestion that the Constitution was not perfect would add to the strength of Anti-Federalism. A similar sentiment was prevalent in Massachusetts where Federalist apathy to the Bill of Rights was grounded on a satisfaction with the Constitution as it was, unamended, whereas the anti-Federalists were more interested in amendments which would strengthen the states at the expense of the national government, rather than amendments restricted to safeguarding personal liberties. Caught between conflicting party interests in Massachusetts, the Bill of Rights simply died of inaction in that state.[112]

In Madison's state, however, the Federalists went all out to ratify, while the Anti-Federalists, the victims of a dilemma of their own making, first sought to sabotage the Bill of Rights and then, having held up ratification for nearly two years, irresolutely acquiesced. In the beginning Grayson and Lee reported to the Virginia House of Delegates their hope that a new constitutional convention might be convened to devise amendments that would "secure against the annihilation of the State Governments. . . ."[113] They feared, correctly, that ratification of the Bill of Rights would make impossible the subsequent adoption of what they called "Radical Amendments," while rejection of the Bill of Rights might force Congress or a new constitutional convention to reconsider the whole subject of amendments from the Anti-Federalist standpoint. The Federalists, on the other hand, eagerly supported the Bill of Rights in the knowledge that its adoption would sufficiently appease the public fear generated by the opposition, thereby preventing

[112] Matteson, "Organization of the Government," pp. 325–328.
[113] Quoted *ibid.*, p. 319.

additional amendments that would hamstring the national government. Virginia's lower House, dominated by the Federalists, quickly "and without debate of any consequence," passed the amendments proposed by Congress. But the opposition party controlled the state Senate. That body, as Randolph reported to Washington, "will attempt to postpone them [the amendments]; for a majority is unfriendly to the government."[114] As a member of the Virginia lower House reported to Madison, the Senate was inclined to reject the Bill of Rights, not because of opposition to its guarantees, but from an apprehension "that the adoption of them at this time will be an obstacle to the chief object of their pursuit, the amendment on the subject of direct taxation." [115]

As predicted, the Virginia Senate voted by a bare majority to strike out what are now the First, Sixth, Ninth, and Tenth Amendments until the next session of the legislature, thereby allowing time for the electorate to express itself.[116] The senators in the majority also issued a statement grossly misrepresenting the First Amendment's clauses on speech and press and on an establishment of religion and religious liberty.[117] Madison confidently predicted that this Anti-

[114] Randolph to Washington, Dec. 6, 1789, quoted *ibid.*, p. 321.

[115] Hardin Burnley to Madison, Dec. 5, 1789, quoted *ibid.*, pp. 319-320, and in Irving Brant, *James Madison, Father of the Constitution* (Indianapolis, 1950), p. 286 and p. 491 note 15.

[116] *Journal of the Senate of the Commonwealth of Virginia; Begun and held in the City of Richmond, on Monday the 19th day of October . . . 1789* [the bookbinder's title is *Journal of the Senate, 1785 to 1790*] (Richmond, 1828), p. 51, proceedings of Dec. 8, 1789.

[117] With unbelievable inaccuracy the eight senators asserted as to speech and press, "This amendment does not declare and assert the right of the people to speak and publish their sentiments, nor does it secure the liberty of the press. Should these valuable rights be infringed or violated . . . the people would have no

Federalist tactic would boomerang,[118] and it did. For the senators' statement was not only inaccurate on its face; it came from men who with a single exception did not go to the electorate with clean hands. Like Henry and Lee who planned this Anti-Federalist statement, several of the senators had records of having voted against religious liberty and in favor of taxes for religion. By contrast, Madison had led the fight, in 1784 to 1786, against a state establishment of religion and for religious liberty, and none of his supporters in the Virginia Senate had a record of opposition.[119] In the end, Madison's confidence proved justified. Jefferson, who was displacing Henry as the political leader of Virginia, made his influence felt on behalf of the Bill of Rights, while the Anti-Federalists grudgingly gave ground before public opinion. On December 15, 1791, after a session of inaction, the state Senate finally ratified,

---

avowed principle in the constitution to which they might resort for the security of these rights." The senators also asserted that the amendment "does not prohibit the rights of conscience from being violated or infringed . . . " whereas the amendment positively stipulated that Congress shall not abridge the free exercise of religion; the senators also alleged that notwithstanding the amendment's provision against laws respecting an establishment of religion, "any particular denomination of Christians might be so favored and supported by the general government, as to give it a decided advantage over others. . . ." (*Journal of the Senate of . . . Virginia*, pp. 62–63, proceedings of Dec. 12, 1789.) This is not the place to argue what was then understood to constitute a law respecting an establishment of religion, but despite the present-day controversy over the meaning of an establishment, every historian without exception agrees that a law giving preference to one denomination over others positively was understood to constitute an establishment.

[118] Matteson, "Organization of the Government," p. 323, and Brant, *Madison*, p. 287.

[119] See Brant, *Madison*, pp. 286–287 and 491 note 16 for the voting records.

without a record vote, thereby completing the process of state ratification and making the Bill of Rights part of the Constitution.

But the history of the ratification indicates no passion on the part of anyone to grind underfoot the common law of liberty of the press. Indeed the history of the framing and ratification of the First Amendment and the other nine scarcely manifests a passion on the part of anyone connected with the process. Considering its immediate background, our precious Bill of Rights was in the main the chance result of certain Federalists' having been reluctantly forced to capitalize for their own cause the propaganda that had been originated in vain by the Anti-Federalists for ulterior purposes. Thus the party that had first opposed a Bill of Rights inadvertently wound up with the responsibility for its framing and ratification, while the party that had at first professedly wanted it discovered too late that its framing and ratification were not only embarrassing but inexpedient.

Thanks mainly to the state sovereignty sentiment among the Anti-Federalists, the Bill of Rights imposed limitations upon only the national government. But the First Amendment, when read literally, raises the question whether any special significance should be attached to the fact that the prohibition on power was imposed exclusively upon *Congress* instead of upon the government of the United States. Did the specification of Congress imply that restraints were not intended to be imposed upon other federal authorities? Could the executive arm of the government, through the attorney-general's office and United States marshals, prosecute common-law crimes committed by mere words? Could the federal courts try verbal crimes at common law? Did a federal common law of crimes exist? If it did, the free-speech clause offered merely the shadow rather than the substance of protection by stipulating only a restriction upon Congress.

If an intention to permit abridgments of free speech or press by nonlegislative federal bodies cannot be implied, it does not necessarily follow that the Framers were motivated by a desire to give the utmost latitude to expression. Let us assume that the Framers did not say what they meant; assume, on the authority of Madison and James Wilson, that by "Congress" they meant, more broadly, "the general government." It is also possible that they did not say what they meant in another respect; namely, that not all speech is free speech, or, to put it another way, that there are several classes of speech, some of which were not intended to be categorized under the rubric, "the freedom of speech" or freedom of the press. Did they intend that the federal mails should be open to pornographic statements or that a speaker should be free to incite violence directly and immediately against the United States? Did they intend that malicious calumnies against the government should be free? Madison himself was "inclined to think that *absolute* restrictions in cases that are doubtful, or where emergencies may overrule them, ought to be avoided." [120] It is possible, in other words, that the Framers neither said what they meant nor meant what they said. If they did not intend that literally all speech, without exception, should be free without exception, the crucial question is, where did they mean to draw the line between that speech which was constitutionally protected and that which was not?

Even if we were to assume, as does Professor Alexander Meiklejohn, that the Framers really intended to impose

[120] Madison to Jefferson, Oct. 17, 1788, quoted in Madison's *Writings,* 5:274.

upon the national government "an absolute, unqualified prohibition" [121] — there shall be *no* law abridging free speech — it is possible that the Framers were less motivated by a concern for giving unqualified immunity to all speech than by a solicitude for states' rights and the federal principle. Granting, for the moment, an intention to render the national government utterly powerless to act in any way against oral or printed utterances, there is a question whether it was not a primary purpose of the clause to reserve to the *states* an exclusive authority in the field of speech and press. We have the statement of James Wilson in 1789 — he was the only Framer to express himself directly on this point — that a libel against the government of the United States was criminally punishable, but his point was that verbal crimes, even the immediate and direct verbal incitement of crime against the United States, could be prosecuted only by the *state* in which the libel was made and only under state law. Thus, no matter what the Framers meant or understood by freedom of speech or press, the national government even in the absence of the First Amendment could not make speech or press a legitimate subject of restrictive action. The amendment itself was intended as an assurance that Congress would be limited to the exercise of its enumerated powers and was phrased as an express prohibition against the possibility that those powers might be used to abridge freedom of speech or press. It goes without saying that an express prohibition on power did not vest or create a power, previously nonexistent, to abridge speech or press, for as Madison declared, the Bill of Rights was not framed "to imply powers not meant to be included in the enumera-

[121] Meiklejohn, *Free Speech and Its Relation to Self-Government* (New York, 1948), p. 17.

tion." [122] But in view of the Senate's rejection of the House-approved amendment to prohibit state abridgment of freedom of speech, we cannot doubt that the First Amendment left the states free to act against individual expression, subject only to such restraints as might be laid down in state constitutions. The big question persists, however; even had Congress passed, and the states ratified, an amendment imposing upon the states the same prohibition laid by the First Amendment upon the national government, what did the Framers understand by freedom of speech and freedom of press?

No one can say for certain what the Framers had in mind, for although the evidence all points in one direction there is not enough of it to justify cocksure conclusions. It is not even certain that the Framers themselves knew what they had in mind; that is, at the time of the drafting and ratification of the First Amendment, few among them if any at all clearly understood what they meant by the free speech-and-press clause, and it is perhaps doubtful that those few agreed except in a generalized way and equally doubtful that they represented a consensus. Considerable disagreement existed, for example, on the question whether freedom of expression meant the right to print the truth about government measures and officials if the truth was defamatory or revealed for unworthy motives. There was also disagreement about the function of juries in trials for criminal libel.

What is clear is that there exists no evidence to suggest an understanding that a constitutional guarantee of free speech or press meant the impossibility of future prosecutions of seditious utterances. The traditional libertarian

[122] Madison to Jefferson, Oct. 17, 1788, in Madison's *Writings*, 5:271.

interpretation of the original meaning of the First Amendment is surely subject to the Scottish verdict: not proven. Freedom of speech and press, as all the scattered evidence suggests, was not understood to include a right to broadcast sedition by words. The security of the state against libelous advocacy or attack was always regarded as outweighing any social interest in open expression, at least through the period of the adoption of the First Amendment. The thought and experience of a lifetime, indeed the taught traditions of law and politics extending back many generations, supplied an a priori belief that freedom of political discourse, however broadly conceived, stopped short of seditious libel. As Maitland observed, "Taught law is tough law," [123] and its survival power was sufficient to carry it through the American Revolution with its principles unbroken except for a few feudal relics such as those relating to primogeniture and entail. The fact is scarcely even remarkable since the origins and conduct of the American Revolution were unrelated to any hostility to the common law, and surely not to its doctrines of verbal crime which were given statutory recognition and carried to extremes during the Revolution itself. Moreover, the Sedition Act, passed less than seven years after the ratification of the First Amendment, suggests that suppression of seditious libel was not considered to be an abridgment of freedom of speech or press. Yet the Framers themselves, whatever they understood freedom of speech or press to mean, had given the public specific assurances again and again that neither speech nor press could be the subject of repressive legislation by a government bereft of authority as to that subject.

[123] Frederick Maitland, *English Law and the Renaissance*, p. 18, quoted in Roscoe Pound, *The Formative Era of American Law* (Boston, 1938), p. 144.

And we have that undisputed statement of James Wilson that criminal libels against the United States could be avenged only in the state courts under state law. It was only after the new government had gone into operation and the First Amendment was ratified that many of the Framers and their associates spoke and acted as if freedom of speech and press could be prosecuted in federal courts and be abridged by Congress as well. In this regard both the Sedition Act and the problem whether a federal common law existed deserve attention.

If a federal common law of crimes existed, then the attorney-general's office might prosecute and the federal courts might try nonstatutory crimes against the United States. In other words, the existence of a federal common law meant that the First Amendment could not possibly have been intended to supersede the common law of seditious libel or other branches of the common law of defamation which delimited freedom of expression. *Congress,* in accordance with a literal interpretation of the First Amendment, might not be empowered to enact libel laws — or more precisely, might not abridge freedom of speech or press, but the executive and judicial departments might proceed at common law independently of statutory provisions. The question, then, is whether there was supposed to be a federal common law of crimes. The answer is that the evidence is contradictory.

Charles Warren has shown that the intention of the Judiciary Act of 1789 was to vest the federal courts with common-law jurisdiction,[124] but it is not clear that their jurisdiction was to extend to criminal as well as civil cases,

[124] Charles Warren, "New Light on the History of the Federal Judiciary Act of 1789," in D. B. Maggs *et al.*, eds., *Selected Essays on Constitutional Law* (Chicago, 1938), 3:1246–1254.

except, necessarily, to crimes committed on the high seas. Nor is it clear, if jurisdiction over common-law crimes was intended to be vested in the federal courts, whether the courts were to create a federal common law of crimes or apply the common law of the state in which the crime was committed. Either alternative would comprehend the common law of criminal utterances. If we may extrapolate from Warren's research on section 34 of the Judiciary Act of 1789, the probability is that the Framers of the act intended the state common law to be applied.[125] But the federal judges from the very beginning assumed the existence of a federal common law of crimes. All the early cases, excepting one in which the court split, are on the side of the proposition that there was a federal common law of crimes. Yet in 1812 and again in 1816 the Supreme Court rejected that proposition.[126]

The first judicial pronouncement on the subject seems to have been in *United States* v. *Smith,* 1792, where the federal district court held that it possessed common-law jurisdiction over crimes and therefore might try a person

[125] I am indebted to my colleague, John P. Roche, for this insight which cuts away the ground of the whole controversy whether a federal common law was intended. I doubt, however, that sufficient evidence can be mustered to support the proposition which, though plausible, seems not to have occurred to the federal courts in criminal cases with but one exception. In 1807 U.S. District Judge Pierpont Edwards ruled that in the trial of a common-law crime in a federal court, the law of the state in which the crime occurred was to be applied. Edwards' ruling is discussed below, p. 304. Although Professor Roche's proposition is without the support of other rulings, it is logically and psychologically sound and fits with what we know of the original intentions of the framers of the Judiciary Act of 1789 as to civil cases at common law.

[126] U.S. v. Hudson and Goodwin, 7 Cranch 32 (1812), and U.S. v. Coolidge, 1 Wheaton 415 (1816).

indicted for counterfeiting notes of the Bank of the United States.[127] In Ravara's case, in the following year, Justices Wilson and Iredell, on circuit, ruled that the federal court had jurisdiction of the common-law crime of attempted extortion against a foreign diplomat. At the trial, Chief Justice Jay, sitting with District Judge Peters, ruled that the defendant could be punished at common law by the United States, though no federal statute covered the crime.[128] In the same year, Henfield's case attracted the attention of Washington's cabinet. The accused was indicted for having violated a United States treaty and offending "against the peace and dignity of the said United States" by privateering against a friendly power. Secretary of Treasury Hamilton prepared the indictment which was prosecuted by another Framer, Attorney-General Edmund Randolph. Justice Wilson, with Justice Iredell and Judge Peters concurring, clearly sustained the indictment at least in part on common law grounds.[129] John Marshall, in his *Life of Washington*, noted with regret that Henfield was acquitted by the jury after having been indicted, in part, "at common law, for disturbing the peace of the United States." [130]

In Worrall's case of 1798, where the indictment at common law was for attempted bribery of a United States official, Justice Chase, who viciously enforced the Sedition Act of that year, confounded the bench and bar by announcing his opinion that there was no federal common

[127] Federal Cases #16323, cited by Howe, ed., *Readings,* p. 336 note 2.
[128] "Trial of Joseph Ravara," 2 Dallas 297–299 (1793), in Wharton, ed., *State Trials,* 90–92, discussed in Albert J. Beveridge, *The Life of John Marshall* (Boston, 1919), 3:24–25.
[129] "Trial of Gideon Henfield," 1793, in Wharton, ed., *State Trials,* 49–92, discussed in Charles Warren, *The Supreme Court in United States History* (Boston, 1923, 3 vol. ed.), 1:112–114.
[130] Quoted in Wharton, ed., *State Trials,* p. 88.

law of crimes. But Chase's associate in Worrall's case, Judge Peters, expressed his disagreement, and the jury convicted.[131] Chase's opinion remained unique until it was later adopted by the Supreme Court in 1812.

A few months after Worrall's case, but before the Sedition Act was passed, common-law prosecutions for the crime of seditious libel were begun in the two cases of Benjamin F. Bache and John Burk, editors. Bache died before trial and Burk, an alien, settled his case out of court by promising to quit the country. Bache's trial would have been before Judge Peters; Burk's before Justice Paterson.[132] Earlier, in 1797, there had even been an abortive attempt to try Congressman Samuel J. Cabell of Virginia for seditious libel. A federal grand jury in Richmond, stirred by a charge from Justice Iredell against the "unsettling tendencies" of letters to their constituents published by certain congressmen, presented Cabell for disseminating "unfounded calumnies against the unhappy government of the United States. . . ." Attorney-General Charles Lee prepared a memorandum on "Libellous Publications" in which he first quoted Blackstone and then Mansfield to the effect that the liberty of the press consists in printing without prior restraint, adding, "in this definition I concur with the learned judge." [133] Jefferson and Madison prepared a resolution, adopted by the Virginia House of Delegates, condemning the presentment of Cabell as a violation of the

[131] U.S. v. Worrall, 2 Dallas 384 (1798), in Wharton, ed., *State Trials*, 189–199, discussed in Warren, *Supreme Court*, 1:433–434, and Beveridge, *Marshall*, 3:28 note 2.

[132] Smith, *Freedom's Fetters*, ch. 10, "Common Law Indictments," pp. 188–220, is an excellent discussion of these cases.

[133] July 27, 1797, in Benjamin F. Hall, ed., *Official Opinions of the Attorneys General of the United States* (Washington, 1852), 1:72.

principles of representation and "a subjection of a natural right of speaking and writing freely." [134] As a result of this protest, perhaps, the presentment was allowed to die by the federal authorities; Cabell was never tried. But the incident revealed Justice Iredell's belief that the federal courts possessed jurisdiction over the common-law crime of seditious libel.

Iredell explained his position at great length in 1799 when he announced to a federal grand jury that the First Amendment declared the common law as expounded by Blackstone. Stating that every government in the world possessed a power to punish seditious libel, Iredell added, "It is unquestionably possessed by all the State governments, and probably has been exercised in all of them: sure I am, it has in some. If necessary and proper for them, why not equally so, at least, for the government of the United States. . . ." [135] Turning to the First Amendment, he declared:

> We derive our principles of law originally from England. There, the press, I believe, is as free as in any country of the world, and so it has been for near a century. The definition of it is, in my opinion, no where more happily or justly expressed than by the great author of the commentaries on the laws of England, which book deserves more particular regard on this occasion, because for nearly thirty years it has been the manual of almost every student

[134] On Cabell's case, see Manning J. Dauer, *The Adams Federalists* (Baltimore, 1953), p. 154, and Adrienne Koch and Harry Ammon, "The Virginia and Kentucky Resolutions: an Episode in Jefferson's and Madison's Defense of Civil Liberties," *William and Mary Quarterly*, 3rd ser., 5:152–153 (April 1948).

[135] Charge to the Grand Jury by Iredell, April 11, 1799, in "Trial of the Northampton Insurgents. In the Circuit Court of the United States for the Pennsylvania District," Wharton, ed., *State Trials*, p. 476.

of law in the United States, and its uncommon excellence has also introduced it into the libraries, and often to the favourite reading of private gentlemen; so that his views of the subject could scarcely be unknown to those who framed the Amendments to the Constitution: and if they were not, unless his explanation had been satisfactory, I presume the amendment would have been more particularly worded, to guard against any possible mistake. His explanation is as follows: . . . [long quotation from Blackstone].

It is believed that, in every State in the Union, the common law principles concerning libels apply; and in some of the States words similar to the words of the Amendment are used in the Constitution itself, or a contemporary Bill of Rights, of equal authority, without ever being supposed to exclude any law being passed on the subject. So that there is the strongest proof that can be of a universal concurrence in America on this point, that the freedom of the press does not require libellers shall be protected from punishment.[136]

In the last of the eighteenth-century cases, Chief Justice Ellsworth began an opinion of 1799, sustaining an indictment for violation of a federal treaty, by saying, "The common law of this country remains the same as it was before the Revolution." [137] The chief justice also informed a federal grand jury that they might indict for "acts manifestly subversive of the National Government. . . . An offense consists in transgressing the sovercign will, whether that will be expressed, or obviously implied. Conduct, therefore, clearly destructive of a government or its powers,

[136] *Ibid.*, pp. 478–479.
[137] "Trial of Isaac Williams" (1799), reported originally in the *Connecticut Courant*, Sept. 30, 1799, and reprinted in Wharton, ed., *State Trials*, pp. 652–654. The line quoted is at p. 653. Discussed in Warren, *Supreme Court*, 1:159–160.

which the people have ordained to exist, must be criminal."
He expressly added that the indictable offense need be
defined only by common law, not statute.[138]

Before 1812 there were several other cases in which federal courts accepted jurisdiction over common-law crimes.
The only cases worth mention were those arising in Connecticut where six persons were indicted for the same
offense: seditiously libeling the president of the United
States in speech or press. The prosecution in four of the
cases was ultimately dropped, but the cases of two editors,
on demurrer to the jurisdiction of the federal circuit court,
were brought together before the Supreme Court. Justice
Johnson, speaking for the "majority," ruled in a brief opinion that the question whether the United States courts
"can exercise a common law jurisdiction in criminal cases"
had been "settled in public opinion" which long opposed
such jurisdiction. Moreover, the Constitution had not expressly delegated to the federal courts authority over common-law crimes. "The legislative authority of the Union
must first make an act a crime, affix a punishment to it,
and declare the Court that shall have jurisdiction of the
offense." [139]

Justice Story, who had not made known his dissent at
the time, did so in a circuit opinion the following year,[140]
thus forcing a reconsideration of the rule of the Hudson-
Goodwin case; but on the appeal, in *United States* v. *Cool-*

[138] Quoted in Warren, *Supreme Court*, 1:162, from *Independent Chronicle* (Boston), June 13, 1799.

[139] U.S. v. Hudson and Goodwin, 7 Cranch 32, 34 (1812). W. W.
Crosskey, *Politics and the Constitution* (Chicago, 1953), 2:782,
claims that Chief Justice Marshall and Justices Story and Washington dissented from Johnson's opinion without noting the fact
of their dissent on the record.

[140] U.S. v. Coolidge, 1 Gallison 488 (1813).

idge, decided 1816, Justice Johnson, though noting that the Court was divided, refused to review his own precedent.[141] In both cases it is an extraordinary fact that there were no arguments of counsel. Hence, the great question was decided without reasoned consideration by bench or bar. The decisions of 1812 and 1816, when contrasted with the many federal indictments for common-law crimes, including the crime of seditious libel, leave historians in doubt about the true intentions of the Framers. It is noteworthy that Justices Wilson, Paterson, and Ellsworth, who accepted jurisdiction of common-law crimes, were among a select group of the most influential members of the Constitutional Convention of 1787, while Justices Jay and Iredell, who accepted similar jurisdiction, were major figures closely associated with the Framers. Hamilton and Randolph, who played important roles in the government's prosecution of Henfield, were also giants among the Framers. But no one can prove that in 1787 or 1789 any of them intended the existence of a federal common law of crimes. Indeed, any evidence drawn from the period after 1791, at the latest, should be discounted in any determination of the *original* understanding of the First Amendment.

Among the untrustworthy evidence is that relating to the controversy over the Sedition Act of 1798. It is true that on most questions concerning the meaning of the free speech-and-press clause, one can find a full-dress debate in the *Annals of Congress* for 1798, supplemented by newspaper comment, related tracts and books, the arguments of counsel in Sedition Act trials, the Virginia and Kentucky Resolutions and accompanying debates, and Madison's "Report on the Virginia Resolutions." For the first

[141] U.S. v. Coolidge, 1 Wheaton 415 (1816), discussed in Warren, *Supreme Court*, 1:440.

time our public men of the generation of the Framers expressed themselves with force, clarity, and elaborate detail on the meaning and limitations of freedom of speech and press; on the powers of Congress under the First Amendment; on the reserved powers of the states in reference to seditious and other criminal libels; on the question whether the First Amendment left the common law in force or superseded it; and on the existence of a federal common law of crimes. A full discussion of all these matters may be based on an analysis of the controversy over the Sedition Act. But as a revelation of prior opinion, the debate of 1798 and after is suspect.

Views expressed during that acrimonious time are untrustworthy because they were distinctly *ad hoc* in character and because partisans were even less motivated by principle and precedent than usual. They argued from personal and party interests. Not a single Federalist in the United States is known to have opposed the constitutionality of the Sedition Act, while the only Federalist who doubted the wisdom of the Act was John Marshall.[142] Every Democratic-Republican with the exception of James Sullivan believed it to be unconstitutional.[143] Eminent judges of our own time, including Holmes, Brandeis, Black, Douglas, Jackson, and others, have expressed that opinion.[144] But every member of the Supreme Court in 1798–1800, in rulings on circuit, thought otherwise.[145] It is no coincidence that all members of the Court at that time were Federalists. If Federalist statements of 1798–1800 cannot be accepted

---

[142] Smith, *Freedom's Fetters*, pp. 150–155.

[143] For Sullivan's views, see below, pp. 289–293.

[144] See above, pp. 1–2.

[145] See the index to Smith, *Freedom's Fetters*, under the names of the individual justices, Ellsworth, Chase, Cushing, Iredell, Paterson, and Washington, for citations to cases.

as evidence of opinion in 1791 or earlier, the pronouncements of the Jeffersonians must also be rejected. Had any of the latter declared at any time before 1791, or before the onset of the Sedition Act controversy, some of the opinions which they formed in the party battle of 1798–1800, their later statements would not be as suspect. That they were sincere in 1798 is not to be doubted, but sincerity is no test of prior intention. Nor is it a test of consistency; many of the Jeffersonians, most notably Jefferson himself, behaved when in power in ways that belied their fine libertarian sentiments of 1798. James Madison, the most influential of all the Framers, is possibly the one person of outstanding distinction whose record is clean and consistent. Perhaps Albert Gallatin's name should be joined with Madison's, but there is no proof that any of the libertarian propositions advanced by them during the 1798–1800 period were believed in or thought of by either at an earlier date. Madison's towering authority and integrity, combined with the power of his arguments, could not in any event do more than deadlock the debate, since the admission of his testimony as evidence of prior understanding necessarily requires the admission of Federalist testimony from John Adams, William Paterson, Oliver Ellsworth, and others whose opinions on our fundamental law and the intentions of the Framers can hardly be dismissed. The result of such a constitutional Donnybrook would be inconclusive, leading to the proposition that we do not know what the First Amendment's freedom of speech-and-press clause meant to the men who drafted and ratified it at the time that they did so. Moreover, they themselves were at that time sharply divided and possessed no clear understanding either. If, however, a choice must be made between two propositions, first, that the clause substantially

embodied the Blackstonian definition and left the law of
seditious libel in force, or second, that it repudiated Blackstone and superseded the common law, the known evidence
points strongly in support of the former proposition. Contrary to Justice Holmes,[146] history favors the notion.

[146] In Abrams v. U.S., 250 U.S. 616, 630 (1919), Holmes, with
Brandeis concurring, wrote: "I wholly disagree with the argument
of the Government that the First Amendment left the common law
as to seditious libel in force. History seems to me against that notion." On an earlier occasion, when times were more settled and
Brandeis' influence was not yet felt, Holmes said with greater historical accuracy, in reference to freedom of press clauses: "The main
purpose of such constitutional provisions is to prevent all such
previous restraints as had been practised by other governments,
and they do not prevent the subsequent punishment of such as
may be deemed contrary to the public welfare." (Patterson v.
Colorado, 205 U.S. 454, 462 [1907].)

CHAPTER SIX

ᝍᕪ The Emergence of an American Libertarian Theory

The Sedition Act debates are unreliable as evidence of the Framers' original understanding of freedom of speech and press. But the statute provoked American libertarians to formulate a broad definition of the meaning and scope of liberty of expression for the first time in our history. As usual, however, an avante-garde movement had its origins in England where the trial in 1783 of the Dean of St. Asaph for seditious libel [1] touched off a flurry of libertarian writings. Thomas Erskine, the counsel for the defense who emerged from the case the acknowledged leader of England's libertarians, denied that the press was truly free under prevailing common-law doctrines and procedures:

> For how can it be said that the press is free because everything may be published without a previous licence, if the publisher . . . may be prosecuted by information of the King's Attorney-General, without the consent of the Grand Jury, — may be convicted by the petty jury, on the mere fact of publishing . . . and must then depend upon judges who may be the supporters of the very Adminis-

[1] Howell's *State Trials*, 21:846.

tration whose measures are questioned by the defendant, and who must therefore either give judgment against him or against themselves.[2]

Erskine, as a close reading of his famous argument indicates, never actually proposed more than the power of juries to decide the criminality of the accused's statement, but his exhilarating forensics conveyed the impression that the cause of a free press had found a new David, and the libertarians rallied round him. In 1784 and 1785, books and tracts appeared by Joseph Towers,[3] James Adair,[4] Sir Samuel Romilly,[5] Manasseh Dawes,[6] and Capel Lofft,[7] popularizing the views of Erskine and his great predecessor, Father of Candor.

The new generation of English libertarians mainly championed truth as a defense and the power of juries. Lofft, a rationalist leader who wrote with considerable power, came to the verge of repudiating the concept of seditious libel altogether, an unprecedented step, but drew back from the abyss at the last moment. Having defended the right severely to censure public men and measures, and having denied that "the most artful and daring libeller can shake a Government worthy of public confidence," he declared

[2] "Argument, in the King's Bench, in support of the Rights of Juries," 1784, in *Speeches of Thomas Lord Erskine. Reprinted from the Five Volume Octavo Edition of 1810. With a Memoir of His Life* by Edward Walford (London, 1870), 1:190–191.

[3] *Observations on the Rights and Duty of Juries, in Trials for Libels,* 1784, reprinted in Towers' *Tracts on Political and Other Subjects* (London, 1796), 2:1–174.

[4] *Discussions of the Law of Libels As at Present Received* (London, 1785), 97 pp.

[5] *A Fragment of the Constitutional Power and Duty of Juries Upon Trials for Libels* (London, n. d., [1785]), 16 pp.

[6] *The Deformity of the Doctrine of Libels, and Informations Ex-Officio* (London, 1785), 40 pp.

[7] *An Essay on the Law of Libels* (London, 1785), 110 pp.

that in the code of a free people who share political rights, have full information on the operations of the government, and free investigation of its measures, "it would be no surprize if the very title of Libel were not to be found." [8] Yet when he enumerated his proposed reforms in cases of crown libel, he left the common law intact except for the power of the jury to judge an accused's criminal intent and the libelous character of his utterance. Adair, a Whig member of Parliament and a sergeant-at-law, fleetingly endorsed the view, last proposed by Francis Maseres and Jeremy Bentham, that the bad-tendency test of words should be scrapped and that only "actual" or "positive" injuries to the public rather than "presumed" ones should be punished. [9]

It was Manasseh Dawes, however, who was the first to elaborate on the repressiveness of the bad-tendency test and advocate in considerable detail the overt-acts test in cases of political libel. [10] Comparable remarks by Father of Candor, Bentham, Maseres, and Adair had been brief and undeveloped. Dawes, a Whig barrister of the Inner Temple, made their view the foundation of his whole discussion of the right of political criticism as had Furneaux in respect to religious criticism. Dawes even conscripted Coke as an authority for his proposition that sedition can never be committed by words, but only by "violent act," [11] an achievement in the technique of citing precedents that was

[8] *Ibid.*, pp. 60 and 61.
[9] *Discussions of the Law of Libels*, pp. 27–28.
[10] *The Deformity of the Doctrine of Libels*, pp. 11–24 and 28. Theodore Schroeder, *Constitutional Free Speech* (New York, 1919), pp. 419–421, claims wrongly that Robert Morris in 1770, Joseph Fownes in 1773, and Richard Price in 1777 endorsed the overt-acts test, but wholly ignores Manasseh Dawes.
[11] Dawes, *The Deformity of the Doctrine of Libels*, p. 13.

worthy of some of Sir Edward's own inventions. Although the tenor of Dawes's remarks clashed fundamentally with the very concept of seditious libel, he at no point explicitly rejected it. The only interpretation of his thesis that allows it consistency is that he would not, contrary to his own assertions, restrict punishment to the commission of overt acts only, but would punish verbal incitements resulting in crime. There is no other way to reconcile his endorsement of the overt-acts test with his concern for the procedures to be followed in all trials for seditious libel. His tract must therefore be construed as a proposal for a new standard of criminality that should be the guide in cases of verbal crime against the government. Dawes may not have been the most radical English libertarian of the seventeenth and eighteenth centuries — that accolade belongs to Bentham, but he was nearly so and the most sensible and most modern-minded of all. Only Maseres, whose tract was marred by contradictory propositions, rivals Dawes as one who might be at home among twentieth-century libertarians who defend freedom for all expression that falls short of advocating and causing, directly and immediately, the commission of crime.

The efforts of Dawes, Erskine, and indeed of all the English libertarians since Cato were rewarded in 1792 with the enactment of Fox's Libel Act, which embodied their one most insistent demand, that the jury be empowered to give a general verdict on the whole matter put in issue in trials of criminal libel. The libertarian value of the reform was promptly demonstrated by unjustifiable verdicts of guilty returned by juries in a mass of cases. It is a curious coincidence that in England, as in the United States six years later, the largest wave of prosecutions for seditious libel in the nation's history immediately followed the enactment of the libertarian reform. The explanation, of course, lies with the impact of the ideas of the French Revolution upon public opinion in both Britain and America. The governments in both countries, determined to crush their political opposition, regarded criticism as subversion. There are more trials for seditious utterances reported in the *State Trials* for the two years following Fox's Libel Act than the total number reported for the whole of the eighteenth century before that time.[12] Within a year of Fox's Libel Act the attorney-general declared that he had on file two hundred informations for seditious libel.[13] The most notorious conviction was that against Tom Paine for publishing his *Rights of Man*.[14] Duffin and Lloyd were convicted of seditious libel for having pasted a placard on the door of their debtor's prison alleging that liberty would commence in Great Britain when infamous bastilles, as France had shown, were no longer necessary.[15] A jury voted guilty against John Frost, an attorney, for his remarks, probably uttered when tipsy, that he was for equality, no king, and a better constitution. Frost was disbarred and pilloried as well as imprisoned for his conversation.[16] Winterbotham, a Baptist minister, commented favorably on the French Revolution and condemned oppressive taxes in his sermons, resulting in his conviction for seditious words and a sentence of four years and steep fines. In this case the jury

[12] Sir James Stephen, *A History of the Criminal Law of England* (London, 1883), 2:362–363.
[13] Sir Thomas Erskine May, *The Constitutional History of England* (New York, 1880), 2:142 note 2.
[14] Rex v. Paine, Howell's *State Trials*, 22:357 (1792).
[15] Rex v. Duffin and Lloyd, Howell's *State Trials*, 22:318 (1792).
[16] Rex v. Frost, Howell's *State Trials*, 22:471 (1793).

convicted against the court's recommendation of an acquittal.[17] The cases of Briellat, Hudson, Muir, Palmer, Skirving, Margarot, and Gerrald in 1793 and 1794 were similar to those already mentioned. In each the juries returned verdicts of guilty for seditious words, oral or printed, that were harmless and hardly even intemperate.[18] In a couple of cases, those of Lambert and of Eaton,[19] there were acquittals or verdicts of "guilty of publishing only," but the English sedition trials, like the American ones a few years later, proved conclusively that making juries judges of the criminality of allegedly seditious words did not have the effect of broadening the scope of free discussion, certainly not during times of stress — and there are rarely sedition trials at any other times.[20]

The most notable published protest against these trials was the Reverend Robert Hall's *An Apology for the Freedom of the Press*.[21] Hall's position was that all men should have an absolute liberty of discussing "every subject which can fall within the compass of the human mind," and he meant what he said without any ifs or buts. Like Furneaux and Jefferson, he denied that the magistrate had a power to

[17] Rex v. Winterbotham, Howell's *State Trials*, 22:875 (1793).

[18] Each of the cases, with citations to the *State Trials*, is discussed by May, *Constitutional History of England*, 2:142–150. Muir's case is also discussed in Arthur E. Sutherland, Jr., "British Trials for Disloyal Association during the French Revolution," *Cornell Law Quarterly*, 34:309–315 (Spring 1949).

[19] Rex v. Lambert, Perry, and Gray, Howell's *State Trials*, 22:953 (1793), and Rex v. Eaton, *State Trials*, 22:753 (1793).

[20] The most notable acquittals during the 1790's in England were in cases of treason, not sedition. See the discussion of the trials of Hardy and Tooke in Sutherland, "British Trials," *Cornell Law Quarterly*, 34:316–328.

[21] Issued as a tract in 1793. I used the reprint in John Foster, ed., *The Miscellaneous Works and Remains of the Reverend Robert Hall* (London, 1846), pp. 159–233.

punish the mere expression of opinions, but unlike their statements which appeared in contexts of defending religious opinions, Hall's was particularly concerned with political opinions, as was Dawes's. Distinguishing words, sentiment, and opinion from "conduct" or "behavior," he demanded that only the latter be regarded as criminal.[22] He made an otherwise commonplace point that freedom of expression is to be cherished as a step to the truth by noting that opinions of social value were frequently mixed with error. Publications, he stated, "like every thing else that is human, are of a mixed nature, where truth is often blended with falsehood, and important hints suggested in the midst of much impertinent or pernicious matter; nor is there any way of separating the precious from the vile, but by tolerating the whole." [23] This observation may seem obvious now, but it was original and cogent in its time, when men as sensible as John Adams and William Cushing could agree even in a moment of calm that falsehood was criminal if published against the government. In England, when Hall wrote, and in America after the Sedition Act, men were jailed for snatch phrases or sentences culled from lengthy remarks and condemned as false. Hall's thought must be measured for its courage and libertarianism in the context of the repressive prosecutions that were sweeping England when he wrote:

> [Government] being an institution purely human, one would imagine it were the proper province for freedom of discussion in its utmost extent. It is surely just that every one should have a right to examine those measures by which the happiness of all may be affected. . . . Under pretence of its being seditious to express any disapprobation

[22] *Ibid.*, p. 172.
[23] *Ibid.*

of the *form* of our government, the most alarming attempts are made to wrest the liberty of the press out of our hands. . . . An inquiry respecting the comparative excellence of civil constitutions can be forbidden on no other pretence than that of its tending to sedition and anarchy. This plea, however, will have little weight with those who reflect to how many ill purposes it has already applied; and that when the example has been introduced of suppressing opinions on account of their imagined ill tendency, it has seldom been confined within any safe or reasonable bounds. . . . The law hath amply provided against overt acts of sedition and disorder, and to suppress mere opinions by any other method than reason and argument, is the height of tyranny. Freedom of thought being intimately connected with the happiness and dignity of man in every stage of his being, is of so much more importance than the preservation of any constitution, that to infringe the former, under pretence of supporting the latter, is to sacrifice the means to the end.[24]

Erskine himself in his justly celebrated defense of Paine against a charge of seditious libel provided Hall with an immediate model, for the great lawyer had argued, "His [Paine's] *opinions* indeed were adverse to our system; but I maintain that OPINION is free, and that CONDUCT alone is amenable to the law." This statement had been preceded by the declaration that every man ought to be free to publish "what his own reason and conscience, however erroneously, have dictated to him as truth" on all political subjects.[25] Erskine repeated similar views in Frost's trial,[26] but there as in Paine's trial his further remarks modified his seeming endorsement of the overt-acts test. He regarded the calumny of living magistrates as criminal.

[24] *Ibid.*, pp. 174, 176–177, and 179.
[25] *Speeches of Erskine*, 1:313 and 309.
[26] *Ibid.*, 1:392.

In the same class he placed contumacious private judgment and words spoken with a premeditated design of "undermining" the government. He also believed that "time or occasion" may mix with words and invest otherwise innocent expressions with an "enormous guilt." [27]

But no man in American history had as yet approached Erskine's libertarianism in the cases of Paine and Frost, let alone match Dawes and Hall, or even Maseres and Adair, in their defense of freedom of political criticism against the doctrines of seditious libel. Between the publication of the works of Dawes and Hall in England, America adopted the Constitution and the First Amendment. What American tracts or essays had appeared on the subject of speech and press during that time? Franklin's 1789 essay on the press, discussed in the preceding chapter, was of such a character that it was quoted at length by supporters of the Sedition Act during the House debate in 1798, and no opponent of the Act even tried to explain that the damaging testimony from Franklin meant other than it seemed.[28] The only other American contribution was an anonymous tract of 1789, published in Boston, by "a Friend to Harmony" who addressed himself exclusively to the problem of personal libels against public men.[29] His viewpoint was

[27] *Ibid.*, 1:309–310 (Paine's trial) and 380. (Frost's trial). Erskine's tolerance for political criticism did not extend to religious criticism. In 1797 he abandoned his defense of freedom of the press by prosecuting the publisher of Paine's *Age of Reason,* a defense of Deism which he deemed an unlawful attack upon the Christian religion. Rex v. Williams, Howell's *State Trials,* 26:654 (1797).
[28] *Annals of Congress,* 5th Cong., 2nd session, pp. 2102, 2169.
[29] *Candid Considerations on Libels . . . With Some Observations on the Liberty of the Press.* By a Friend to Harmony (Boston, 1789), 22 pp. The only other American tract which I have found is Samuel Stanhope Smith's *A Sermon on Slander delivered at the church on Brattle St., Boston, Oct. 24, 1790* (Boston, 1791),

certainly a libertarian one, since he insisted that "a law against libels cannot exist without endangering the liberty of the press." [30] The thesis of the tract was that libels, being addressed to public opinion, should be answered in the press, leaving the public to judge the truth. But the writer wholly ignored the problem of libels on the government, with the result that his contribution to libertarian thought on the subject of seditious utterance was slight. Nor was the American contribution in formal debates any greater than in publications, for we have seen that the recorded pronouncements of the members of state ratifying conventions who defined freedom of the press were Blackstonian in character, as in the outstanding case of James Wilson.

Not until 1798 did any Americans rival the libertarianism of their English counterparts. The reason for the sudden if belated emergence of a sharply articulated body of "Jeffersonian" thought on freedom of speech and press was the threat that the government of the United States under the Adams administration might attempt to eliminate political criticism, create a one-party press in the country, and by controlling public opinion insure a Federalist victory in the elections of 1800. The Sedition Act made criminal "any false, scandalous and malicious" writings, utterances, or publications against the government, Congress, or the president, with intent to defame them, bring them into contempt or disrepute, or excite against them the hatred of the people. A defendant in any prosecution under the bill was permitted to give in evidence the truth of the

---

24 pp. Smith, the Vice President and Professor of Moral Philosophy at Princeton, was concerned with slander as a sin rather than as a crime. He rejected the notion that truth is not slanderous.

[30] *Candid Considerations,* p. 20.

matter charged as a libel, while the jury was empowered to determine the law and facts of the case.[31] In the course of the House debates, advocates of the bill clearly manifested their belief that the political opinion of the opposition party constituted seditious libel, subject to prosecution under the bill.[32] Representative Albert Gallatin of Pennsylvania accurately summed up the situation when he declared:

> This bill and its supporters suppose, in fact, that whoever dislikes the measures of Administration and of a temporary majority in Congress, and shall, either by speaking or writing, express his disapprobation and his want of confidence in the men now in power, is seditious, is an enemy, not of Administration, but of the Constitution, and is liable to punishment . . . this bill must be considered only as a weapon used by a party now in power in order to perpetuate their authority and preserve their present places. [33]

Under the pressure of the Sedition Act, which ironically was passed by the Senate on July 4, writers of the Jeffersonian party were driven to originate so broad a theory of

[31] *Statutes at Large*, 1:596–597, reprinted in J. M. Smith, *Freedom's Fetters; The Alien and Sedition Laws and American Civil Liberties* (Ithaca, 1956), Appendix, pp. 441–442.

[32] See, *e.g.*, Speech of Rep. Allen of Connecticut, July 5, 1798, *Annals of Congress*, 5th Cong., 2nd session, pp. 2093–2100; speech of Rep. Harper of South Carolina, July 5, *ibid.*, pp. 2102–2103.

[33] Speech of July 5, 1798, *ibid.*, p. 2110. On July 10, Gallatin observed that the bill's supporters admitted that its true object was "to enable one party to oppress the other. . . . Is it not their object to frighten and suppress all presses which they consider as contrary to their views; to prevent a free circulation of opinion; to suffer the people at large to hear only partial accounts, and but one side of the question; to delude and deceive them by partial information, and, through those means, to perpetuate themselves in power?" (*Ibid.*, p. 2162.) See also the speech of Nicholas of Virginia, pp. 2140–2141.

freedom of expression that the concept of seditious libel was, at last, repudiated.

In the Congressional debates the libertarians did not go that far, although they denounced the Federalist theory of freedom of expression as much too narrow, unwise, and contradictory to the First Amendment. Otis of Massachusetts had represented the Federalist theory when he delivered a speech based on the following theme: "This freedom . . . is nothing more than the liberty of writing, publishing, and speaking, one's thoughts, under the condition of being answerable to the injured party, whether it be the Government or an individual, for false, malicious, and seditious expressions, whether spoken or written; and the liberty of the press is merely an exemption from all previous restraints." [34] John Nicholas of Virginia denied, however, that there could be any satisfactory way of distinguishing liberty from "licentiousness" without abridging liberty itself; he rejected any distinctions based on "truth" versus "falsehood": offensive criticism of the government would invariably be deemed false. Printers, as a result, "would not only refrain from publishing anything of the least questionable nature, but they would be afraid of publishing the truth, as, though true, it might not always be in their power to establish the truth to the satisfaction of a court of justice." [35]

Gallatin, agreeing with Nicholas, may not have had history on his side but his reasoning now seems persuasively logical. Speaking of the First Amendment, he declared that

---

[34] Speech of July 10, *ibid.*, p. 2148. For similar statements by other Federalists, see pp. 2097 (Allen), 2102 and 2167–2168 (Harper), and 2112 (Dana).

[35] Speech of July 10, *ibid.*, pp. 2140–2141.

he and his friends understood it to mean that Congress could not pass *any* law punishing "any real or supposed abuse of the press." He continued:

The construction given to it by the supporters of the bill was, that it did not prevent them to punish what they called the licentiousness of the press, but merely forbade their laying any previous restraints upon it. It appeared to him preposterous to say, that to punish a certain act was not an abridgement [*sic*] of the liberty of doing that act. It appeared to him that it was an insulting evasion of the Constitution for gentlemen to say, 'We claim no power to abridge the liberty of the press; *that*, you shall enjoy unrestrained. You may write and publish what you please, but if you publish anything against us, we will punish you for it. So long as we do not prevent, but only punish your writings, it is no abridgment of your liberty of writing and printing.'

. . . That amendment [the First] provided against the passing of any law abridging either the liberty of the press or the freedom of speech; and a sound construction must be such as to be applicable to both. But that contended for, to wit, that the only prohibition was that of passing any law laying previous restraints upon either, was absurd, so far as it related to speech; for it pre-supposed that Congress, by the Constitution, as it originally stood, might have passed laws laying such restraints upon speech; and what these possibly could have been, he was altogether at a loss to conceive, unless gentlemen chose to assert that the Constitution had given Congress a power to seal the mouths or to cut the tongues of the citizens of the Union; and these, however, were the only means by which previous restraints could be laid on the freedom of speech. Was it not evident, that, as speech could not be restrained, but might be punished, a Constitutional clause forbidding any abridgment of the freedom of speech must necessarily mean, not that no laws should be passed laying previous restraints upon it, but that no punishment should by law be inflicted upon it? [36]

Gallatin also supported Nicholas in answering the Federalist argument that the true liberty of the press was bounded by truth, that the bill reached only falsehoods, and that therefore it did not abridge the only kind of political criticism that the First Amendment protected. Animadversions on the government and its measures, replied Gallatin, almost always intermixed facts and opinions. "And how could the truth of opinions be proven by evidence?" If one who thought as he did, that the bill was unconstitutional and intended for party purposes, should publish that opinion and were prosecuted for doing so, a jury sympathetic with the administration would not hesitate to judge his opinion ungrounded, "or, in other words, false and scandalous" and therefore malicious.[37]

Gallatin and Nicholas were the first Americans on record to have rejected "truth" as an inadequate protection for the freedom of political opinion in cases of seditious libel; to put the thought another way, they were the first to discard "false" and "licentious" on ground that these were not meaningful or usable standards for the guidance of a jury weighing the lawfulness of an alleged verbal crime against the government. In this respect the remarks of the two congressmen were as sound as could be. So, too, was Gallatin's scornful repudiation of the Blackstonian definition of liberty of the press as grossly unprotective. He was also accurate in pointing out that the "no prior restraints" concept could never have applied to freedom of speech,[38]

[36] *Ibid.*, pp. 2160–2161.
[37] *Ibid.*, p. 2162.
[38] Later writers who have made the same point are Thomas M. Cooley, *Treatise on Constitutional Limitations Which Rest Upon*

although no one literally meant that it ever could have. The point of the Federalist argument on freedom of speech was not that it meant the absence of prior restraints but that one might say what he pleased subject to being responsible for malice, falsehood, sedition, and the like; in other words, that freedom of speech did not imply exemption from subsequent punishment for the abuse of "licentious" use of that freedom. The intolerable narrowness of this view of freedom of speech is unquestionable today, but it was not publicly questioned in America before Gallatin did so.[39] His exposure of the frailty of the argument that freedom of political expression implied freedom for "truth" only was an enormous achievement in spurring a "breakthrough" in American libertarian thought, as was his exposure of the repressive connotations of the Blackstonian "no prior restraints" formula.

Gallatin and his congressional colleagues did not, however, define the scope of permissible political expression. True enough, they hammered away at their main point

the *Legislative Power of the States,* ed. V. H. Lane (Boston, 1903, 17th ed.), pp. 603–604, and W. R. Vance, "Freedom of Speech and of the Press," *Minnesota Law Review,* 2:250 (March 1918). Vance, however, goes on to say, quite correctly, that freedom of speech, as originally understood, was "intended to mean that a citizen's right to express publicly his opinions concerning public men and events was to be unrestricted save as he might render himself liable to civil action for slander or criminal prosecution for treason or sedition in accordance with then existing common law rules." (*Ibid.*) I agree with Vance's statement except as to its reference to treason which the Framers did not regard as a crime that could be committed by words. I believe Vance was also wrong in concluding at p. 259 that the Framers intended the United States as well as the states to have the power to enact legislation against seditious utterances.

[39] William Cushing, in his private correspondence with John Adams, in 1789, had questioned the prior restraints concept but only in reference to political "truths." See above, pp. 193–195.

that under the First Amendment Congress could not enact any law effecting any degree of a restraint on speech or press, and they denied insistently that there was any jurisdiction in the federal courts over seditious libels. But they did not repudiate the concept of seditious libel and did not deny the power of the states to control speech and press. Gallatin, for instance, in the same speech in which he denounced "the law of political libels" as an instrument of tyranny and advocated open discussion as the only proper means of combatting error, admitted that prior to the bill under debate, "the cognizance of offences of this nature had exclusively belonged to the State courts. . . ."[40] Nicholas agreed.[41] Nathaniel Macon of North Carolina said of liberty of the press, "The States have complete power on the subject. . . ."[42] The last of the principal speakers against the bill made the point unanimous; Edward Livingston of New York declared, "There is a remedy for offenses of this kind in the laws of every State in the Union. Every man's character is protected by law, and every man who shall publish a libel on any part of the Government, is liable to punishment."[43] A moment later, however, Livingston added that there "ought to be" no power to protect the United States Government from verbal abuse; moreover that "when gentlemen speak of slanders against the Government, he knew of no such thing."[44] From the passage in which this statement appears, it seems that Livingston meant that there ought to be no power in the *national* government to protect itself from slander, for he was

[40] Speech of July 10, in *Annals of Congress*, 5th Cong., 2nd session, p. 2163.
[41] *Ibid.*, p. 2142.
[42] *Ibid.*, p. 2152, and see also p. 2106.
[43] *Ibid.*, p. 2153.
[44] *Ibid.*, p. 2154.

paraphrasing and answering the Federalist claim that the
Sedition Act was needed so that the United States could
protect itself against seditious libel. When he alleged that
he knew of no slanders against the United States, he was
simply denying that the Federalists' illustrations of slanders,
drawn from the Jeffersonian press, were slanderous.[45] It
is possible, of course, that the opponents of the Sedition
Act argued for an exclusive state jurisdiction over political
libels not because they believed in or wanted state prosecutions, but because such an argument was tactically useful as
a means of denying federal jurisdiction.[46] Nevertheless, an

[45] Smith, *Freedom's Fetters*, p. 149, states that Livingston meant
to repudiate the concept of seditious libel. He claims that Livingston was discussing "the nature of free speech," which is not so,
and like the other Republican speakers intended his arguments
against seditious libel to be applied "to state governments as well
as the federal government. . . . They made clear their belief that
political libels had been withdrawn from the realm of prosecution
by either the state or federal government." (*Ibid.*, p. 149.) Smith
states that until the Sedition Act was brought forward the cognizance of libels belonged exclusively to the state courts, a proposition supported in part by a citation to Gallatin's speech of July 10,
at p. 2164 of the *Annals*, 5th Cong., 2nd session. Smith does not
quote Gallatin's remark but confidently assures us at p. 148 note 21
that he "referred not to seditious libels, which he claimed could
not exist under a free government, but to defamatory libels against
personal reputations, obscenity, etc." These statements by Smith
are insupportable. Gallatin was explicitly discussing seditious libel
and no other kind and had just finished quoting the proposed
Sedition Act when he stated, "Heretofore the cognizance of
offences of this nature had exclusively belonged to the State
courts . . ." I find no statement by Gallatin that seditious libels
could not exist under a free government.

[46] See, *e.g.*, the case of the Jeffersonian theorist, Tunis Wortman,
in his *Treatise Concerning Political Enquiry, and the Liberty of
the Press* (New York, 1800), pp. 229–230, where he alleged that if
the coercion of libels be necessary or proper "our state legislatures
and tribunals are possessed of sufficient authority to remedy the
evil . . . the States respectively should solely exercise the power

assertion of state control over speech and press is scarcely compatible with a supposed intention to exempt either from subsequent punishment for abuse.

The Kentucky Resolutions of 1798, drafted by Jefferson, affirmed, for instance, that no power over the freedom of speech or press having been delegated to the United States by the Constitution, "nor prohibited by it to the states, all lawful powers respecting the same did of right remain, and were reserved to the states, or to the people; that thus was manifested their determination to retain to themselves the right of judging how far the licentiousness of speech, and of the press, may be abridged without lessening their useful freedom. . . ."[47] Madison in 1799 said of the Sedition Act that "from the existence of state law, it is inferred that Congress possess a similar power of legislation," an inference of a "concurrent power" which he denounced as a "death-wound on the sovereignty of the States." The laws for the correction of calumny were not defective, he added, because, "Every libellous writing or expression might receive its punishment in the State courts. . . ."[48] Jefferson himself cleared away any doubt about his opinion on this issue when he wrote, in 1804:

---

of controuling the conduct of their own citizens in such cases. . . ." Yet it is not questionable that Wortman opposed the concept of seditious libel and would never support a prosecution for mere words. For a discussion of Wortman, see below, pp. 283–288.

[47] Reprinted in Jonathan Elliot, ed., *The Debates in the Several State Conventions . . . and Other Illustrations of the Constitution* (Philadelphia, 1941, 2nd ed., rev.), 4:540–541.

[48] "Address of the General Assembly to the People of the Commonwealth of Virginia," Jan. 23, 1799, a document accompanying the Virginia Resolutions of 1799, in *The Writings of James Madison*, ed. Gaillard Hunt (New York, 1900–1910), 6:333–334. Whether "Every libellous writing" was meant to include libels against the government and Constitution as well as against public officers is not clear from the context of the statement.

Nor does the opinion of the unconstitutionality and consequent nullity of that law [the Sedition Act] remove all restraint from the overwhelming torrent of slander which is confounding all vice and virtue, all truth and falsehood in the US. The power to do that is fully possessed by the several state legislatures. It was reserved to them, and was denied to the general government, by the constitution according to our construction of it. While we deny that Congress have a right to controul the freedom of the press, we have ever asserted the right of the states, and their exclusive right to do so.[49]

Thus even as the Jeffersonians flatly repudiated the Blackstonian and Federalist theories of freedom of speech and press, they seemed to have reservations about the unlimited application of their own theory in the realm of state law. It would be misleading not to represent their theory of freedom of expression as inextricably part of their theory of federalism. In other words, that they believed a federal common-law prosecution for seditious libel to be illegal did not mean that they also believed a similar prosecution in the state courts to be illegal; that they argued the unconstitutionality of the Sedition Act did not mean that they would have deemed unconstitutional a similar statute enacted by a state legislature. More than likely, however, they would have regarded such a statute as unwise and dangerous public policy, whether constitutional or not.

The widely reported speeches of Gallatin, Livingston, Macon, and Nicholas, during the House debates on the Sedition Act, and the Virginia and Kentucky Resolutions launched the emergence of a new libertarianism in Amer-

[49] Jefferson to Abigail Adams, Sept. 4, 1804, in *The Writings of Thomas Jefferson*, ed. Paul Leicester Ford (New York, 1892–1899), 10:90.

ica. In its initial phase it was expressed in brief, disjointed fashion in the rapid fire of parliamentary give-and-take. But reflective and systematic expositions of considerable length were soon published in the form of tracts or books. The one exception was the scholarly argument of George Blake, counsel for Abijah Adams who was tried at common law for seditious libel against the Commonwealth of Massachusetts in 1799. Blake's argument, which has been summarized in a preceding chapter, filled several long columns in each of eight consecutive issues of the Boston *Independent Chronicle*.[50] His thesis was that the concept of seditious libel, being repugnant to the spirit and genius of a republican form of government, could not have been received with the main body of the common law in a state whose constitution guaranteed freedom of the press. Shortly before the publication of Blake's argument, George Hay wrote *An Essay on the Liberty of the Press*.[51] Early in 1800 appeared James Madison's lengthy *Report* for the Virginia House of Delegates on the Alien and Sedition Acts.[52] In the

[50] Issues of the *Chronicle* dated from April 8–11 through April 29–May 2, 1799, summarized above, pp. 210–211. Each issue of the *Chronicle* carried a dateline covering a four-day period, the interval between issues.

[51] Hortensius, *An Essay on the Liberty of the Press. Respectfully Inscribed to the Republican Printers Throughout the United States* (Philadelphia, 1799), 51 pp. The first time that I consulted this tract, I used the original edition just cited; my references, however, are to the 1803 Richmond reprinting to which I had easier access for the purpose of note-taking. The reprinting was set in smaller type (30 pp.), but is otherwise the same as the original edition.

[52] The *Report* appeared originally as a tract of over eighty pages. I looked at the copy in the Langdell Treasure Room, Harvard Law Library, which is bound together with the 1799 issue of Hay's *Essay*, but have used and cited the reproduction in Elliot, ed., *Debates*, 4:546–580, under the title, "Madison's Report on the Virginia Resolutions . . . Report of the Committee to whom

same year Tunis Wortman published his *Treatise Concerning Political Enquiry, and the Liberty of the Press.*[53] In the following year appeared James Sullivan's *A Dissertation upon the Press in the United States of America*[54] and John Thomson's *An Enquiry, Concerning the Liberty, and Licentiousness of the Press, and the Uncontroulable Nature of the Human Mind.*[55] In 1803 Hay republished his tract of 1799 and a completely new one with a similar title,[56] while St. George Tucker devoted an appendix of his edition of Blackstone's *Commentaries* to the subject of freedom of speech and press.[57]

Blake's newspaper argument, the tracts by Hay, Sullivan, and Thomson, and the book by Wortman are quite rare and little known among historians. Tucker's appendix and to a much greater degree Madison's *Report* are easily accessible, but have infrequently been referred to. Taken together these are the sources which compose the main body of original and significant Jeffersonian thought on freedom of speech-and-press.

Hay, a member of the Virginia House of Delegates and

---

were referred the Communications of various States, relative to the Resolutions of the last General Assembly of this State, concerning the Alien and Sedition Laws." The Report is also available in *The Writings of Madison*, 6:341–406, and in a number of early printings. The *Report* was written by Madison in late 1799, adopted by the state legislature on Jan. 11, 1800, and published immediately after.

[53] (New York, 1800), 296 pp.
[54] Published anonymously "By an Impartial Citizen" (Boston, 1801), 54 pp.
[55] New York, 1801), 84 pp.
[56] *An Essay on the Liberty of the Press, Shewing, That the Requisition of Security for Good Behaviour from Libellers, is Perfectly Compatible with the Constitution and Laws of Virginia* (Richmond, 1803), 48 pp.
[57] Philadelphia, 1803), I, part II, note G, pp. 11–30 of Appendix.

son-in-law of James Monroe, became a United States attorney under Jefferson, gained fame as the prosecutor in Burr's trial for treason, and later was appointed to the federal bench. Two thirds of his first essay on the liberty of the press was a carefully wrought attack on the constitutionality of the Sedition Act. The last third of the essay is of greater interest since he addressed himself to the intentions of the Framers of the First Amendment and the meaning of freedom of political expression. As a libertarian theorist, Hay was an absolutist, one of the earliest of the new-style American radicals for whom the concept of a verbal political crime was abhorrent. Jefferson himself was to provide their standard when he declared in his First Inaugural Address, "If there be any among us who would wish to dissolve this Union or to change its republican form, let them stand undisturbed as monuments of the safety with which error of opinion may be tolerated where reason is left free to combat it." Hay might have regarded this statement as too moderate, for he explicitly favored complete freedom for licentiousness, falsehood, and error, even if maliciously motivated and harmful.[58] Of freedom of speech he wrote, "A man may say every thing which his passions suggest; he may employ all his time, and all his talents, if he is wicked enough to do so, in *speaking* against the government matters that are false, scandalous, and malicious . . ." without being subject to prosecution.[59] Although the statement appeared in the context of a passage on the First Amendment, Hay believed in the same scope of freedom under state law. His second essay on the subject focused on the law of Virginia, and in that context he

[58] *An Essay on the Liberty of the Press* (1799), pp. 22–23, 25, and 27 of the 1803 edition.
[59] *Ibid.*, p. 25.

claimed that no person could be punished for his opinions, however absurd "or immoral in their tendency" on any subject whatever, nor for malicious untruths. One was "safe within the sanctuary of the press" even if he condemned republican institutions, censured the state government and every officer of it, ascribed its measures and their conduct to the basest motives, and lied outright in doing so. These, said Hay, were all matters of public concern affecting the rights and interests of the people, and were therefore placed by the free-press clause of the state constitution "in the open field of discussion" without any limits. Those who had framed that constitution knew "that this field would be often occupied by folly, malignity, treachery, and ambition; but they knew too that intelligence and patriotism would always be on the spot in the hour of danger, and to make *their* entrance at all times easy and secure, it was left open to all." [60] Hay drew the line only at libels of private reputations.

Observing that there were only two kinds of freedom, "absolute" or "uncontrouled" versus "qualified or abridged," Hay attempted to prove as a matter of logic but without the grace of historical evidence that the Framers must have intended the former freedom when guaranteeing freedom of speech and press. A qualified freedom, he explained, meant a privilege, not a right, that might be restrained or regulated by law as the public good might require in the opinion of the legislature. If the Framers meant that, "they meant nothing" and the First Amendment was superfluous, "the grossest absurdity that was ever conceived by the human mind." What they did mean, as to speech, was that all citizens should have the same right to express themselves as congressmen themselves had, totally

[60] *An Essay on the Liberty of the Press* (1803), p. 29.

exempt from the control of any law or the jurisdiction of any court. As to the press, the Framers intended "a total exemption from any law making any publication whatever criminal," even if the result was "mischief." [61] Truth and facts had no greater protection under the First Amendment than the worst falsehoods and opinions, regardless of their tendency. The latter were as equally uncontrollable as the former. To rest the defense of the press on truth as a defense was to protect only the "morally right" and to ignore that fact and opinion were often indistinguishable and that opinions were not provable as true. And there were "many truths, important to society, which are not susceptible of that full, direct, and positive evidence, which alone can be exhibited before a court and jury." A policy of permitting full scope to licentiousness, Hay admitted, might result in harm, but the evil was far less than that resulting from any effort to restrain it. [62]

Hay concluded his essay with a contemptuous glance at the definition of a free press as simply an exemption from previous restraints. If that definition were accepted, he declared, a man might be put to death for what he published provided that no notice was taken of him before he published it. That might be the case in England, "But this definition does not deserve to be transplanted into America." There was no basis for introducing "British doctrine" here where, unlike the case of England, there was a written constitution, a limitation on the legislative power, and its object was to secure the freedom of the press. [63] Such was the character of Hay's essay; his second one, in 1803, did

---

[61] *An Essay* (1799), pp. 23–26 of the 1803 edition.
[62] *Ibid.*, pp. 26–28.
[63] *Ibid.*, p. 29. See also the 1803 *Essay*, p. 32.

not differ in any vital respects when he traversed much of the same ground, examining state rather than federal law. The only notable change, perhaps, was his much stiffer stand against personal defamation. It remained the only exception to his belief in "absolute" freedom, but in 1803 he accepted the validity of a criminal proceeding, by information or indictment, against a notorious libeler of a private person, while earlier he had believed that the injury sustained should be redressable civilly only by a suit for damages.[64]

The *Report* of 1800 by the Virginia House of Delegates contained little on the First Amendment that had not been in Gallatin's speeches, Blake's argument, or Hay's first essay; but since the *Report* came from the hand of the "Father" of the Constitution and of the Bill of Rights it carries an uncommon authority, not on the original meaning of the First Amendment but on the meaning that it ought to have. Madison advanced the following propositions in a characteristically brilliant exposition: that the Sedition Act was unconstitutional; that the United States possessed no jurisdiction over common-law crimes; that a popular, or free, republican government cannot be libeled; that the First Amendment was intended to supersede the common law on speech and press; and that the freedom guaranteed by the amendment was absolute, so far as the federal government was concerned, because it could not be abridged by any authority of the United States.

Following an elaborate examination and rejection of the arguments that had been advanced by the Federalists in support of the existence of a federal common law of

[64] Compare the 1799 *Essay*, p. 23, with the 1803 *Essay*, pp. 10–11, 24, 28.

crimes,[65] Madison next enlarged on the absence of any power in Congress to enact a sedition law. Concluding that such a law could not be constitutionally justified by either the enumerated or implied powers, he turned his attention to the First Amendment and the contention that its protection of the freedom of the press connoted the common-law definition of that term. Were the contention valid, a sedition law that did not establish a prior restraint would not abridge the freedom of the press, and Congress might regulate the press short of abridging it. By way of answer Madison followed Gallatin, Blake, and Hay in denouncing the prior-restraints definition; "this idea of the freedom of the press can never be admitted to be the American idea of it" since a law inflicting penalties would have the same effect as a law authorizing a prior restraint. "It would seem a mockery to say that no laws should be passed preventing publications from being made, but that laws might be passed for punishing them in case they should be made." [66]

At this point Madison discoursed on the "essential difference between the British government and the American constitutions" to support his view. In England, he pointed out, the danger of encroachments on the rights of the people was understood to be confined to the king, while Parliament, being considered as the guardian of those rights against violation from the executive, possessed unlimited power. Under such a government an exemption of the press from prior restraints by licensers appointed by the king was all the freedom that could be achieved. But the case of the United States was altogether different. The people, not the

[65] "Madison's Report on the Virginia Resolutions," Elliot, ed., *Debates*, 4:561–567. On this point, see also Gallatin's speeches. *Annals of Congress*, 5th Cong., 2nd sess., pp. 2137, 2157–2158; and Hay's first *Essay on the Liberty of the Press* (1799), pp. 15–18.

[66] "Madison's Report," Elliot, ed., *Debates*, 4:569.

government, possessed "the absolute sovereignty" and placed the legislature as well as the executive under limitations of power by constitutions that were paramount to legislative acts. As a result, the security of the press required that it should be exempt "not only from previous restraint of the executive, as in Great Britain but from legislative restraint also; and this exemption, to be effectual must be an exemption, not only from the previous inspection of licensers, but from the subsequent penalty of laws. The state of the press, therefore, under the common law, cannot, in this point of view, be the standard of its freedom in the United States." [67] On behalf of this conclusion, Madison advanced a second and related theoretical point. In England, with its hereditary and nonresponsible monarch, it was a maxim that the king can do no wrong, and Parliament, two thirds of whose membership was also hereditary and nonresponsible, claimed omnipotence. In America, however, the executive was not held to be infallible nor the legislature unlimited, and both, being elective, were responsible. Necessarily, therefore, a different degree of freedom of the press was contemplated by American constitution-makers. An elective, limited, and responsible government required a much greater freedom of animadversion than might be tolerated by such a government as that of Great Britain. And since the electoral process was the essence of a free and responsible government, a wide latitude for political criticism was indispensable to keep the electorate free, informed, and capable of making intelligent choices. The relationship of the press to the elective principle required that the press, "checkered as it is with abuses," be exempt from punishment. Abuse was inseparable from the proper use of anything, but it was the better

[67] *Ibid.*, 4:569-570.

part of wisdom to leave the press's "noxious branches to their luxurious growth, than, by pruning them away, to injure the vigor of those yielding the proper fruits." [68]

To these considerations Madison added another which he thought proved that the common law could not be permitted to explain the terms used in the First Amendment. That amendment also protected freedom of religion, and it could never be admitted that its English meaning limited its meaning in the United States. The "liberty of conscience and freedom of the press," Madison affirmed, "were equally and completely exempted from all authority whatever of the United States." [69] The principle of the First Amendment rather than a studied discrimination of its words and phrases should dictate an understanding of it. Some persons had argued that there was a notable difference in the protections afforded the various First Amendment freedoms. Congress, for example, was to make no law *respecting* an establishment of religion but was merely enjoined against *abridging* freedom of speech and press, from which fact the conclusion had been drawn that Congress might make a law respecting but not abridging freedom of speech and press.[70] Madison, who had drafted the amendment, regarded such reasoning as specious for it would also yield the impossible conclusion that freedom of religion might be abridged by Congress although not prohibited:

> For, if Congress may regulate the freedom of the press, provided they do not abridge it, because it is said only, 'they shall not abridge it,' and it is not said 'they shall make no

[68] *Ibid.*, 4:570–571, 575–576.

[69] *Ibid.*, 4:576, 571.

[70] See, *e.g.*, Justice Iredell's Charge to the Grand Jury, April 11, 1799, in the "Trial of the Northampton Insurgents," in Francis Wharton, ed., *State Trials of the United States during the Administrations of Washington and Adams* (Philadelphia, 1849), p. 478.

law respecting it,' the analogy of reasoning is conclusive, that Congress may *regulate*, and even *abridge*, the free exercise of religion, provided they do not *prohibit it;* because it is said only, 'they shall not prohibit it;' and is *not* said, 'they shall make no law *respecting*, or no law *abridging* it.' [71]

The amendment, Madison declared, was intended to have the broadest construction as to freedom of the press as well as of religion. It "meant a positive denial to Congress of any power whatever on the subject." [72]

In support of this proposition, he reviewed the immediate history of the amendment, noting that although the Framers of the Constitution had invariably urged that any power exercised over speech and press would be a "manifest usurpation," the people had demanded express assurance "to prevent misconstruction or abuse" of the powers vested. The purpose of the First Amendment had been to give that assurance by an explicit guarantee that would extend the ground of public confidence in the government. Here Madison raised and directly answered a crucial question:

> Is then, the federal government, it will be asked, destitute of every authority for restraining the licentiousness of the press, and for shielding itself against the libellous attacks which may be made on those who administer it?
>
> The Constitution alone can answer this question. If no such power be expressly delegated, and if it be not both necessary and proper to carry into execution an express power; above all, if it be expressly forbidden by a declaratory amendment to the Constitution,—the answer must be, that the federal government is destitute of all such authority.[73]

[71] Madison's Report," Elliot, ed., *Debates*, 4:577.
[72] *Ibid.*, 4:571.
[73] *Ibid.*, 4:572–573.

In other striking passages Madison lent his great authority to the view, becoming prevalent in American libertarian thinking, that the privilege of giving in evidence the truth of the matter contained in political writings was of little value if any.[74] He also depreciated the supposed protection inhering in the requirement that a political libel cannot be proved against an accused without proof of his malicious or criminal intent to defame or bring into contempt, disrepute, or hatred. The intent was simply inferred from the publication, and its punishment necessarily struck at the right of freely animadverting on the government, its measures and officers. To prohibit the intent was to prohibit the excitement of unfavorable sentiments against the government, and to do that was "equivalent to a prohibition of discussions having that tendency and effect; which again, is equivalent to a protection of those who administer the government, if they should at any time deserve the contempt and hatred of the people, against being exposed to it, by free animadversions on their characters and conduct." [75]

Since no man knew better than Madison what the First Amendment was intended to mean, the problem naturally arises whether his exposition of 1800 should be regarded as a reliable account of a prior understanding or as a hindsight interpretation that demonstrated the formulation of a new libertarian theory in response to the Sedition Act. The problem cannot be satisfactorily resolved, since the evidence is negative in character. There is simply no record of Madison's views during the period of the framing, except on the point that the national government was to have no authority whatsoever over speech and press. That being

[74] *Ibid.*, 4:575.
[75] *Ibid.*

so, it made no difference on a national level what was meant
by freedom of speech or press. Yet if Madison's views of
1800 represented his earlier understanding, it passes belief
that he would have remained silent in the Virginia ratifying
convention of 1788 when George Nicholas, one of his
closest supporters, defined freedom of the press as the
absence of a licensing act. Significantly, no one at the convention, not even the demagogic Patrick Henry and those
of his party who clamored for a written guarantee for
freedom of the press, took issue with Nicholas' definition.
Even if that definition, which was the common law's, had
not been the only one known, it was the most widely
known and believed, making necessary on Madison's part
an explanation to the First Congress — he offered none —
that his proposed amendment for a guarantee of the freedom of the press comprehended a rejection of the common
law's restraints in order to secure a greatly enlarged scope
for the freedom.

Moreover, in 1800 Madison construed the amendment as
implying a bar on all federal authority respecting speech
or press. That that was his intention in 1789 is granted, but
his draftsmanship left much to be desired as an expression
of that intention. He did not employ the emphatic language
of the Virginia ratifying convention's recommendation
that the liberty of the press "cannot be cancelled abridged
restained or modified by any authority of the United
States." [76] As he originally introduced the amendment it
read, "shall not be deprived or abridged," [77] but omitted the
significant phrase, "by any authority of the United States,"
which would have included the executive and judiciary, as

[76] Charles C. Tansill, ed., *Documents Illustrative of the Formation
of the Union of the American States* (Washington, 1927), p. 1027.
[77] *Annals of Congress*, 1:451.

well as Congress, and would have implied a prohibition on the exercise by the federal courts of any jurisdiction over a common law of criminal libels. As originally drafted, Madison's proposed amendments had separate articles on religion and speech-and-press,[78] a fact which weighs against his argument in 1800 that since all were protected in the same amendment, the inapplicability of the common-law definition of freedom of religion implied the inapplicability of the common-law definition of freedom of speech-and-press. No part of that argument was worthy of Madison. The English common law on freedom of religion could scarcely have been intended, since America had no national church, and also because there had been a long history of American thought and experience on freedom of religion proving a clear rejection of the common law in this respect. But American thought and experience on freedom of speech and press had been the same as England's, indicating that the common-law definition in that respect did apply. If anything, English thought on the necessity for

[78] *Ibid.* The separate articles on religion and on speech-and-press were joined together as clauses in the same article or amendment by a select committee of the House to whom Madison's recommendations were assigned, but as passed by the House the clauses were once again separated and made into distinct articles. The Senate, on receiving the separate articles, rejoined them as clauses of a single article, and the joint committee of House and Senate that finally agreed on the wording of the amendments retained the compressed form. For a very convenient collection of the various drafts of the Bill of Rights, from Madison's initial draft through the draft approved by the joint conference committee for submission to the states, see Edward Dumbauld, *The Bill of Rights and What It Means Today* (Norman, Okla., 1957), Appendices 5–9, pp. 206–222. For a narrative of the adoption of the First Amendment by Congress, see Milton R. Konvitz, *Fundamental Liberties of a Free People* (Ithaca, 1957), pp. 345–361.

repudiating the common law as to speech and press had been far more vigorous than American thought which tended to be quiescent or acquiescent by comparison.

The mere fact that a common-law right, such as the liberty of the press, had been elevated to constitutional status in America did not argue that its meaning had changed. That would be implying a great deal from nothing. Why then did so many of the first state constitutions guarantee liberty of the press? The most probable answer is disconcerting: the history of the writing of American bills of rights does not warrant a presupposition that the process was a very rational one. In the glorious act of reverting from a state of nature to a civil government by framing a social compact, Americans tended simply to draw up a glittering catalogue of "rights" that satisfied their urge for an expression of first principles. It was a terribly important and serious task, but was executed in an incredibly haphazard fashion that verged on ineptness. Of the eleven original states that framed constitutions, two passed over freedom of the press; four ignored the right of a defendant to be represented by counsel in a criminal trial; six failed to protect the right against unreasonable searches and seizures; six omitted a provision against compulsory self-incrimination; six, incredibly, neglected the right to the writ of habeas corpus; six, again, took no notice of a right to indictment by grand jury; and eight made no provision against bills of attainder. The right to trial by jury was probably the only one universally secured by the first American state constitutions, unless freedom of religion be added to the list despite the fact that five states constitutionally permitted or provided for an establishment of religion in the form of tax supports for churches. Too many of the bills of rights gave constitutional status to a variety of common-law rights, unchanged in their meaning, to warrant the belief that the guarantee of a free press originally intended a repudiation of its common-law meaning. In the national Bill of Rights, for example, the guarantee of the right against self-incrimination simply declared the common law, as indeed was the case as to almost every provision of the Bill of Rights. The conclusion must be that Madison's exposition of 1800 was not a reliable statement of the understanding prevalent at the time of the framing and ratification of the First Amendment. It was, rather, a major step in the evolution of the meaning of the free speech-and-press clause.

The work of St. George Tucker borrowed so heavily and openly from Madison's *Report* that it may be best reviewed at this point. Tucker was a professor of law at the College of William and Mary and a member of the Virginia high court. He habitually used the word "absolute" as a prefix to the right of speaking, writing, and publishing, which he described as "unlimited as the human mind," subject to the penalties of the law only for personal defamation. He claimed that the First Amendment freedoms had been purposely undefined so that they could be transmitted to future generations unshackled and unlimited. In his rejection of the constricted concept of freedom in the common law, Tucker enlarged on Madison's comparison of political theory in England and America by noting that in America the government, whether state or federal, was the servant of the sovereign people, making indispensably necessary that the people have the broadest freedom of inquiring into and criticizing the conduct of its servant. Freedom in England was so much narrower because the locus of sovereignty and the relationship between rulers and subjects differed.[79] Tucker's exposition, although adding very little to Madison's, was enormously important to the emergence of an American libertarianism because his absolutist theory of freedom of discussion appeared in his scholarly edition of Blackstone, for many years the standard edition used by the American bench and bar. A more strategically significant place for the repudiation of the Blackstonian concept of "no prior restraints" could not be imagined.

Tunis Wortman, a New York lawyer who was prominent in Tammany politics, contributed pre-eminently to the emergence of an American libertarianism in his book of 1800, *A Treatise Concerning Political Enquiry, and the Liberty of the Press*.[80] It is, in a sense, the book that Jefferson did not write but should have. Devoid of party polemics and of the characteristically American preoccupation with legal and constitutional problems, it is a work of political philosophy that systematically presents the case for freedom of expression. "The freedom of speech and opinion," wrote Wortman in his preface, "is not only necessary to the happiness of Man, considered as a Moral and Intellectual Being, but indispensably requisite to the perpetuation of Civil Liberty. To enforce and advocate that inestimable right, is the principal object of the present Treatise." [81] The outstanding characteristics of the book are its philosophic approach and its absolutist theses.

Always preoccupied with first principles, Wortman be-

[79] Tucker's *Blackstone* (1803), I, part II, note G, pp. 11, 15, 16, 17, 20, and 29.

[80] (New York, 1800), 296 pp. Eugene Perry Link, *Democratic-Republican Societies, 1790–1800* (New York, 1942), mentions Wortman at p. 115 as one of the "leading American democrats" of the time. See also Isaac Q. Leake, *Memoir of the Life and Times of General John Lamb* (Albany, 1850), p. 345. No sketch of Wortman appears in the *Dictionary of American Biography*.

[81] *Treatise Concerning Political Enquiry*, p. iv.

gan with the premise of the Declaration of Independence that government, particularly a representative system, is founded for the good of the whole people to secure their liberties. From the right of the people to dissolve their government whenever public opinion deemed essential, Wortman implied the existence of an "unlimited right" in both the individual and society to express political opinions. Any attempt by the government to coerce opinion or abridge the freedom of inquiry "materially violates the most essential principles of the social state." [82] The right of the individual would also be violated, for Wortman believed, "There is no natural right more perfect or more absolute, than that of investigating every subject which concerns us." [83] He drew that right from a psychological explanation of the way the human mind worked in gaining knowledge and forming beliefs.[84]

It was the "prerogative of intellect" and the nature of the mind to extend its operation into every subject, since thoughts spring uncontrolled and spontaneously in response to environment. Once the intellect begins, its direction cannot be diverted, and the association of ideas leads with astonishing rapidity from subject to subject and reflection to reflection, making it impossible, even stupid, to prescribe bounds to the "empire of thought." Nor would bounds on the formation of opinion be desirable, even if possible, for the mind, given access to knowledge and the habits of reason, could be sufficiently enlightened to overcome passion. From the standpoint of a society interested in the progression of knowledge and truth, intellectual

[82] *Ibid.*, pp. 28–29.
[83] *Ibid.*, p. 33.
[84] *Ibid.*, pp. 32–43.

intercourse should remain "entirely unshackled," so that the mass of error will be subjected to continued diminution as investigation continues free and unrestricted. But opinions among men vary on all subjects and fortunately so, since diversity engenders argument which tends in the long run to correct errors, remove prejudices, and strengthen perceptions. Thus, the habit of open debate enables society to form the wisest decisions in the management of human affairs, particularly on matters of government.[85] Wortman devoted several chapters to the development of this Jeffersonian thesis that man is capable of wisely governing himself in his political as well as personal and social life, on condition that the expression of opinion be unfettered.[86]

The first half of the book stressed the right of society to freedom of expression. Wortman then turned to the importance of freedom to the individual himself and to the social benefits of individual freedom. All prospects of general improvement, he argued, depend on the industry and imagination of the individual, whose contribution, in turn, depends on the unlimited liberty of exercising his faculties. But without the "liberty of enquiry, and the right of disseminating our opinions," the individual is crippled. Society suffers with him because his disability diminishes public enlightenment and holds forth the specter that tyranny might replace free government. The alternative is to regard knowledge as a "general fund of which all have a right to participate: it is a capital which has the peculiar property of increasing its stores in proportion as they are used. We are entitled to pursue every justifiable method of increasing our perceptions and invigorating our faculties. We are

[85] *Ibid.*, pp. 122–123.
[86] *Ibid.*, pp. 47–113.

equally entitled to communicate our information to others." He drew the line only at the "point at which our conduct becomes injurious." [87]

Turning to the problem of willful and false libels against private persons or against the government, Wortman presented in detail the thesis that prosecution is most inadvisable even for an undoubted abuse of freedom of expression that should be regarded as criminal.[88] Coercion, he argued, is a destructive and self-defeating corrective; force can never conquer falsehood, nor is it necessary. The worst misrepresentation of the government cannot result in public disrespect for it, nor in a breach of peace. To believe to the contrary libels society by assuming that the people cannot differentiate truth from error when given the facts. To invoke the penal code against seditious libelers is invariably attended with the most pernicious consequences to society, far exceeding the dangers of the "most unbounded licentiousness."

"How then," Wortman asked, "shall erroneous opinions or wilful misrepresentations be combated [*sic*] by the wise and provident legislator? The proper answer to this enquiry is, That Government should by no means interfere unless by affording such information to the public as may enable them to form a correct estimate of things." A libel might be willfully false and injurious. "Admitted. But how shall such opinion be destroyed, or its farther propagation prevented? By fair and argumentative refutation, or by the terrible dissuasive of a statute of sedition? By the convincing and circumstantial narrative of the Truth, or by the terrors of Imprisonment and the singular logic of the Pil-

[87] *Ibid.*, pp. 140–148 *passim.*
[88] *Ibid.*, pp. 150–182.

lory?" [89] Falsehood might temporarily triumph, but never for long if the remedy of "Reason and Argument" be relied upon. A society accustomed to thinking, talking, and writing freely will become experienced in judgment; "confidence should be reposed in the wisdom and virtues of the people." [90] Their discernment, being strengthened by habits of political discussion, is sufficient to detect and condemn misrepresentations. Only a government whose administration and policies cannot survive investigation needs to resort to the punishment of seditious utterances, although coercion can never vindicate the character of a government or its officers, nor can it remove an erroneous impression. That can be achieved only by representation of the truth, full publication of government transactions, a good record, and reliance upon public opinion.

For the government to proceed by criminal prosecutions in order "to punish men for their assertions respecting itself, ever has been, and ever will be, subject to the most odious oppression." Sedition laws make it impossible "to attempt to estimate the precise extent of prohibition, or ascertain what we are permitted to speak, and at what point we are compelled to silence." Men whose only guilt consists of credulity, zeal, prejudice, mistaken opinion, or "imbecility of understanding" are victimized by prosecutions, with the result that the free formation of public opinion is destroyed and a pernicious silence creeps over society. This is the history of prosecutions for libel. They fail, however, to achieve their underlying purpose of establishing public tranquillity, and they can never effect a cure of the complaints that give rise to libels. Indeed, by damming up dis-

[89] *Ibid.*, pp. 159, 160.
[90] *Ibid.*, p. 161.

content and removing the possibility of its verbal expression, prosecutions make a resort to violence more likely. The worsening of the situation would compel the government either to fortify its powers by introducing "Military Despotism" or to relax its suppressive measures. The wise government understands that free speech is a preventative of revolutions. In a representative system of government, which Wortman believed to be functionally dependent upon freedom of political discussion, prosecutions for seditious libel subvert the constitution.[91]

In the final chapters of his book, he addressed himself to legal and constitutional problems in the United States. He traversed minutely the ground covered by Madison and others on the constitutionality of federal sedition laws, the meaning of the First Amendment's freedom of speech-and-press clause, the question whether a federal common law of criminal libel existed, and the invalidity of relevant Blackstonian concepts. In the course of his presentation of the Madisonian argument, Wortman endorsed the overt-acts test[92] and concluded that the entire law of criminal libel was the "offspring of a Monarchy"; it could "never be reconciled to the genius and constitution of a Representative Commonwealth." [93] In the whole of Wortman's book there was probably not an argument that could not be traced to some earlier writer, but the same point can be made as to the "originality" of other classics in libertarian literature, from Milton's *Areopagitica* to Mill's *On Liberty*. Wortman's treatise is surely the pre-eminent American classic, because of its scope, fullness, philosophical approach,

[91] This paragraph summarizes pp. 162–192 of Wortman. The quoted lines are at pp. 163 and 170.
[92] *Ibid.*, p. 253.
[93] *Ibid.*, p. 262.

masterful marshaling of all the libertarian arguments, and uncompromisingly radical view.

The tract written by James Sullivan in 1801 on liberty of the press[94] should be noticed because its author was the leader of the Democratic-Republican party in Massachusetts. The party's perennial candidate for governor, he was finally elected in 1807 after many years of service as attorney-general of the state. During the controversy over the adoption of the Constitution he had been closely associated with the Federalists. From his record and a reading of his tract on liberty of the press one would never know that he had become one of the foremost Jeffersonian politicians in New England.[95] As attorney-general, Sullivan had successfully prosecuted Abijah Adams in 1799 for a seditious libel against the state legislature and had advanced the same Blackstonian argument as in his earlier prosecution of Freeman, in 1791.[96] His tract of 1801 was considerably more moderate, conspicuously omitting any reference to the "no prior restraints" concept, but in tone and content was alien to the newly emergent libertarianism of Gallatin, Wortman, Hay, Madison, Tucker, and other Jeffersonians, a fact that may have accounted for the tract's anonymous publication.

Calling himself an "Impartial Citizen," Sullivan wrote a narrowly legalistic analysis that attempted to reconcile freedom of the press and the common law of criminal libel. He defined that freedom as meaning the right to publish

[94] *A Dissertation upon the Constitutional Freedom of the Press in the United States of America.* By an Impartial Citizen (Boston, 1801), 54 pp.

[95] J. T. Adams, "Sullivan, James," *DAB.* For a full-length study, see Thomas Coffin Armory, *The Life of James Sullivan* (Boston, 1859).

[96] See above, pp. 208 and 211.

any political opinions in the absence of such restraints "as shall prevent a free and necessary communication of ideas, for the preservation of liberty and the support of the principles of the constitution." Sullivan believed that although a few states had accepted the defense of truth, they had not changed the common-law principle of freedom of the press which had been "adopted and uniformly acknowledged in the country; nor do they differ essentially from those [constitutions] of the other states." [97] As a matter of policy he would not allow truth as a defense in trials for criminal libel against public officers. He reasoned, interestingly, that if the charge against an official warranted impeachment or indictment, he should not be censured until after a fair trial and an opportunity of being heard in his own defense. To charge him in a gazette would prejudice public opinion against him, reverse the presumption of his innocence, and injure his chance of being judged by an impartial jury. Permitting truth as a defense simply encouraged attacks on public officials by their enemies, usually for causes not criminal, with the result that the people's servants would be constantly having to defend themselves against accusations that would never be produced against them by grand juries.[98]

Sullivan insisted that freedom of the press was broad enough to permit the exposure of an official's weakness, impropriety, bad policies, and even unconstitutional acts, without charging him with crime or defaming his character. He realized that representative government depended upon open political debate as a means of enabling the public to form its opinions on an administration for the purpose

[97] *Dissertation upon Freedom of the Press,* p. 20.
[98] *Ibid.,* pp. 21–25.

of voting; and he would not invoke the common law against any writer whose criticism of the government was mistaken. Anyone had a right to give his opinion, however wrong. "Some men," wrote Sullivan, "may form wrong conclusions with very honest hearts, while others form the same from wrong heads and seditious minds; but there can be no way, in which a just, and exact scrutiny can be made, and therefore, there can be no punishment in such cases, without a dangerous infringment [*sic*] on the right of private judgment, in public concerns." People reasoned in different ways; to punish wrong reasoning or error would mean "an end of all free inquiry on the measures of administration." [99]

Sullivan drew a line, however, against seditious libel as he understood it: "But if the false publications proceed from *malice* to the government, or its officers, or from a seditious temper against the powers of the state, and the fact published be in itself false, there can be no reason why the author and publisher should not receive adequate and condign punishment." [100] Criminal prosecution was not warranted in the case of a libel against an officer of the government, even for an act done in his official capacity, on the theory that the libel was against the person privately; the remedy in that case must be the same as in the case of an ordinary citizen: a civil suit for damages in the courts of the state in which the libel was published, even if the injured party be an officer of the United States government. But a false and malicious libel against such an officer made "with an intent to subvert the government of the United States, to bring it into hatred or contempt . . .

[99] *Ibid.*, p. 34. See also pp. 31 and 54.
[100] *Ibid.*, p. 31.

must in itself be a crime against the government, and ought to be punished." [101] In cases of seditious libel Sullivan would permit truth as a defense.

In his discussion of federal powers against seditious libel, he endorsed the view that a federal common law of crimes necessarily existed as a means of preserving the government of the United States. Whatever had "a tendency to overthrow the constitution and civil authority" he believed to be a crime against the government punishable "without any act of Congress for the purpose." [102] As for the Sedition Act of 1798, he thought that it "was intended to have been passed on proper principles, and the Congress had an undoubted right to pass an act against seditious libels. . . ." [103] A power to punish a libel against the government itself was implicit from the inherent right of self-protection. To argue, as some had, Sullivan declared, that the state governments would preserve and defend the federal government was absurd, "because a government, depending upon another government for its existence, is merely a corporation — it can have no sovereignty — and can be no band of union for a nation." [104] The Sedition Act of 1798, however, was not drawn on "rules of prudence" nor was it enforced with a discretion that merited the confidence of the people.[105] In one provision, moreover, it was unwarranted by the Constitution, for it outlawed libels against the president personally as well as libels against him published with intent to injure or subvert the government itself. Only the latter case was constitutionally punishable by

[101] *Ibid.*, p. 33.
[102] *Ibid.*, p. 41.
[103] *Ibid.*, p. 31.
[104] *Ibid.*, p. 50.
[105] *Ibid.*, p. 31.

the United States; yet some of the actual prosecutions under the act were for libels against the president that belonged to the exclusive jurisdiction, civil or criminal, of the states.[106] This distinction between a libel on the officer and a libel on the office, or any institution of the government itself, may have been a lawyer's hairsplitting, but it would have prevented a majority of the prosecutions that did in fact occur under the Sedition Act.

Nevertheless, Sullivan's mild criticism of the statute would not warrant classifying him among the new libertarians. He could differentiate fact from opinion and tolerate opinion even if "wrong" or erroneous, a feat that John Adams could not accomplish; but Sullivan's tract placed him apart from the Jeffersonian theorists. His independence of mind led him to an endeavor that holds the same fascination for the reader as for one who watches a man trying to keep his balance while straddling two stools that are placed too far apart. No amount of reasoning could keep Sullivan from falling between the common law of seditious libel and the freedom of the press in his effort to keep both securely under control. He really passed judgment on himself when first he recognized that the virtual impossibility of separating "wrong" but "honest hearts" from "seditious minds" made prosecution a dangerous infringement on liberty, and then went ahead to endorse prosecutions for malicious or seditious utterances against the government. Sullivan's tract deserves to be remembered as an example of the failure to find a middle way between the old Blackstonian views and the newer Jeffersonian ones.

In the same year that Sullivan's tract appeared, John Thomson of New York published his slim book on the

[106] *Ibid.*, pp. 27–28, 33, 48, 51–52.

press,[107] a trenchant and comprehensive discussion that represented the same viewpoint as Wortman's and inevitably duplicated it in many respects. Thomson began with a cogent analysis of the meaninglessness of the term "licentiousness" when used as a test to gauge the criminality of the press. He concluded that it was an undefinable term used by those "who evidently wished nobody to enjoy the Liberty of the Press, but such as were of their opinion." [108] Not only was it impossible to define the opinions which were dangerous to the peace and good order of society; it was mischievously misleading even to make the attempt since all opinions should be allowed an equal freedom of expression and none could actually alienate the affections of the people from their government or injure them.[109] "Political opinions," he claimed, "could never be destructive of social order, or public tranquility, if allowed a free operation." The law protected against "actions injurious to the peace of the community";[110] opinion should never be punished, not even if false.

Error, granted Thomson, would circulate widely under a policy of "free and unrestrained Liberty of Speech and Press," but even error had its use as a step toward public enlightenment.[111] To make "truth" the bound of permissible freedom cut society off from the better understanding of truth that developed from collision with error, fixed the understanding of truth at its present stage of development,

---

[107] *An Enquiry, Concerning the Liberty, and Licentiousness of the Press, and the Uncontroulable Nature of the Human Mind* (New York, 1801), 84 pp. I have been unable to locate biographical data on Thomson.

[108] *Ibid.*, p. 7.

[109] *Ibid.*, pp. 8, 77, 79, 84.

[110] *Ibid.*, p. 79.

[111] *Ibid.*, p. 83.

and ignored the fact that opinions could not be proved: "how are *their* truth or falsehood to be determined? A decision in this case, would be as absurd as deciding which was the most palatable food, agreeable drink, or beautiful color." [112] The real danger did not come from erroneous opinions or misrepresentations of fact, which could be corrected in the public mind by counterargument. The real danger derived from the "Government interfering in the direction of public opinion," [113] as Thomson sought to prove by reviewing the recent history of prosecutions for sedition in England and America. "Let not Government interfere," he declared, not even in a case of malicious falsehood. "In no case whatever use coercive measures. . . . Coercion may silence," he concluded, "but it can never convince." [114]

Such was the gist of Thomson's book. In the course of it, he restated the traditional theory that freedom of expression was responsible for myriad benefits in the realm of art, science, religion, and philosophy as well as in politics and government, benefits that far outweighed its disadvantages. He also rehearsed many of the arguments that Madison, Wortman, and others had recently made. But he added two arguments that were unjaded and provocative.

The first of these had been suggested rather obliquely as early as 1704 by Matthew Tindal,[115] when he claimed that members of Parliament should not deny to others the right they themselves possessed of publishing their debates. Hay was the first American to contend that a guarantee of free-

---

[112] *Ibid.*, p. 68.
[113] *Ibid.*, p. 74.
[114] *Ibid.*, p. 83.
[115] *Reasons against Restraining the Press* (London, 1704), p. 10.

dom of speech meant that citizens should have the same right of unlimited expression possessed by their representatives.[116] Others had discoursed on the relation between unfettered public discussion and a representative system of government, but not even Madison or Wortman went on to draw the related conclusion that Hay and Thomson did. It was Thomson, however, who buttressed the point with a reasoned argument.

He noted that Article One, Section Six, of the Constitution provided that members of Congress "shall not be questioned," that is, held legally liable, for any speech they might make; their remarks were clothed with an immunity that gave them the right to say whatever they pleased in their legislative capacities. Thomson then reasoned that if freedom of discussion was necessary for them, it was equally necessary, indeed more so, for their sovereigns, the people whom they represented. The electorate must pass judgment on the proceedings of Congress and insure that the government operated for the benefit of the government. For the fulfillment of their electoral duties and their responsibility to protect themselves, the people could not be denied access to any viewpoint. The agents of the people were accordingly powerless to abridge the freedom of speech or press. The intention of the framers of the First Amendment, Thomson concluded, was to guarantee that the people possessed "the same right of free discussion" as their agents.[117] His argument was logically, if not historically, convincing; it went far to show the invalidity of the concept of seditious libel in a republican form of government.

[116] *An Essay on the Liberty of the Press* (1799), p. 26 of the 1803 ed.
[117] Thomson, *Enquiry*, pp. 20, 22.

Thomson's second unusual thesis was no less thorough-going in its implications, far more subtle, and the most interesting in the entire libertarian armory. In essence it was that opinion is not punishable because it is involuntary, an idea traceable to Locke and Jefferson and even to the common-law requirement that a criminal intent must be present before a crime can be said to exist. The idea, whether valid or not, also went far to provide immunity for political expression.

The emergence of a body of libertarian thought among the Jeffersonians did not, however, result in a union of principle and practice when they achieved power. Prosecutions for verbal crime had been reprehended as a shocking betrayal of natural and constitutional rights when the victims were the party faithful. But the accession to power stimulated a fresh understanding of the dangers of seditious libel from an uncontrolled opposition press. Measures to protect the government and public opinion suddenly seemed necessary, even salutary. New York, the home of Wortman and Thomson, as well as of Zenger and James Alexander, was the scene of the first Jeffersonian assault on liberty of the press. The Federalists of New York reacted by revealing that they too had chameleon-like qualities; they played the role of defenders of freedom of expression — against Jeffersonian despoliation.

When Jefferson became president, his most powerful ally in New York, George Clinton, once again became governor of that state after a Federalist interregnum. In 1803 Clinton's administration obtained a common-law indictment for seditious libel against Harry Croswell, editor of a Federalist publication, *The Wasp*. His crime was an accusation that Jefferson had paid James T. Callender to denounce Washington as "a traitor, a robber, and a perjurer" and Adams as "a hoary-headed incendiary." [118] Croswell was convicted at a trial presided over by Chief Justice Morgan Lewis, a Democrat, who was to succeed Clinton as governor. Lewis denied a request that the trial be postponed long enough for the defendant to subpoena Callender as a witness to prove the truth of his accusation against Jefferson. "His honor," says the report of the case, "then read to the jury the opinion of Lord Mansfield, in the case of The Dean of St. Asaph . . . and charged them, that the law therein laid down was the law of this state. . . ." The jury, in other words, was instructed that truth was not a defense against a charge of seditious libel, and that its only duty was to find whether the defendant had in fact published the statement charged.[119]

On appeal to the highest court of the state, Croswell was represented by Alexander Hamilton, who eloquently championed the cause of a free press in an argument that recalled Andrew Hamilton's defense of Zenger. The great Federalist leader demanded that the court grant Croswell a new trial and the defense of truth, so that the people might know whether President Jefferson had been guilty of the "foul" act attributed to him. Hamilton maintained "that the common law applied to the United States," but construed it to empower the jury to decide the criminality of an alleged libel. Freedom of the press, he declared, "consists in the right to publish, with impunity, truth, with good motives, for justifiable ends, though reflecting on government, magistracy, or individuals." [120] Attorney-General Ambrose

[118] People v. Croswell, 3 Johnson's (N.Y.) Cases 336, 337–339 (1804).

[119] *Ibid.*, at p. 341.

[120] Hamilton's argument is reported in People v. Croswell, at pp. 352–361. The quoted words are at pp. 352–353, 357, and 358.

Spencer, a Democrat, argued for the state that a libel was punishable not because of its falsity, "but because of its evil tendency; its tendency to a breach of the peace" which existed whether true or false. Blackstone and Mansfield were his guides.[121]

The Court of Errors, reporting its opinions in 1804, was equally divided, although it is certain that if Ambrose Spencer, newly appointed to the court, had not disqualified himself, there would have been a majority ruling adopting the most reactionary views on freedom of the press. Those views were re-expressed by Chief Justice Lewis, joined by Judge Brockholst Livingston, whom Jefferson would appoint to the Supreme Court of the United States in 1806. Hamilton's argument was restated in the opinion of Judge James Kent, a Federalist, joined by Smith Thompson, a Democrat who had studied law with Kent. As a result of this case, the state legislature enacted a bill in 1805 allowing the jury to decide the criminality of an alleged libel and permitting truth as a defense if published "with good motives and for justifiable ends." [122]

President Jefferson's opinion of this prosecution for seditious libel is unknown, but there is reason to believe that he approved of the Clinton administration's effort to vindicate his name. Indeed it would not be surprising if one day there should be discovered a letter from Jefferson to Clinton advising that the scurrilous Federalist press be muzzled by the common law. Such a letter exists in an analogous case in Pennsylvania, addressed by Jefferson in 1803 to Clinton's counterpart, Governor McKean, the same McKean who when chief justice of his state had ruled that

[121] Spenser's argument is reported in People v. Croswell, at pp. 348–352, the quoted words at p. 349.
[122] Lewis' opinion is reported in People v. Croswell, at pp. 394–411; Kent's at pp. 363–394; the statute of 1805 at pp. 411–413.

Pennsylvania's clause on freedom of speech-and-press had merely declared the common law.[123] First informing McKean that patronage appointments would be coming his way, Jefferson then cautioned the Democratic governor to keep confidential his remarks on the subject of libel prosecutions. The Federalists, he noted, having failed to destroy the freedom of the press "by their gag law, seem to have attacked it in an opposite form, that is by pushing its licentiousness and its lying to such a degree of prostitution as to deprive it of all credit." Jefferson was not without a suggestion for the melioration of the condition of the press: "I have therefore long thought that a few prosecutions of the most eminent offenders would have a wholesome effect in restoring the integrity of the presses." But he warned McKean not to begin a "general prosecution, for that would look like a persecution: but a selected one. The paper I now inclose, appears to me to offer as good an instance in every respect to make an example of, as can be selected." [124]

Although we do not know what paper Jefferson enclosed with his letter, singling out his intended victim, in all probability it was a clipping from *The Port Folio*, a Philadelphia journal of literature and politics edited by Joseph Dennie, an arch-Federalist and onetime secretary to Timothy Pickering, Adams' secretary of state, who had directed the enforcement of the Sedition Act. Dennie made a practice of satirizing Jefferson unmercifully. McKean took no action, however, until two months after the president's letter, when *The Port Folio* published an essay calling democracy "contemptible and vicious" and predicting that it would bring the country to civil war, despotism, and

---

[123] See above, pp. 204–207.
[124] Jefferson to McKean, Feb. 19, 1803, in Jefferson's *Writings*, 9:451–452.

anarchy: "No wise man but discerns its imperfections, no good man but shudders at its miseries, no honest man but proclaims its fraud, and no brave man but draws his sword against its force." [125] The essay led to Dennie's indictment in Pennsylvania for a seditious libel against both the state and national governments. The indictment charged him with maliciously intending to "condemn the principles of the revolution, and revile, depreciate and scandalize the characters of the revolutionary patriots and statesmen, to endanger, subvert, and totally destroy the republican constitutions and free governments of the United States" and similar crimes.[126] The case was not tried for more than two years. Judge Jasper Yeates, a Federalist, instructed the jury that although the defendant was accountable to the law for an abuse of his constitutional privilege to speak and write freely, "The enlightened advocates of representative republican government pride themselves in the reflection that the more deeply their system is examined, the more fully will the judgments of honest men be satisfied that it is the most conducive to the safety and happiness of a free people." [127] The jury acquitted.

Although Jefferson had written in 1804 that he had always asserted an "exclusive" right in the states "to controul the freedom of the press," [128] he was ready to concede a concurrent right in the United States to prosecute seditious

[125] Respublica v. Dennie, 4 Yeates' (Penn.) Reports 267 (1805).

[126] *Ibid.*, at p. 268.

[127] *Ibid.*, at p. 270. Judge Yeates's charge was modeled on Hamilton's argument in the Croswell case. Yeates, however, drew a line against "malicious" publications which have a "tendency to anarchy, sedition, and civil war." He left it to the jury to decide whether the defendant had gone to "unwarrantable lengths" in his essay.

[128] Letter to Abigail Adams, Sept. 4, 1804, quoted in full above, at pp. 266–267.

libel at common law when Federalist control of a state government stymied state punishment of his critics. The prosecutions in the United States courts in Connecticut, during Jefferson's presidency, are quite revealing. A Federalist partisan referred to them as Jefferson's "reign of terror." [129] The story begins with the president's appointment of a trusted political lieutenant, Pierpont Edwards, as United States district judge for Connecticut in 1806. Justice Paterson being ill at the time, Judge Edwards conducted the United States Circuit Court alone. In an address to the grand jury handpicked by a Jeffersonian marshal, Edwards asked for common-law indictments against the publishers of libels against the United States, on ground that they would, if not restrained, "more effectually undermine and sap the foundations of our Constitution and Government, than any kind of treason that can be named." [130] The federal grand jurors returned indictments in 1806 for seditious libel against Judge Tapping Reeve of the Connecticut Superior Court for articles he had published in *The Litchfield Monitor*, a Federalist paper; against Thomas Collier, publisher of the *Monitor;* and against Thaddeus Osgood, a candidate for the ministry. A few months later, Hudson and Goodwin, editors of the Federalist *Connecticut Courant* of Hartford, and the Reverend Azel Backus were also indicted. The charge against each of the six defendants was the same: seditious libel of President Jefferson.

---

[129] "Hampden," *A Letter to the President of the United States, touching the Prosecutions under his Patronage, before the Circuit Court in the District of Connecticut* (New Haven, 1808), p. 28.

[130] The *Litchfield* (Conn.) *Witness*, April 30, 1806, as quoted by William A. Robinson in his sketch of Edwards in the DAB.; quoted also in variant form by William W. Crosskey, *Politics and the Constitution* (Chicago, 1958), 2:771. Crosskey deserves credit for breaking first ground on this story.

Backus and Osgood had committed the alleged crime in the course of preaching sermons; the other defendants in newspaper print.[131]

Jefferson, in 1809, informed a friend that the prosecutions "had been instituted, and had made considerable progress, without my knowledge, that they were disapproved by me *as soon as known,* and directed to be discontinued." [132] The prosecutions may have been instituted without Jefferson's knowledge, but he learned of them in December of 1806, nearly four months before they were scheduled for trial, and he approved of them until expediency dictated his disapproval some months later. Thomas Seymour, a Connecticut Democrat, informed the president, in a letter of December 20, that the party faithful in Connecticut supported "the prosecutions depending before the Circuit Court in this District for libels against the President and Administration of the General Government. . . ." Without naming the indicted parties, Seymour described them as "a Judge, two political priests, and three Federal printers." [133] Jefferson was also probably apprised of the facts by Gideon Granger, his cabinet officer from Connecticut, who kept close watch on political developments at home. Moreover, Congressman Samuel W. Dana, a Connecticut Federalist, on January 2, 1807, described the prosecutions to the House of Representatives in order to obtain support for his abortive bill making truth a defense in federal criminal-libel trials.[134] Jefferson himself replied to

[131] "Hampden," *A Letter to the President,* pp. 8–12.
[132] Jefferson to Wilson Carey Nicholas, June 13, 1809, in Jefferson's *Writings,* 9:253. Italics added.
[133] "From the Citizens of Hartford," Seymour and others to Jefferson, in W. C. Ford, ed., *Thomas Jefferson, Correspondence Printed from the Originals in the Collections of William K. Bixby* (Boston, 1916), pp. 137, 139.
[134] *Annals of Congress,* 9th Cong., 2nd sess., p. 247.

Seymour in a letter dated February 11, 1807, acknowledging the "prosecutions in the Court of the U S" and recommending that if truth be admitted as a defense, the effect could "not lessen the useful freedom of the press." He himself had never troubled to contradict the calumnies against him, he declared, and he would "leave to others"— Judge Pierpont Edwards and the federal jury?—the task of recalling the press to truth.[135] By curious coincidence Judge Edwards then decided that section 34 of the Judiciary Act of 1789 required him to follow state law in common-law trials in the courts of the United States, with the consequence that a Connecticut statute of 1804, allowing truth as a defense, was held to be applicable to the forthcoming trials.[136] This ruling ultimately led to the undoing of the government's position.

Excepting the case against Judge Reeve, which was not prosecuted because he was related by marriage to Judge Edwards, who refused to issue a warrant of arrest, the trials were scheduled for the April session of the court in 1807. The petty jurors were personally selected by the marshal instead of by lot as was customary. Defense counsel objected, of course, to the proceedings. They stated that it was their intention to argue that the federal courts had no jurisdiction over crimes at common law; they therefore requested a postponement of the cases until Edwards was joined in the following year by a member of the Supreme Court on circuit duty. Edwards, however, declared that it was against the public peace of the state to let the cases lie over another year, particularly since the public had a right to have a determination "as to the facts charged." But

---

[135] Jefferson to Seymour, Feb. 11, 1807, in Jefferson's *Writings*, 9:30.
[136] "Hampden," *A Letter to the President*, iii.

his eagerness to try the cases immediately was frustrated by the discovery of defects in the indictments, necessitating a postponement until the September session of the court. In September Edwards behaved in a manner that caused counsel to express "surprise at the unexpected turn the case had taken. . . ." Each of the defendants, except the Reverend Azel Backus, having renewed a demurrer to the jurisdiction of the court, Edwards promptly reserved decision on their demurrers until he should be joined by another judge. The effect of this move postponed the trials until, if necessary, the Supreme Court itself would finally rule on the question of jurisdiction. Backus, however, insisted upon being tried immediately, while Edwards insistently sought to convince him that it would be a hardship to him to have to stand trial before the jurisdictional point was settled. In the end, Backus' trial was postponed against his wishes.[187]

Quite obviously, Edwards had changed his mind between April and September of 1807 about going ahead with the prosecutions. The explanation for his change of mind reveals why Backus was so eager to be tried for seditious libel. Jefferson had learned for the first time the exact nature of Backus' libel, knew that it could be proved to be true, and commanded Gideon Granger to secure "an immediate dismission of the prosecution." [188] The libel in question

---

[187] *Ibid.*, pp. 14–20, quoting at pp. 16–20 an article from the *Connecticut Courant* (Hartford), Sept. 30, 1807.

[188] Jefferson to W. C. Nicholas, June 13, 1809, in Jefferson's *Writings*, 9:253. Jefferson claimed in this same letter that he had first told Granger to dismiss the suit against Backus at an unspecified earlier date, before he had learned the nature of the minister's libel. But he also said that it was not until *after* his second command to dismiss the suit that he learned there were other prosecutions, which is simply not true. The president admitted, however, that he was writing from memory and was uncertain of his details. His statements that he disapproved the prosecutions as soon as he

concerned "the Walker affair" of 1768, when Jefferson
seems to have attempted the seduction of a friend's wife.
The incident had become a "public scandal" in 1805, forcing the president to confess, to a member of his cabinet, the
"incorrectness" of his conduct: "when young and single
I offered love to a handsome lady." [139] Since Backus had the
facts on his side and had already subpoenaed the lady's
husband as well as James Madison and others from Virginia
to testify to the truth of his accusation against the president, the decision to prevent the trial from coming off was
understandable. In April of 1808 the government withdrew
the prosecutions against Backus and the other defendants
excepting Hudson and Goodwin.[140] Their case, prior to
trial, was appealed to the Supreme Court for a decision on
the question whether federal tribunals possessed jurisdiction
over the common-law crime of seditious libel; the decision,
handed down in 1812, was against federal common-law
jurisdiction.[141]

Regardless of Jefferson's personal complicity in the Connecticut prosecutions, the very fact that they could have
been instituted in the federal courts under his own administration suggests that the libertarian arguments of the Sedi-

heard about them and ordered the dismissal of Backus' suit before
knowing the nature of the latter's libel are not consistent with his
cordial letter more than two years earlier to Thomas Seymour,
when he wrote that the prosecutions could not lessen the useful
freedom of the press if truth be vindicated. Moreover, Judge Edwards' conduct at the April 1807 session of the court, two months
after the letter to Seymour, additionally indicates that expediency,
rather than principle, motivated Jefferson's orders to Granger.

[139] Jefferson to Robert Smith, July 1, 1805, quoted in Dumas
Malone, *Jefferson the Virginian* (Boston, 1948), p. 448. See Malone,
pp. 447–451 for a discussion of the Walker affair.

[140] "Hampden," *A Letter to the President*, p. 23.

[141] U.S. v. Hudson and Goodwin, 7 Cranch (U.S.) 32 (1812).

tion Act period were *ad hoc* and novel in character. The prosecutions against Croswell and Dennie additionally indicated that Jeffersonian principles respecting freedom of political expression depended upon whose ox was being gored by the common law of seditious libel.[142]

Neither Hay, Wortman, nor Thomson should be regarded as the theorist of Jeffersonianism in power; the honor belongs, rather, to a greater writer than any of them, a man who was the foremost pamphleteer in the English language, a friend of the radicals in England and France as well as in America, a condemned seditionist, Thomas Paine. In 1806, after the indictments for seditious libel had been returned in Judge Edwards' court, Paine published an essay on "Liberty of the Press" in a New York newspaper.[143] He began by criticizing the "licentiousness" of Federalist editors and noted that nothing was more common than "the continual cry of the *Liberty of the Press.*" Undertaking to define the term, since it was being used "without being understood," Paine drew from English history a Blackstonian conclusion that the abolition of previous censorship made the press only as free as speech had always been. He ended:

[142] Worthington Chauncey Ford, summarizing his study of "Jefferson and the Newspaper," concludes, "he had lashed himself into a fine frenzy over the temporary sedition laws as a gag upon free speech and an attack upon a free press, yet would have the state permanently apply the same remedy; he had wished to reform journalism, but his idea of reformation was that of the character in Beaconsfield's novel of the agreeable man — 'one who agrees with me'; and he had begun by wishing for a sheet of intelligence without advertisements, ending by using a sheet of advertisements without news." *Records of the Columbia Historical Society*, 8:110 (1905).

[143] *The American Citizen* (N.Y.), Oct. 20, 1806, reprinted in *The Life and Works of Thomas Paine*, ed. William M. Van der Weyde (New Rochelle, 1925), 10:287–290.

A man does not ask liberty beforehand to say something he has a mind to say, but he becomes answerable afterwards for the atrocities he may utter.

In like manner, if a man makes the press utter atrocious things he becomes as answerable for them as if he had uttered them by word of mouth. Mr. Jefferson has said in his inaugural speech, that '*error of opinion might be tolerated, when reason was left free to combat it.*' This is sound philosophy in cases of error. But there is a difference between error and licentiousness.

Some lawyers in defending their clients . . . have often given their opinion of what they defined the liberty of the press to be. One said it was this, another said it was that, and so on according to the case they were pleading. Now these men ought to have known that the term *liberty of the press* arose from a FACT, the abolition of the office of Imprimateur [*sic*], and that opinion has nothing to do with the case. The term refers to the fact of printing *free from prior restraint*, and not at all to the matter printed, whether good or bad. The public at large—or in case of prosecution, a jury of the country—will be judges of the matter.[144]

Paine's views in this respect represented those of the Framers.

But the Framers had a genius for studied imprecision. They were conscious of the need to phrase the Constitution in generalized terms and without a lexicographical guide, for they meant to outline an instrument that would serve future generations. Like Martin Chuzzlewit's grandnephew who had no more than "the first idea and sketchy notion of a face," the Constitution was purposely made to embody first ideas and sketchy notions. Detailed codes, which become obsolete with a change in the particular circumstances for which they were adopted, are avoided by men

[144] *Ibid.*, 10:289–290.

trained in the common law. They tend rather to formulate principles that are expansive and comprehensive in character. The principles and not their framers' understanding and application of them are meant to endure. The Constitution, designed by an eighteenth-century rural society, serves as well today as ever because an antiquarian historicism that would freeze its original meaning has not guided its interpretation and was not intended to.

The First Amendment's injunction, that there shall be no law abridging the freedom of speech or press, was boldly stated if narrowly understood. The bold statement, not the narrow understanding, was written into the fundamental law. "It is far better," as Tunis Wortman wrote, "to err on the side of Latitude than on that of Restraint." [145] On this point the Framers would probably have agreed with Wortman. He and Blake, Hay, Madison, Gallatin, Tucker, and Thomson originated a libertarian philosophy that ought to define the content of the free speech-and-press clause. They were addressing the future, not the past. Their insistence that they were simply clarifying the past's original understanding reflected an Anglo-American habit of going forward while facing backwards: rights that should exist are established on the fictitious pretense that they have ever existed, and arguments are concocted to give to the fiction the appearance of both reality and legality. But there is no evidence to warrant the belief, nor is there valid cause or need to believe, that the Framers possessed the ultimate wisdom and best insights on the meaning of freedom of expression. It is enough that they gave constitutional recognition to the principle of freedom of speech and press in unqualified and undefined terms. That they were Blackstonians does not mean that we cannot be Brandeisians.

[145] Wortman, *Treatise Concerning Political Enquiry*, p. 205.

APPENDIX
BIBLIOGRAPHY
INDEX

ᐬᕃ The "Psychology of Freedom"

The introductory clause of the preamble to the Virginia Statute of Religious Freedom, as originally drafted by Jefferson, was: "Well aware that the opinions and beliefs of men depend not upon their own will, but follow involuntarily the evidence proposed to their minds. . . ."[1] Professor Mark Howe has suggested that this Jeffersonian thought provides a clue which might enable us to understand the original meaning of the First Amendment, not by a textual analysis but by examining a presupposition of the generation that bequeathed it to us. Howe's hypothesis is that the amendment, having been broadly intended to protect belief by granting its expression immunity from government penalty, embodied a "psychology of freedom" which, valid or not, was popular at the time. "Beyond the constitution," he declared, "lay a rationalized body of experience known as the common law and a theory of knowledge, conceived by John Locke. The body of experience and the theory of knowledge, in combination produced a theory of liberty, or if you will, a psychology of freedom, outside the Bill of Rights."[2]

[1] *The Papers of Thomas Jefferson*, ed. Julian P. Boyd, *et al.* (Princeton, 1950–), 2:545. The clause did not appear in the final version of the bill as adopted by the state legislature.

[2] Mark DeWolfe Howe, "The Psychology and Language of Freedom," a paper delivered in 1955 at a conference sponsored by the American

The contribution of the common law to this libertarian concept reflected the fundamental premise of an ancient jurisprudence of crimes. From time beyond legal memory, English jurists had regarded the individual as a free moral agent possessing a will to act lawfully or unlawfully by choosing between right and wrong. Only such a person could justly be held criminally responsible for his acts, because only the exercise of a free and rational will could cause a crime. No act, however reprehensible or even fatal its consequences, could be punished unless its doer knowingly intended a criminal deed; he must, that is, possess a malicious or criminal intent which Blackstone sometimes termed the "vicious will." Blackstone, a reliable guide to the Framers' understanding on this point, formulated it as follows:

> All the several pleas and excuses, which protect the committer of a forbidden act from the punishment which is otherwise annexed thereto, may be reduced to this single consideration, the want or defect of *will*. An involuntary act, as it has no claim to merit, so neither can it induce any guilt: the concurrence of the will, when it has its choice either to do or to avoid the fact in question, being the only thing that renders human actions either praiseworthy or culpable. Indeed, to make a complete crime cognizable by human laws, there must be both a will and an act. . . . And, as a vicious will, without a vicious act is no civil crime, so, on the other hand, an unwarrantable act without a vicious will is no crime at all. So that to constitute a crime against human laws, there must be, first, a vicious will; and, secondly, an unlawful act consequent upon such vicious will.

Where there is a "defect of understanding," Blackstone added, ". . . there is no discernment, there is no choice; and

Council of Learned Societies and printed in a pamphlet entitled *Progress and Survival: Present-Day Relevance of Eighteenth-Century Thought*, which is a transcript of the several brief addresses by participants. The pamphlet is unpaginated, undated, and does not state the name of a publisher or place of publication. I am indebted to Professor Howe for bringing the pamphlet to my attention and lending me his copy at an early stage of my research, thereby alerting me to be on the lookout for expressions of the "psychology of freedom" in Anglo-American libertarian thought.

where there is no choice, there can be no act of will. . . ." [3]

Blackstone apparently did not believe that the formation and expression of an opinion sprang from a want of will. The first person to state that idea was William Walwyn, the English Leveller whose thought was original in many respects. Walwyn even joined the idea to the common-law principle that criminal intent must be present to constitute a crime, with the result that he originated the libertarian concept that opinions cannot be criminal because they are involuntary. His statement appeared in the context of an argument in 1644 on behalf of freedom of conscience. That freedom should not be violated, he contended,

> Because of what judgment soever a man is, he cannot chuse but be of that judgement, that is so evident in it selfe, that I suppose it will be granted by all, whatsoever a mans reason doth conclude to be true or false, to be agreeabe or disagreabe to Gods Word, that same to that man is his opinion or judgement, and so man is by his own reason necessitated to be of that mind he is, now where there is a necessity there ought to be no punishment, for punishment is the recompense of voluntary actions, therfore no man ought to be punished for his judgment.[4]

John Locke unquestionably deserves to be credited with developing the theory of knowledge that Walwyn had earlier taken as self-evident. In *An Essay Concerning Human Understanding*, having detected "something unreasonable in most men," because they would not assent to proofs "as clear as daylight," Locke explained that individual differences in education and prejudice could not fully account for the phenomenon. He attributed it to the "association of ideas" resulting not from logic but "chance or custom" which "settles habits of thinking in the understanding, as well as of determining in the will. . . ." [5] Ideas once accidentally connected "afterwards kept company together in that man's mind, as if

---

[3] *Commentaries*, 4:20–21.

[4] "The Compassionate Samaritane," in William Haller, ed., *Tracts on Liberty in the Puritan Revolution, 1638–1647* (New York, 1933), 3:67–68.

[5] Book II, ch. 33, sections 1–6, at p. 316 in the London ed. of 1879.

they were but one idea."[6] The result was that the mind operated in a nonrational manner that had slight relation to one's will and was the greatest cause of error as well as diversity of opinion. Men could convince themselves that falsehood was truth because the chance association of ideas resulting from their personal experiences "blinds their understandings" and "captivates their reasons. . . ."[7] Words, being very imperfect tools of thought, additionally confused the mind, making clear thinking difficult, particularly as to the truths of law, government, and religion.[8] Little wonder, then, that knowledge and belief are only "partly voluntary"; indeed, Locke continued, "our will hath no power to determine the knowledge of the mind one way or another . . ." as to opinions and beliefs as well as external objects.[9]

In his discussion of "Wrong Assent, or Error," he asserted that "assent is no more in our power than knowledge . . . it is not in our choice to take which side we please, if manifest odds appear on either.[10] The odds were fixed for every man by forces beyond his control. The "greatest part of mankind" were enslaved by their mean condition, their lives worn out trying to "still the croaking of their own bellies. . . ." Lacking the opportunity of knowledge and inquiry, they could not be responsible for opinions dumbly held.[11] Others, with leisure and education, either lacked the intelligence or inclination to question their opinions. Engaged in a "hot pursuit of pleasure, or constant drudgery in business," their thought was elsewhere engaged, so they contented themselves by taking on trust the opinions they found convenient and fashionable.[12] All men labored mentally under the influence of passion and self-interest that blunted reason. The unknowing victims of

[6] *Ibid.*, sect. 7, p. 317.
[7] *Ibid.*, sect. 18, p. 320.
[8] Book III, ch. 10, sect. 12, p. 401–402.
[9] Book IV, ch. 13, sections 1–3, pp. 552–553.
[10] *Ibid.*, ch. 20, sect. 16, 605–606.
[11] *Ibid.*, sect. 2, p. 597.
[12] *Ibid.*, sect. 6, p. 600.

"authority"—the opinions of parents, friends, party, and country—they simply inherited their first principles from childhood. These were fastened in the mind by degrees until "riveted there, by long custom and education, beyond all possibility of being pulled out again." In maturity, their opinions were the "unavoidable consequence" of "reasoning from received traditional principles." [13] Even the educated, with the time and inclination to weigh the proofs of their opinions, reasoned from "received hypotheses" in which they had developed a stake that paralyzed their freedom of understanding. But nothing contributed as much to that result as the helpless association of ideas.

This exposition by Locke on the involuntary formation of opinion depicted men as puppets pulled by a hundred strings. They had free will to act only on the basis of their understanding, but their understanding lacked volition or freedom. Thus, Locke concluded in his *Letter Concerning Toleration* that "it is absurd that things should be enjoined by laws, which are not in men's power to perform; and to believe this or that to be true, does not depend upon will." [14] That this Lockian theory when combined with the common law of criminal intent produced what Mark Howe called a libertarian "psychology of freedom" cannot be doubted, for we have the testimony of Jefferson's thought. That he voiced a presupposition of the eighteenth century is, however, debatable. Presuppositions tend to be elusive because they are characteristically avowed only on rare occasions. This particular presupposition remained almost entirely inarticulated for about a century after Locke. However, J. B. Bury, in *A History of Freedom of Thought*, wrote that in the period during which the cause of toleration was fought for and won—a period not defined by Bury—the argument that the advocates of toleration "generally used was the injustice of punishing a man for opinions which he honestly held and *could not help holding, since con-*

[13] *Ibid.*, sections 8–9, p. 601. See also sections 11, 12, and 17, pp. 603, 606.
[14] *The Works of John Locke* (London, 1812, 11th ed.), 4:39–40.

viction is not a matter of will; in other words, the argument that error is not a crime and that it is therefore unjust to punish it."[15] Bury neglected, though, to offer a single illustration of any person's having endorsed the notion expressed in the italicized words. Illustrations by the score can be adduced to demonstrate the widely held view of the eighteenth century that error is not a crime. Many writers, Hume preeminently, also believed that custom structured one's notions; but only Locke's faithful disciples, William Trenchard and John Gordon, in their *Cato's Letters,* articulated the belief that "Men's Thoughts are not subject to their own Jurisdiction."[16]

It is not unreasonable, however, to assume that Locke's theory of involuntary belief had entered the thinking of educated men of the eighteenth century. Yet only Tunis Wortman and John Thomson, in 1800 and 1801 respectively, expressed the theory. Thomson developed it quite elaborately in order to "attempt a definition of what I mean by the liberty of the press. . . ." Wortman, too, had found it necessary in the same connection to present a psychological explanation of the way the mind operated to form beliefs and opinions. What he had implied,[17] Thomson made explicit:

> All men are endowed, by nature, with the power of thinking; yet have they no controul over their thoughts. As no individual can prevent the operation of this principle within himself, much less can he direct those of any other person . . . therefore, no association of men, however numerous or respectable, can ever have a right to say you shall not think this, or you shall think that: this being a power which does not exist among mankind. Consequently it must follow, that men should be allowed to express those thoughts, with the same freedom that they arise.

[15] (Home University ed., Oxford University Press, 1952 printing), p. 188. Italics added.
[16] *Cato's Letters* (London, 1755, 6th ed.), 2:247. See also 4:42 and 53.
[17] Tunis Wortman, *Treatise Concerning Political Enquiry and the Liberty of the Press* (New York, 1800), p. 32.

In other words — speak, or publish, whatever you believe to be truth.[18]

Thomson followed with an explanation, which he derived from Locke, beginning with the proposition that the mind at birth "is a total blank . . . like a sheet of blank paper, upon which you may write whatever you please." A variety of factors, which differed in the life of each individual, influenced what was written upon his mind and accounted for the propensity of mankind to differ in opinions. Pleasure and pain might be the immediate determining motives in the formulation of one's thoughts, but "man has no controul over his thoughts." A proposition might be put to two men who view it in opposite lights, each believing his own opinion to be the most agreeable to reason. "This arises entirely from the different point of view in which it appears to them," Thomson explained, "And, it follows of course, that neither party has any controul over his own thought; on the contrary, it is his thought which controuls him." He could not, therefore, be justly held criminally responsible for the expression of his opinions. Nor could the government possess a power to punish him for an involuntary belief. "As man individually has no controul over his own mind," Thomson concluded, "so it must follow of course, that he never could have delegated that to a government, which he did not himself possess." [19] Wortman, in expressing the lack of volition in the process of forming opinions, had stressed the manner in which thoughts sprung to the mind spontaneously in response to the environment under the irresistible influence of the "doctrine of association," a Lockian concept of the involuntary and chance association of ideas. But Wortman, unlike Thomson, also stressed the point that greater knowledge and habits of reason-

[18] John Thomson, *An Enquiry, Concerning the Liberty, and Licentiousness of the Press, and the Uncontroulable Nature of the Human Mind* (New York, 1801), pp. 11–12.
[19] *Ibid.*, pp. 12–15 *passim.*

ing increased the degree of volition in the thinking process.[20] The importance which Thomson gave to the idea that opinions are not formed by an act of will is evident in his inclusion of the phrase, "the Uncontroulable Nature of the Human Mind," in his title.

The idea that opinion is not punishable because it is involuntary is fascinating. It may illuminate the kind of thinking that resulted in a broadened, libertarian understanding of freedom of speech and press after the First Amendment was adopted. But even to assume that the Amendment was originally understood by its framers and by the American public to reflect Locke's theory does not warrant the conclusion that the expression of seditious libels was intended to be provided an immunity from prosecution. Such a conclusion would be giving greater weight to a fugitive thought in Jefferson and to the later statements of Wortman and Thomson than to all the evidence mustered in the preceding chapters. Professor Howe's insight that a "psychology of freedom, outside the Bill of Rights" must have existed has greater validity when applied to the period after the Sedition Act had provoked the emergence of a body of American libertarian thought. If dated by its actual expression in the United States, the psychology of freedom was a nineteenth-century contribution.[21]

[20] Wortman, *Treatise Concerning Political Enquiry*, pp. 32, 38–41, and 43.

[21] In addition to Wortman's statement of 1800 and Thomson's of 1801, see the elaborate statement in the "Preface" of Thomas Cooper's *A Treatise on the Law of Libel and the Liberty of the Press* (New York, 1830). See also Thomas Herttell, *The Demurrer* (New York, 1828), pp. 14–16, and Samuel Bailey, *Essays on the Formation and Publications of Opinions and Other Subjects* (London, 1826, 2nd ed.), Essay I, cited by Howe.

◆§ Bibliography

This bibliography includes only sources that I have cited in the footnotes. Scores of libertarian tracts were examined without yielding material for this book and are therefore omitted, including works by such writers as Isaac Backus, Joel Barlow, Thomas Cooper, Joseph Fownes, John Leland, Richard Price, Joseph Priestly, John Toland, and David Williams. The abbreviation "N.Y.P.L." after a tract indicates that I used the copy in the New York Public Library after failing to locate one in the Boston-Cambridge area.

ORIGINAL TRACTS, ESSAYS, BOOKS AND COLLECTED WORKS

[Adair, James]. *Discussions of the Law of Libels As at Present Received* (London, 1785), 97 pp.

Adams, John. *Works; with a Life of the Author,* ed. Charles Francis Adams (Boston, 1850–1856), 10 vols.

Addison, Joseph. See Anon. *Thoughts of a Tory Author . . .*

Alexander, James. Untitled essay on freedom of speech, in *Philadelphia Gazette,* Nov. 17–Dec. 8, 1737, numbers 466–469 (Photostated by courtesy of the Historical Society of Pennsylvania).

[Asgil, John]. *An Essay for the Press* (London, 1712), 8 pp. N.Y.P.L.

Anon. *Another Letter to Mr. Almon, in Matter of Libel* (1770), in *A Collection of Scarce and Interesting Tracts* (London, 1788, 4 vols., editor unnamed), 4:5–157.

——— *A Second Postscript in a Late Pamphlet, Entitled, A Letter to Mr. Almon, in Matter of Libel,* in *A Collection of Scarce and Interesting Tracts* (London, 1788, 4 vols., editor unnamed), 4:158–196.

Anon. *Arguments Relating to a Restraint upon the Press in a Letter to a Bencher, from a Young Gentleman of the Temple* (London, 1712), 52 pp. N.Y.P.L.

Anon. *Candid Considerations on Libels . . . Wtih Some Observations on the Liberty of the Press.* By a Friend to Harmony (Boston, 1789), 22 pp.

Anon. *Common Sense: or, the Englishman's Journal* (London, 1738), a letter to the editor, Jan. 7, 1738, pp. 331–341, and an editorial, Jan. 21, 1738, pp. 349–354.

Anon. *The Craftsman's Doctrine and Practice of the Liberty of the Press* (London, 1732), 61 pp.

Anon. *The Doctrine of Innuendo's Discuss'd; Or The Liberty of the Press Maintain'd* (London, 1731), 26 pp.

Anon. *An Enquiry into the Doctrine, Lately Propagated, concerning Libels, Warrants, and the Seizure of Papers . . . in a Letter to Mr. Almon from the Father of Candor* (London, 1764), 135 pp.

Anon. "Hampden." *A Letter to the President of the United States, touching the Prosecutions under his Patronage, before the Circuit Court in the District of Connecticut* (New Haven, 1808), 28 pp.

Anon. *The Juryman's Touchstone; or, A Full Refutation of Lord Mansfield's lawless opinion in Crown Libels.* By The Censor General (London, 1771), 93 pp. N.Y.P.L.

Anon. *A Letter Concerning Libels, Warrants, the Seizure of Papers, and Sureties for the Peace of Behaviour . . . With the Postscript and Appendix* (London, 1771), 164 pp., in *A Collection of Interesting Political Tracts,* ed., probably, by John Almon (London, 1773, 8 vols.), 1:1–164. Separately paged.

Anon. *A Letter from Candor to the Public Advertiser* (1764), in *A Collection of Interesting Political Tracts,* ed., probably, by John Almon (London, 1773, 8 vols., reprinting Candor's 3rd ed. 1770), 1:1–40. Separately paged.

Anon. *Letters on the Subject of the Proper Liberty of the Press.* By an Englishman (London, 1790), 58 pp. N.Y.P.L.

Anon. *The Liberty of the Press* (London, n.d.), [ca. 1763], 58 pp. N.Y.P.L.

Anon. *Literary Liberty Considered; in a Letter to Henry Sampson Woodfall* (London, 1774), 32 pp.

Anon. *A Narrative of a New and Unusual American Imprisonment of Two Presbyterian Ministers: And Prosecution of Mr. Francis Mackemie* (1704), by a Learner of Law, and Lover of Liberty, in Peter Force, ed. *Tracts and Other Papers* . . . , vol. 4, no. 4.

Anon. *The Press Restrained: A Poem* (London, 1712), 16 pp. N.Y.P.L.

Anon. *State Law: Or, the Doctrine of Libels, Discussed and Examined* (London, n.d., [1729], 2nd ed.), 136 pp. N.Y.P.L.

Anon. *The Thoughts of A Tory Author, Concerning the Press: With the Opinion of the Ancients and Moderns, about Freedom of* SPEECH *and* WRITING (London, 1712), 33 pp. [Uncertainly ascribed to Joseph Addison].

[Austin, Benjamin]. *Mr. Otis' Speech in Congress, on the Sedition law, with remarks by the "Examiner" on this important subject* (Boston, n.d.), [1798], 35 pp.

Bentham, Jeremy. *A Fragment on Government* (London, 1776), 208 pp.

Blackstone, Sir William. *Commentaries on the Laws of England* (1765–1769), (New York, 1836, 18th ed., 2 vols.).

Bl[o]unt, Charles. *A Just Vindication of Learning and the Liberty of the Press* (London, 1695), 27 pp.

Blount, Charles. *Reasons Humbly Offered for the Liberty of Unlicens'd Printing* (London, 1693), 32 pp.

[Bollan, William]. *The Freedom of Speech and Writing upon Public Affairs, Considered, with an Historical View* (London, 1766), 160 pp.

Bollan, William. *Essay on the Right of Every Man in a free*

State to Speak and Write Freely (London, 1772), 49 pp. An abridgment of Bollan's book of 1766.

Brown, John. *Thoughts on Civil Liberty, on Licentiousness, and Faction* (London, 1765), 168 pp.

[Burgh, James]. *Political Disquisitions: Or, An Enquiry into Public Errors, Defects and Abuses* (London, 1775), 3 vols. Chapter VI of vol. 1 and ch. IX of vol. 3 are related to speech and press.

Busher, Leonard. *Religious Peace: or A Plea for Liberty of Conscience* (London, 1614; reprinted 1646), in Edward Bean Underhill, ed. *Tracts on Liberty of Conscience and Persecution, 1646–1661* (London, 1846), pp. 1–81.

Caribbeana (London, 1741), 2 vols.

Chauncy, Charles. *The only Compulsion proper to be made Use of in the Affairs of* Conscience *and* Religion. *A Sermon* (Boston, 1739), 26 pp.

A Collection of Scarce and Interesting Tracts (London, 1788, 4 vols., editor unnamed), vol. 4.

[Collins, Anthony]. *A Discourse of Free Thinking* (London, 1723), 178 pp.

────── *A Discourse of the Grounds and Reasons of the Christian Religion* (London, 1724), 285 pp. preface iii–lxii.

────── *A Discourse concerning Ridicule and Irony in Writing* (London, 1729), 77 pp.

Cooper, Thomas. *A Treatise on the Law of Libel and the Liberty of the Press* (New York, 1830), 184 pp.

[Cushing, William, and Adams, John]. "Hitherto Unpublished Correspondence Between Chief Justice Cushing and John Adams in 1789," [ed. Frank W. Grinnell], *Massachusetts Law Quarterly*, 27:12–16 (October 1942).

Dawes, M[anasseh]. *The Deformity of the Doctrine of Libels, and Information Ex Officio* (London, 1785), 40 pp.

[Defoe, Daniel]. *A Vindication of the Press* (London, 1718), 36 pp. N.Y.P.L.

Erskine, Thomas Lord. *Speeches of Thomas Lord Erskine. Reprinted from the Five Volume Octavo Edition of 1810.*

With a Memoir of His Life by Edward Walford (London, 1870), 2 vols.

Force, Peter, ed. *American Archives: Consisting of a Collection of Authentic Records* (Washington, 1837 ff.), 4th series, 6 vols.

———— *Tracts and Other Papers Relating Principally to the Origin . . . of the Colonies in North America* (New York, 1947 ed.), 4 vols.

Ford, Paul Leicester, ed. *Essays on the Constitution of the United States* (Brooklyn, 1892).

Ford, Worthington, C., ed. *Thomas Jefferson Correspondence Printed from the Originals in the Collection of William K. Bixby* (Boston, 1916).

Fowle, Daniel. *A Total Eclipse of Liberty* (Boston, 1755), 32 pp.

Franklin, Benjamin. *The Writings of Benjamin Franklin,* ed. Albert Henry Smyth (New York, 1905–1907), 10 vols.

Furneaux, Phillp. *Letters to the Honourable Mr. Justice Blackstone, Concerning His Exposition of the Act of Toleration . . . in His Celebrated Commentaries on the Laws of England* (London, 1770; 2nd ed., 1771).

———— *An interesting appendix to Sir William Blackstone's Commentaries on the laws of England* (Philadelphia, 1773).

———— *The Palladium of Conscience* (Philadelphia, 1773).

Gorton, Samuel. "Simplicities Defence against Seven-Headed Policy" (1646), in Peter Force, ed., *Tracts and Other Papers Relating Principally to the origin . . . of the Colonies in North America* (New York, 1947 ed.), 4 vols. no. 6.

Hall, Robert. *An Apology for the Freedom of the Press, and for General Liberty* (1793), in John Foster, ed. *The Miscellaneous Works and Remains of the Reverend Robert Hall* (London, 1846), pp. 159–233.

Haller, William, ed. *Tracts on Liberty in the Puritan Revolution, 1638–1647* (New York, 1933), 3 vols.

Haller, William, and Davies, Godfrey, eds. *The Leveller Tracts, 1647–1653* (New York, 1944).

[Hay, George]. Hortensius. *An Essay on the Liberty of the Press, Respectfully Inscribed to the Republican Printers Throughout the United States* (Philadelphia, 1799), 51 pp. Reprinted in Richmond, 1803, in a 30 pp. edition.

Hay, George. *An Essay on the Liberty of the Press, Shewing, That the Requisition of Security for Good Behaviour from Libellers, is Perfectly Compatible with the Constitution and Laws of Virginia* (Richmond, 1803), 48 pp.

[Hayter, Thomas Bishop]. *An Essay on the Liberty of the Press, Chiefly as It Respects Personal Slander* (London, n.d.) [late 1750's], 47 pp.

Hopkinson, Francis. *The Miscellaneous Essays and Occasional Writings of Francis Hopkinson* (Philadelphia, 1792), 3 vols.

Hume, David. *Essays Moral, Political, and Literary*, ed. T. H. Green and T. H. Grose (London, 1898), 2 vols.

Jefferson, Thomas. *The Papers of Thomas Jefferson*, ed. Julian P. Boyd, et al. (Princeton, 1950–   , series in progress).

——— *The Writings of Thomas Jefferson*, ed. Paul Leicester Ford (New York, 1892–1899), 10 vols.

[Keith, George, and Budd, Thomas]. *New England's Spirit of Persecution Transmitted to Pennsilvania, And the Pretended Quaker Found Persecuting the True Christian-Quaker, in the Tryal of Peter Boss, George Keith, Thomas Budd and William Bradford, . . . 1693. Giving an Account of the most Arbitrary Procedure of that Court* (Philadelphia, 1693, printed by William Bradford), 38 pp.

Kippis, Alexander. *A Vindication of the Protestant Dissenting Ministers* (London, 1773), 123 pp.

Locke, John. *Letters on Toleration*, in *The Works of John Locke* (London, 1812, 11th ed., 10 vols.), vol. 6.

——— *An Essay Concerning Human Understanding* (written 1671, first published 1690), (London, 1879, Tegg and Co.).

[Lofft, Capel]. *An Essay on the Law of Libels* (London, 1785), 110 pp. N.Y.P.L.

Madison, James. *The Writings of James Madison*, ed. Gaillard Hunt (New York, 1900–1910), 9 vols.

[Marshall, John]. *Address of the minority in the Virginia Legislature to the people of that state; containing a vindication of the constitutionality of the Alien and Sedition laws* (n.p., 1799), 16 pp.

[Maseres, Francis]. *An Enquiry Into the Extent of the Power of Juries, on Trials of Indictments or Informations, for Publishing Seditious, or other Criminal Writings, or Libels. Extracted from a Miscellaneous Collection of Papers that were Published in 1776, Intitled, Additional Papers Concerning the Province of Quebec* (Dublin, 1792), 48 pp. N.Y.P.L.

Maule, Thomas. See Philanthes, Theo.

Mayhew, Jonathan. "A Discourse Concerning Unlimited Submission" (1750), in Perry Miller and Thomas H. Johnson, eds., *The Puritans* (New York, 1938), 277–280.

McPherson, Elizabeth, ed. "Unpublished Letters from North Carolinians to James Madison and James Monroe," *North Carolina Historical Review*, 14:157–169 (1937).

Milton, John. *The Works of John Milton*, ed. Frank A. Patterson, *et al* (New York, 1931–1938, 18 vols. in 21); vol. 4, ed. William Haller, contains: *Areopagitica* (1644); *A Treatise of Civil power in Ecclesiastical causes* (1659); and *Of True Religion, Heresie, Schism, and Toleration* (1673).

Morris, Robert. *A Letter to Sir Richard Aston . . . Containing . . . some Thought on the Modern Doctrine of Libels* (London, 1770), 68 pp.

Paine, Thomas. *The Life and Works of Thomas Paine*, ed. William M. Van der Weyde (New Rochelle, 1925), 10 vols.

Philanthes, Theo. *New-England Persecutors Mauld With their own Weapons . . . Together with a brief Account of the*

Imprisonment and Tryal of Thomas Maule of Salem, for publishing a Book, entitled, Truth held forth and maintained, &c. (New York, 1697), 62 pp. [by Maule, Thomas].

[Raynor, John]. *A Digest of the Law concerning Libels. By a Gentleman of the Inner-Temple* (Dublin, 1778), 139 pp. N.Y.P.L.

Ratcliffe, Ebenezer. *Two Letters Addressed to the Right Rev. Prelates* (London, 1773), 123 pp.

[Romilly, Sir Samuel]. *A Fragment of the Constitutional Power and Duty of Juries upon Trials for Libels* (London, n.d.), [1785], 16 pp. N.Y.P.L.

Smith, Samuel Stanhope. *A Sermon on Slander delivered at the church on Brattle St., Boston, Oct. 24, 1790* (Boston, 1791), 24 pp.

Smith, William. *Historical Memoirs from 16 March 1763 to 9 July 1776 of William Smith*, ed. William H. W. Sabine (New York, 1956).

Spinoza, Benedict de. *The Chief Works of Benedict de Spinoza*, trans. R. H. M. Elwes (London, 1883), 2 vols.

[Sullivan, James]. *A Dissertation upon the Constitutional Freedom of the Press in the United States of America*. By an Impartial Citizen (Boston, 1801), 54 pp.

Thomson, John. *An Enquiry, Concerning the Liberty, and Licentiousness of the Press, and the Uncontroulable Nature of the Human Mind* (New York, 1801), 84 pp.

Tindall, Matthew. *A Letter to a Member of Parliament, shewing that a restraint on the press is inconsistent with the Protestant religion, and dangerous to the liberties of the nation* (London, 1698), 32 pp.

—— *A Letter to a Friend: Occasioned by the presentment of the grand jury for the county of Middlesex, of the author, printer and publisher of a book entitled the rights of the christian church asserted* (London, 1708), 24 pp.

—— *Reasons against Restraining the Press* (London, 1704), 15 pp.

Towers, Joseph. *Observations on the Rights and Duty of Juries, in Trials for Libels,* 1784, reprinted in Towers' *Tracts on Political and Other Subjects* (London, 1796), 3 vols.), 2:1–174.

[Towers, Joseph]. *An Enquiry into the Question, Whether Juries are, or are not, Judges of Law, as well as of Fact; With a particular Reference to the case of Libels* (London, 1764), 31 pp.

[Trenchard, John, and Gordon, William]. *Cato's Letters: Or, Essays on Liberty, Civil and Religious* (London, 1755, 6th ed.), 4 vols.

Tucker, St. George. "Of the Right of Conscience; And of the Freedom of Speech and of the Press," in Tucker's *Blackstone's Commentaries: with Notes of Reference, to the Constitution and Laws, of the Federal Government of the United States; and of the Commonwealth of Virginia* (Philadelphia, 1803, 5 vols.), Appendix to Vol. 1, Part II, Note G., pp. 1–30.

Underhill, Edward Bean, ed. *Tracts on Liberty of Conscience and Persecution, 1614–1661* (London, 1846).

[Wilkes, John]. *English Liberty . . . containing the Private Correspondence, Public Letters, Speeches, and Addresses, of John Wilkes* (London, n.d. [1769], 2 vols. in 1), 391 pp.

——— *The North Briton* (Dublin, 1766), 2 vols.

Williams, Elisha. *A seasonable Plea for the Liberty of Conscience, and the Right of private Judgment, in Matters of Religion, without any Controul from human Authority. By a Lover of Truth and Liberty* (Boston, 1744), 66 pp. Signed "Philalethes" on p. 66.

Williams, Roger. *The Writings of Roger Williams.* Publications of the Narragansett Club (Providence, 1866–1874), 6 vols.

Winslow, Edward. *Hypocrasie Unmasked, A True Relation of the Proceedings of the Governor and Company of the*

Massachusetts Bay against Samuel Gorton of Rhode Island (1646), ed. Howard Millar Chapin (Providence, 1916).

Winthrop, John. *The History of New England from 1630 to 1649*, ed. James Savage (Boston, 1853), 2 vols.

Wolfe, Don M., ed. *Leveller Manifestoes of the Puritan Revolution* (New York, 1944).

[Woodfall, Henry]. Phileleutherus Anglicanus. *A Summary of the Law of Libel. In Four Letters* (1770), in *A Collection of Scarce and Interesting Tracts* (London, 1788, 4 vols., editor unnamed), 4:197–221.

Wortman, Tunis. *Treatise Concerning Political Enquiry, and the Liberty of the Press* (New York, 1800).

DEBATES, TRIALS, AND OTHER PUBLIC RECORDS

[Alexander, James]. *A brief Narrative of the Case and Tryal of John Peter Zenger, Printer of the New-York weekly Journal* (1736), in Rutherford, Livingston. *John Peter Zenger . . . Also a Reprint of the First Edition of the Trial* (New York, 1941).

Andrews, Charles M., ed. *Narratives of the Insurrections, 1675–1690* (New York, 1915).

[Annals of Congress]. *The Debates and Proceedings in the Congress of the United States* (Washington, 1834 ff).

Brown, William Hand, et al., eds. *Archives of Maryland* (Baltimore, 1883–1952), 65 vols.

Chandler, Peleg W., ed. *American Criminal Trials* (Boston, 1844), 2 vols.

Documentary History of the Constitution of the United States of America, 1786–1870. Derived from Records, Manuscripts, and Rolls Deposited in the Bureau of Rolls and Library of the Department of State (Washington, 1894–1905), 5 vols.

Elliot, Jonathan, ed. *The Debates in the Several State Conventions on the Adoption of the Federal Constitution . . . and Other Illustrations of the Constitution* (Philadelphia, 1941, 2nd ed., rev.), 5 vols.

Ford, Worthington C., *et al.*, eds. *Journals of the Continental Congress 1774–1789* (Washington, 1904–1937), 24 vols.

Hall, Benjamin, ed. *Official Opinions of the Attorneys General of the United States* (Washington, 1852), 2 vols.

Hening, William Waller, ed. *The Statutes at Large Being a Collection of All the Laws of Virginia (1619–1792)* (Richmond, 1809–1823), 13 vols.

Howe, Mark DeWolfe, ed. *Readings in American Legal History* (Cambridge, Mass., 1949).

Howell, Thomas Bayly, comp. *A Complete Collection of State Trials to 1783*. Continued by T. J. Howell to 1820 (London, 1816–1828), 34 vols.

Independent Chronicle (Boston), 1791, for the trial of Edward Freeman; 1799, for the trial of Abijah Adams.

The Journal of the First Session of the Senate of the United States of America (New York, 1789).

Journal of the Senate of the Commonwealth of Virginia: Begun and held in the City of Richmond, on Monday the 19th day of October . . . 1789 (Richmond, 1828). [Journal of the Senate, 1785 to 1790]

Journal of the Votes and Proceedings of the General Assembly of the Colony of New-York, 1691–1765 (New York, 1764–1766), 2 vols.

MacKinney, Gertrude, and Hoban, Charles F., eds. *Votes and Proceedings of the House of Representatives of the Province of Pennsylvania (1682–1776)*, in *Pennsylvania Archives*, 8th ser. (n.p., 1931–1935), 8 vols.

McIlwaine, H. R., and Hall, W. L., eds. *Executive Journals of the Council of Colonial Virginia, 1680–1754* (Richmond, 1925–1945), 5 vols.

McIlwaine, H. R., and Kennedy, J. P., eds. *Journals of the House of Burgesses of Virginia, 1619–1776* (Richmond, 1805–1915), 13 vols.

McMaster, John Bach, and Stone, Frederick D., eds. *Pennsylvania and the Federal Constitution, 1787–1788* (Philadelphia, 1888).

Minutes of the Provincial Council of Pennsylvania (Harrisburg, 1838–1840), 3 vols.

O'Callaghan, E. B., ed. *Documentary History of the State of New York* (Albany, 1849–1851), 4 vols.

O'Callaghan, E. B., and Fernow, B., eds. *Documents Relative to the Colonial History of the State of New York* (Albany, 1856–1887), 15 vols.

Quincy, Josiah, Jr., ed. *Reports of Cases Argued and Adjudged in the Superior Court of Judicature of the Province of Massachusetts Bay, Between 1761 and 1772* (Boston, 1865).

Rutherfurd, Livingston. *John Peter Zenger, His Press, His Trial and a Bibliography of Zenger Imprints. Also a Reprint of the Edition of the Trial* (New York, 1904).

Saunders, William L., ed. *The Colonial Records of North Carolina (1662–1776)* (Raleigh, 1886–1890), 10 vols.

Shurtleff, Nathaniel B., ed. *Records of the Governor and Company of the Massachusetts Bay in New England (1628–86)* (Boston, 1853–1854), 5 vols.

Tansill, Charles, C., ed. *Documents Illustrative of the Formation of the Union of the American States* (Washington, 1927).

Thorpe, Francis Newton, ed. *The Federal and State Constitutions, Colonial Charters, and Other Organic Laws* (Washington, 1909), 7 vols.

Toppan, Robert Noxon, ed. *Edward Randolph* (Boston, 1898–1900, 7 vols.), vol. 4 for the trial of John Wise.

The Virginia Report of 1799–1800, Touching the Alien and Sedition Laws; together with the Virignia Resolutions of December 21, 1798, The Debates and Proceedings thereon, in the House of Delegates in Virginia (Richmond, 1850). Valuable for the Virginia debates on the Sedition Act, at pp. 22–161, although adding little to the earlier debate on the same subject by the House of Representatives. Madison's *Report* is at pp. 189–237.

Wharton, Francis, ed. *State Trials of the United States during* the *Administrations of Washington and Adams* (Philadelphia, 1849).

SECONDARY SOURCES

Allen, J. *English Political Thought, 1603-1660* (London, 1938), 2 vols.
Amory, Thomas Coffin. *The Life of James Sullivan* (Boston, 1859), 2 vols.
Becker, Carl Lotus. *The History of Political Parties in the Province of New York 1760-1776* (Madison, Wis., 1909).
Beveridge, Albert J. *The Life of John Marshall* (Boston, 1919) 4 vols.
Biddle, Francis. *The Fear of Freedom* (New York, 1951).
Brant, Irving. *James Madison, Father of the Constitution* (Indianapolis, 1950).
Brown, David Paul. *The Forum: Or, Forty Years Full Practice at the Philadelphia Bar* (Philadelphia, 1856), 2 vols.
Brown, Robert E. *Middle-Class Democracy and the Revolution in Massachusetts, 1691-1780* (Ithaca, 1955).
Buckingham, Joseph T. *Specimens of Newspaper Literature* (Boston, 1852), 2 vols.
Buranelli, Vincent. "Peter Zenger's Editor," *American Quarterly*, 7:174-181 (1955).
———— *The Trial of Peter Zenger* (New York, 1957).
Bury, J. B. *A History of Freedom of Thought* (Home University sity ed., Oxford University Press, 1952 printing).
Carroll, Thomas F. "Freedom of Speech and of the Press in the Federalist Period: The Sedition Act," *Michigan Law Review*, 18:615-651 (May 1920).
Chafee, Zechariah, Jr. *Free Speech in the United States* (Cambridge, 1948).
———— *Three Human Rights in the Constitution of 1787* (Lawrence, Kan., 1956).
Clarke, Mary Patterson. *Parliamentary Privilege in the American Colonies* (New Haven, 1943).

Clyde, William C. *The Struggle for the Freedom of the Press from Caxton to Cromwell* (London, 1934).

Cobb, Sanford, H. *The Rise of Religious Liberty in America* (New York, 1902).

Cook, Elizabeth Christine. *Literary Influences in Colonial Newspapers* (New York, 1912).

Cooley, Thomas M. *Treatise on the Constitutional Limitations Which Rest Upon the Legislative Power of the States*, ed. V. H. Lane (Boston, 1903, 7th ed.).

Corwin, Edward S. "Freedom of Speech and Press under the First Amendment: A Resume," in Douglas B. Maggs *et al.*, eds. *Selected Essays on Constitutional Law* (Chicago, 1938, 5 vols.), 2:1060–1068.

Cranston, Maurice. *John Locke, A Biography* (London, 1957).

Crosskey, William W. *Politics and the Constitution* (Chicago, 1953), 2 vols.

Dauer, Manning J. *The Adams Federalists* (Baltimore, 1953).

Davidson, Philip. *Propaganda and the American Revolution, 1763–1783* (Chapel Hill, 1941).

DeArmond, Anna Janney. *Andrew Bradford, Colonial Journalist* (Newark, Del., 1949).

Dillon, Dorothy Rita. *The New York Triumvirate* (New York, 1949).

Dumbauld, Edward. *The Bill of Rights and What It Means Today* (Norman, Okla., 1957).

Duniway, Clyde Augustus. *The Development of Freedom of the Press in Massachusetts* (New York, 1906).

Ford, Paul Leicester, ed. *The Journals of Hugh Gaine, Printer* (New York, 1902), 2 vols.

Fraenkel, Osmond K. *Our Civil Liberties* (New York, 1944).

Frank, Joseph. *The Levellers* (Cambridge, Mass., 1955).

Gegenheimer, Albert Frank. *William Smith* (Philadelphia, 1943).

Goebel, Julius and Naughton, T. Raymond. *Law Enforcement in Colonial New York* (New York, 1944).

Hall, Ford W. "The Common Law: An Account of Its Reception in the United States," *Vanderbilt Law Review*, 4:791–825 (1951).

Hanson, Lawrence. *Government and the Press, 1695–1763* (Oxford, 1936).

Henry, William Wirt. *Patrick Henry: Life, Correspondence and Speeches* (New York, 1891), 3 vols.

Howe, Mark DeWolfe. "Juries as Judges of Criminal Law," *Harvard Law Review*, 52:582–616 (February 1939).

——— "The Psychology and Language of Freedom," in *Progress and Survival: Present-Day Relevance of Eighteenth Century Thought*. A pamphlet reproducing papers delivered at a conference sponsored by the American Council of Learned Societies (n.pg., n.d., n.pb.).

Hulme, Harold. *The Life of Sir John Eliot* (New York, 1957).

——— "The Winning of Freedom of Speech by the House of Commons," *American Historical Review*, 61: 825–853 (July 1956).

Hurst, Willard. "Treason in the United States," *Harvard Law Review*, 58:226–272, 395–444, and 806–857 (1944–1945).

Jones, Matt Bushnell. *Thomas Maule, The Salem Quaker and Free Speech in Massachusetts Bay* (Salem, 1936), 42 pp. Reprinted from Essex Institute Historical Collections, vol. 72, no. 1, January 1936.

Jones, Thomas. *History of New York During the Revolutionary War*, ed. E. F. de Lancey (New York, 1879), 2 vols.

Jordan, W. H. *The Development of Religious Toleration in England* (Cambridge, Mass., 1934–1940), 4 vols.

Judson, Margaret. *The Crisis of the Constitution* (Rutgers, 1949).

Kelly, John. "Criminal Libel and Free Speech," *Kansas Law Review*, 6:295–333 (1958).

King, Lord. *The Life and Letters of John Locke* (London, 1858 ed.).

Koch, Adrienne, and Ammon, Harry, "The Virginia and Kentucky Resolutions: An Episode in Jefferson's and

Madison's Defense of Civil Liberties," *William and Mary Quarterly*, 3rd ser., 5:145–176 (1948).

Konvitz, Milton, R. *Fundamental Liberties of a Free People* (Ithaca, 1957).

Leake, Isaac Q. *Memoir of the Life and Times of General John Lamb* (Albany, 1850).

Levy, Leonard W. *The Law of the Commonwealth and Chief Justice Shaw* (Cambridge, 1957).

———— "Did the Zenger Case Really Matter?" *William and Mary Quarterly*, 3rd ser., 17:35–50 (1960).

Lincoln, Anthony. *Some Political and Social Ideas of English Dissent, 1763–1800* (Cambridge, Eng., 1938).

Link, Eugene Perry. *Democratic-Republican Societies, 1790–1800* (New York, 1942).

Malone, Dumas. *Jefferson the Virginian* (Boston, 1948).

Masson, David. *Life of Milton* (London, 1858–1880), 6 vols.

Matteson, David M. "The Organization of the Government under the Constitution," in Sol Bloom, Director General, *History of the Formation of the Union under the Constitution* (Washington, 1943), 141–508.

May, Thomas Erskine. *The Constitutional History of England* (New York, 1880), 2 vols.

McAnear, Beverly, ed. "James Parker *versus* New York Province," *New York History*, 32:321–330 (1941).

McCrady, Edward. *The History of South Carolina under the Royal Government 1719–1776* (New York, 1899).

McRee, Griffith J. *Life and Correspondence of James Iredell* (New York, 1857–1858), 2 vols.

Meiklejohn, Alexander. *Free Speech and Its Relation to Self-Government* (New York, 1948).

Miller, John C. *Crisis in Freedom. The Alien and Sedition Acts.* (Boston, 1952).

———— *Origins of the American Revolution* (Boston, 1943).

Morgan, E. M. "The Privilege Against Self-Incrimination," *Minnesota Law Review*, 34:1–45 (1949).

Mott, Rodney L. *Due Process of Law* (Indianapolis, 1926).
Neale, J. E. "The Commons' Privilege of Free Speech in Parliament," in R. W. Seton-Watson, ed. *Tudor Studies* (London, 1924), pp. 258–286.
Nobbe, George. *The North Briton* (New York, 1939).
Ould, Herman, ed. *Freedom of Expression. A symposium . . . to Commemorate the Tercentary of the Publication of Milton's "Areopagitica"* (London, 1944).
Paterson, James. *The Liberty of the Press, Speech, and Public Worship* (London, 1880).
Patterson, Giles J. *Free Speech and a Free Press* (Boston, 1939).
Pomerantz, Sidney I. "The Patriot Newspaper and the American Revolution," in Richard B. Morris, ed., *The Era of the American Revolution* (New York, 1939), 305–331.
Postgate, Raymond. *That Devil Wilkes* (New York, 1929).
Pound, Roscoe. *The Formative Era of American Law* (Boston, 1938).
Pritchitt, C. Herman. *The American Constitution* (New York, 1959).
Radin, Max. "Freedom of Speech in Ancient Athens," *American Journal of Philology*, 48:215–230 (1927).
Realey, C. B. "The *London Journal* and Its Authors 1720–1723," *University of Kansas Humanistic Studies*, vol. V, no. 3 (December 1935).
Riddell, William Renwick. "Libel on the Assembly: A Pre-revolutionary Episode," *The Pennsylvania Magazine of History and Biography*, 52:176–192, 249–279, and 342–360 (1928).
Robinson, Laura. *Free Speech in the Roman Republic* (Baltimore, 1940).
Roche, John P. "American Liberty: An Examination of the 'Tradition' of Freedom," in M. R. Konvitz, and C. Rossiter, eds., *Aspects of Liberty: Essays Presented to Robert E. Cushman* (Ithaca, 1958), pp. 129–162.

Rossiter, Clinton. *Seedtime of the Republic* (New York, 1953).

Rutland, Robert Allen. *The Birth of the Bill of Rights, 1776–1791* (Chapel Hill, 1955).

Schlesinger, Arthur M. *Prelude to Independence: The Newspaper War on Britain, 1764–1776* (New York, 1958).

Schofield, Henry. "Freedom of the Press in the United States," in Schofield's *Essays on Constitutional Law and Equity* (Boston, 1921, 2 vols.), 2:510–571.

Schroeder, Theodore. *Constitutional Free Speech Defined and Defended in an Unfinished Argument in a Case of Blasphemy* (New York, 1919).

—— *A Free Speech Bibliography* (New York, 1922).

—— *Constitutional Free Speech* (New York, 1919).

Schuyler, Livingston Rowe. *The Liberty of the Press in the American Colonies before the Revolutionary War* (New York, 1905), 85 pp.

Siebert, Frederick S. *Freedom of the Press in England, 1476–1776* (Urbana, 1952).

Slafter, Edmund F. *John Checkley; or, the Evolution of Religious Tolerance in Massachusetts Bay* (Boston, 1897), 2 vols.

Smith, Horace Wemyss. *Life and Correspondence of the Reverend William Smith* (Philadelphia, 1879), 2 vols.

Smith, James Morton. *Freedom's Fetters: The Alien and Sedition Laws and American Civil Liberties* (Ithaca, 1956).

Spaulding, E. Wilder. *His Excellency, George Clinton* (New York, 1938).

Stephen, Sir James Fitzjames. *A History of the Criminal Law of England* (London, 1883), 3 vols.

Stephen, Leslie. *History of English Thought in the Eighteenth Century* (London, 1876), 2 vols.

Stevens, David Harrison. *Party Politics and English Journalism, 1702–1742* (Chicago, 1916).

Sutherland, Arthur E., Jr. "British Trials for Disloyal Association during the French Revolution," *Cornell Law Quarterly,* 34:309–315 (Spring 1949).

Terwilliger, W. Bird. "William Goddard's Victory for the Freedom of the Press," *Maryland Historical Magazine,* 36:139–149 (1941).

Thomas, Isaiah. *The History of Printing in America* (Worcester, 1810), 2 vols.

Thomson, Mark A. *The Secretaries of State, 1681–1782* (Oxford, 1932).

Vance, W. R. "Freedom of Speech and of the Press," *Minnesota Law Review,* 2:239–260 (March 1918).

Van Tyne, Claude H. *The Loyalists in the American Revolution* (New York, 1902).

Veeder, Van Vechten. "History of the Law of Defamation," in *Select Essays in Anglo-American Legal History,* comp. and ed. by a Committee of the Association of American Law Schools (Boston, 1909, 3 vols.), 3:446–473.

Walett, Francis J. "The Massachusetts Council, 1766–1774," *William and Mary Quarterly,* 3rd ser., 6:605–627 (1949).

Wallace, John William. *An Address Delivered at the Celebration by the New York Historical Society, May 20, 1863, of the Two Hundredth Birth Day of Mr. William Bradford* (Albany, 1863).

Warren, Charles, "New Light on the History of the Federal Judiciary Act of 1789," in D. B. Maggs, *et al,* eds., *Selected Essays on Constitutional Law* (Chicago, 1938, 5 vols.), 3:1246–1254.

——— *The Supreme Court in United States History* (Boston, 1923), 3 vols.

Whipple, Leon. *Our Ancient Liberties* (New York, 1927).

Williams, J. B. *A History of English Journalism* (London, 1908).

Wittke, Carl. *The History of English Parliamentary Privilege,* Ohio State University Bulletin, vol. 26, no. 2 (Columbus, 1921).

Index